DON'T PANIC

DON'T PANIC

Taking Control of Anxiety Attacks

R. REID WILSON, Ph.D.

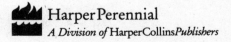

HarperPerennial
A Division of HarperCollins*Publishers*

A hardcover edition of this book was published by Harper & Row in 1986.

First PERENNIAL LIBRARY edition published 1987.

Designer: Sidney Feinberg

Library of Congress Cataloging-in-Publication Data

Wilson, R. Reid.
  Don't panic.

  "Perennial Library."
  Bibliography: p.
  Includes index.
  1. Panic attacks.   2. Anxiety.   3. Self-help techniques.   I. Title.
RC531.W48   1987   616.85'223   85-45670
ISBN 0-06-091438-6 (pbk.)

95 96 RRD (H) 20 19 18 17 16

Dedicated to Dale,
who guides the light

Contents

Acknowledgments

Pursuing a career in clinical psychology fulfills two of my most cherished lifelong dreams: to continually explore the world of ideas as an eager and naive student and, simultaneously, to give to others in a way that makes a difference. This book is a reflection of a lifetime of learning, and I hope it in some small way honors those who have nourished and inspired me. Theoretically, it is a synthesis of the work of hundreds of dedicated professionals in a surprisingly broad spectrum of fields. Their names can be found in this book's bibliography.

Over the past fifteen years I have had the distinct privilege of directly studying under the mentorship of six professionals. Their wisdom and example will remain as powerful influences in my professional life: Takey Crist, MD, Ed Gurowitz, PhD, Michio Kushi, Emily Ruppert, MSW, Daniel Rutrick, MD, and Stephen Lankton, MSW. My three lifelong friends—Phillip Wilson, Leif Diamant, and William "Bud" Garrison—have joined me in adventures that have opened my heart, expanded my perception of the potential of life, and given me the gift of self-love. Through his example, Robert Wilson taught me the value in determination, precision, and intellectual curiosity.

A number of people directly contributed to the existence of this book. Stephen Lankton, MSW, gave me endless encouragement, prodded me to address my self-doubts, and pointed me inward toward my creativity. Richard Bush, PhD, guided me through the logistics of book publishing and continually reminded me that I could succeed. I am indebted to Carol Houck Smith for her suggestions in redirecting the early drafts of this book. Dale Pratt-Wilson, RN, not only offered useful editorial suggestions but sustained me during the times when my faith wavered. John Ware, my agent, arrived at just the right time with just the right support. I wish to express my appreciation to four dedicated and skilled physicians who reviewed and enhanced the medical information in this book: David Savitz, MD, for the physical causes of panic-like symptoms; James Donohue, MD, for panic within chronic obstructive lung diseases; James Harper, MD, for panic within cardiac disorders; and Daniel Rutrick, MD, for the use of medications. Kathie Ness and Margaret Wimberger gently presented significant editorial contributions in the final draft. Special thanks to Melissa Hochschild, Martha Lappen, Elizabeth Gates Diamant, and Millie Johnson for processing the many drafts of this book and to Ann Wilson for proofreading the final manuscript. I am grateful to the staff of Harvard University Medical School's Countway Library and the University of North Carolina's Health Sciences Library for the use of their valuable resources.

Foreword

Hope and guidance are often sought in the pages of books, and on occasion a volume generously rewards the seeker with a sense of comfort and direction. Dr. Wilson's *Don't Panic* is one of those books for people with repeated panic attacks. In preparing this volume, Dr. Wilson has drawn deeply on his experience in helping people with panic and on the scientific literature that deals with panic-related problems. He provides readers with the full understanding they need to begin to recover from debilitating and demoralizing anxiety disorders.

Panic attacks involve strong physical experiences that may badly frighten the sufferers and discourage them from going about usual activities. Often they consult family doctors and medical specialists in an attempt to come to grips with the problem, but are left without satisfying explanations for the troubling attacks, effective techniques for coping with them, or plans for putting life back in order. In those cases in which a medical condition seems to have played a role in the development of the panic problem, the patients may have an even harder time deciding how best to go about helping themselves. Not infrequently, confusion and fear take over, and patients may feel they are truly "losing control."

Dr. Wilson's book will help to dispel much of this fear and confusion. It is sensibly divided into two parts. Part I is packed with much-needed but hard-to-come-by information that will help the panic sufferer identify the components of his or her particular problem. In an invaluable first chapter, Dr. Wilson reviews the physical sensations that are commonly associated with panic and shows that these sensations are a part of the body's normal systems for dealing with emergencies. He explains how a number of factors—physical illness, dramatic or frightening events, current demands and responsibilities, psychological difficulties—can produce panic-like symptoms, and describes how fear of a repetition of these symptoms can lead to severe anxiety.

In the succeeding chapters of Part I, Dr. Wilson discusses the various psychological and medical problems to which panic symptoms may be related and the complications produced by such problems as premenstrual syndrome, hypoglycemia, depression, and alcoholism. He gives clear advice on how to sort the physical and psychological aspects of the problem. Perhaps most intriguing, he takes a look at the thoughts, beliefs, and behavior patterns he has observed in people with panic disorders and agoraphobia, and begins to suggest a plan for recovery.

In Part II, Dr. Wilson presents tools and techniques for overcoming panic disorders and phobias. Correctly emphasizing the loss of self-confidence that is so much a part of these problems, Dr. Wilson maps a path toward more independent functioning. An essential part of his plan is to help panic sufferers recognize the workings of the internal "observer"—that part of us that takes in information about a situation, assesses it, and decides what to do about it.

When people have had repeated panic attacks, according to Dr. Wilson, they are likely to be listening to a "worried observer," a "hopeless observer," or a "critical observer," rather than an objective, patient inner voice. These "negative observers" rapidly interpret and "comment" on events: "I'll get dizzy . . . I'll be embarrassed . . . I've failed . . . I can't handle it . . . Why bother?" The "contaminated observers" see panic as the enemy, and their commentary heightens and intensifies panic attacks. Passivity and avoidance also result from the decisions of these observers. In Dr. Wilson's words, "they invite you to surrender into helplessness, to stop trying, to wave the white flag."

The antidote for these troublesome influences is to nourish and strengthen an "independent" or "supportive" internal observer. This inner friend and ally takes its time gathering information about a situation; it looks for ways to restore calm without retreating. The supportive observer reminds us that it is no advantage to be harshly self-critical or overly preoccupied with symptoms. It sets reasonable goals and strives to meet them but grants the freedom to make a wide variety of choices at any given time. This observer recognizes negative thoughts and images but clears them from the mind, concentrating instead on facts, goals, or physical surroundings.

Dr. Wilson's "supportive observer" has at its disposal an array of techniques to calm the body and mind. Thus, *Don't Panic* includes clear and complete instructions for a number of relaxation methods, including abdominal breathing, muscle relaxation, and meditation, and a concise review of the medications that may be prescribed. The use of paradoxical techniques in controlling panic attacks is explained with lucidity and conviction. Dr. Wilson's readers will also have their calm observers reinforced by reading, and probably rereading, The Guide (Chapter 18)—a soothing script for relaxation that is filled with images of comfort and safety. The Guide reminds panic sufferers of the self-nurturing, self-trusting attitudes they need to learn in order to feel stable and secure in new ventures and adventures.

For years, people with panic attacks and agoraphobia have found reassurance and encouragement in the writings of Claire Weekes. *Don't Panic* continues in the tradition of Dr. Weekes, expanding her advice and integrating the experience of behavior therapists, cognitive therapists, and psychopharmacologists to design a promising strategy for recovery.

Aaron T. Beck, MD
University Professor of Psychiatry
University of Pennsylvania

PART I

IDENTIFYING
THE PROBLEM

Don't Panic is factually accurate,
except that all the names and identifying
characteristics of the individuals discussed
in the book have been changed.

1

Introduction

The Panic Attack

It is as though the symptoms jump you from behind. With little warning the heart begins its rapid pumping, a cold perspiration beads the forehead, trembling hands want to hide from view. The throat attempts in vain to swallow while any remaining moisture in the mouth disappears.

Your mind races to save some semblance of control. "Just relax! Stay calm!" is the silent command. But you place little faith in such words. And why should you? They have always failed to relieve the anarchy of the body in the past.

The more you grip to keep control, the less control you feel. Panic! Seconds pass like minutes as your mind is pulled in two directions. First, to the past: "This is like last month, when I became so weak that I almost fainted." Then, to the body with a mind of its own: "I can't catch my breath. I'm trying. I can't!" The future rushes to the present: "What if this keeps up? I could pass out. If my heart beats any faster I could have a heart attack."

At that same moment the fear of humiliation crowds the noise of the mind. "Everyone's going to see me collapse. I've got to get out of here." With the same suddenness that started this attack, you make your escape out of the door of the conference room or the movie theater, the doctor's office or the grocery store. The farther you get from the scene, the more comfortable you feel.

This scenario portrays what I call *the moment of panic:* an internal experience, supported by physical sensations, that the person has

3

immediately and dangerously lost control of his circumstances. The changes in the body and mind take place so rapidly and unconsciously that they are experienced as an "attack" of panic or anxiety.

All of us have experienced the physical sensations of anxiety. We get "butterflies" in the stomach before we give a speech, or a throbbing headache after hours of caring for rambunctious kids. But the experience of general anxiety is quite distinct from the overwhelming sensations of a panic attack.

For example, have you ever faced a physical emergency alone, one which you were ill prepared to deal with? Imagine opening your cellar door to the sound of water splashing onto the concrete floor. You run down the stairs, half guided by your feet, half carried by your arms pushing off the hand rails. How fast do you size up the situation? How many options do you rule out in the first thirty seconds? "Can I stop it with my hand? No. . . . How about tying it with a rag? Is there a rag around? Won't work! Where's this pipe coming from? Where's the main valve?" Your eyes move rapidly, absorbing every detail which might play a role in reducing the damage caused by a flooding basement. "Grandma's chest of drawers, it's getting ruined! Should I move it? Stop the water first. Where is that valve?! There's the trash can. No use, it's spraying too broadly. Who can I call?"

If you could freeze the action of this scene at this precise moment, you would recognize in yourself many of the physical symptoms found in what we call a panic attack or anxiety attack. The muscles are tense, ready to respond immediately to any directions from the brain ("Get down those stairs—*now!*") The blood is rushing to the brain to stimulate the thought processes. The heart and respiration rates both rapidly increase to produce the essential shifting of blood throughout the body.

Each of us should be thankful for the incredible ability of our body and mind to instantly and automatically respond in such an emergency. How many of us have been saved from injury or death on the highway because our right foot slammed on the brake while our hands pulled on the steering wheel—all this before we had time to even subvocalize the command, "Watch out for that car!"

Brilliant as this built-in emergency system is, something can go awry. During panic, the body responds with many of the same physiological changes that take place during an emergency. However, panic is an exaggeration of our emergency response. Instead of taking advantage of the body's rapidly increased strength, the individual experiencing panic becomes overwhelmed by a variety of symptoms. The more he focuses his attention on these internal changes, the more anxious he becomes, and the less able he is to reassure himself.

A panic attack causes the fastest and most complex reaction known within the human body. It immediately alters the functioning of the eyes, several major glands, the brain, heart, lungs, stomach, intestines, pancreas, kidneys and bladder, and the major muscle groups. For instance, within the cardiovascular system, the heart increases its rate of contractions, the amount of blood it pumps with each contraction, and the pressure it exerts as blood is pumped into the arteries. The blood vessels in the arms, legs, and other parts of the body begin to constrict, reducing blood flow in those areas. At the same time, the vessels which channel blood into the vital organs and skeletal muscles expand, increasing their blood flow.

While this is taking place, your rate of respiration increases. The pupils dilate to improve distance vision. Within the gastrointestinal system, all digestive activity is diminished. Metabolism (the conversion of foods into energy) is enhanced, and an increased amount of sugars and fatty acids are secreted into the bloodstream.

Your subjective experience during a panic attack can vary greatly. Certain sensations (such as noticing your heart rate) are directly related to the physiological changes I have just mentioned. Others (such as the fear that you are dying) are produced by your mental and emotional response to these sensations. Listed below are a variety of symptoms associated with panic. Generally speaking, the more symptoms you have during the panic attack and the greater the intensity of each symptom, the more devastated you will feel by this assault.

The head: Decreased blood flow to the brain, caused by hyperventilation, may result in a feeling of lightheadedness or dizziness, as though your head is "swimming." You may feel faint.

The body: You begin to perspire, have hot and cold flashes, feel numb, or experience prickling or tingling. You feel as though you are whirling about (vertigo). The whole body feels fatigued or depleted.

The mind: You feel disoriented, confused, or unable to concentrate. You feel cut off or far away from your surroundings (derealization). Your body can feel unreal, as though you are in a dream (depersonalization). You become irritable or short-tempered. Common fears are of fainting, going crazy, having a heart attack, dying, making a scene, or becoming trapped.

The eyes: Your eyes flicker or twitch. You may have difficulty focusing on objects, or objects might appear blurry. Figures such as numbers on a page "jump around" or appear reversed.

The mouth and throat: Your mouth becomes dry. You have difficulty swallowing, feel as if there is a lump in your throat or as if you might choke. The muscles in your throat feel tight. As you speak, your voice trembles.

The heart: You may notice that your heart has increased its rate of contractions. The pumping of the heart feels quite strong and pounding, as though it could jump out of your chest. Your heart may seem to skip a beat or two. You experience pain or discomfort in your chest.

Respiration: Your rate of breathing increases and becomes more shallow, possibly leading to hyperventilation. You feel as though you cannot take a full, deep breath. You might have difficulty catching your breath, may painfully gasp for air or feel as if you will smother.

The stomach: Your stomach feels full of "butterflies," or "tied in knots." You might feel nauseous.

The muscles: The muscles throughout your body feel tense, especially in the neck and shoulders. If you are driving, you may notice that your hands are gripping the steering wheel so tightly that your knuckles are white and your arms are stiff. In another situation, you may be unconsciously squeezing your hands into fists. Or, your muscles may feel weak, your legs unable to keep you standing. Your hands and legs tremble, feel cold, clammy, and sweaty, or feel numb.

In essence, your body, which has been fairly trustworthy over the years, begins to mutiny. And if you experience panic attacks with any frequency, this lack of control slowly erodes your self-confidence and your self-esteem. You begin to restrict your activities in order to ward off these attacks. Familiar situations become threatening.

- If panic hits you before or during speeches, you begin to turn down speaking engagements.
- If panic hits you while traveling, you begin to find excuses for canceling out-of-town business meetings and become "just too busy" to take a vacation with the family.
- If panic hits you in groups of people, you begin turning down invitations to parties and other gatherings, preferring to stay at home.

- If panic hits you in stores or restaurants or at the hairdresser's, you begin to avoid each location which might stimulate a recurrence of your symptoms.
- If panic hits you while you are involved in physical exertion, you begin to avoid any activity that exercises your respiratory or cardiovascular system.
- And if panic hits you only while you are alone, you begin to cling to your husband or wife, friends, even your children, to ensure safety and protection from this assault by your body.

You may think that your panic attack came "out of the blue" the first time or continues to "jump you from behind." After you experience several panics, a certain doubt creeps into your mind: "What is wrong with me? Why is this happening? Am I crazy? Is this the beginning of a nervous breakdown? Are these responsibilities [of the job/marriage/new baby/house purchase] too much for me to handle? Do I have a thyroid condition [or heart problem/cancer/high blood pressure]?" For many people, these moments of high excitement or extreme anxiety, of dramatic and sudden changes in the body, are the most frightening and troublesome events of their lives.

It is difficult to pinpoint the causes of panic, and complicating the situation is the fact that panic can be found in several psychological disorders and panic-like symptoms can be found in dozens of physical disorders. An exact diagnosis is often difficult to make, and the treatment approaches can differ greatly. Occasionally the symptoms elude a positive diagnosis.

Panic can take place in several arenas:

Physical Illness. There are a number of physical disorders which produce symptoms resembling extreme anxiety or panic. If an illness remains undiagnosed or misdiagnosed, the individual can grow fearful of these unexpected, dramatic changes in his body. This lack of understanding and the fearful anticipation that results lead to panic because the person becomes increasingly preoccupied with his body. However, once the illness is diagnosed and properly treated, these panic-like symptoms disappear.

Some patients with a diagnosed physical problem become susceptible to panic. For instance, patients who have suffered from a heart attack often are cautious of any activity which might place stress on their heart. If they feel their heart increase its pumping action or if they notice a shortness of breath, their worried thoughts can turn to panic: "Oh, no, I've overstressed my heart. Is there any tingling in my arm like before? My chest is beginning to feel tight." Soon, these fearful thoughts themselves can produce such strong symptoms that the patient rushes to the hospital emergency room for evaluation. Similar problems arise in those diagnosed with angina, stroke, mitral valve prolapse, asthma, and hypertension.

Such fears during or after a physical illness can have significant repercussions. It has been reported that 95 percent of patients who have had a heart attack begin to suffer from anxiety. Of those discharged from a coronary care unit, 70 percent are given medication to cope with anxiety. In one study of post–heart attack patients who never returned to work, 80 percent remained at home because of psychological reasons. Similarly, a study of patients with chronic lung diseases such as emphysema and bronchitis found that 96 percent had disabling anxiety, 74 percent were seriously depressed, and 78 percent were overly preoccupied with their bodies. The fear of becoming breathless seemed to be at the root of most of their problems.

Dramatic, Frightening Events. Imagine that in the course of one week at the local swimming pool with your young child, you twice watch the lifeguards pull near-drowning children out of the pool. You might notice within yourself sensations of anxiety the next time you take your child swimming. This would be a normal response to such an event. Some people have a more extreme response to that same situation. Their minds become full of horrible fantasies about losing their children. They have strong physical reactions when they consider approaching a pool in the future. This is the type of panic that can arise after a person is involved in any traumatic or frightening event, such as the death of a loved one, a serious accident, the diagnosis of a serious illness, or an emergency such as a fire or a stuck elevator. When a person reacts with dread or panic in a harmless situation and begins to avoid all similar situations, this is defined as a phobia.

Current Demands and Fearfulness of the Future. Panic may result from fear of the future, regardless of what has actually happened in the past. For many people this occurs when they are faced with an increase in demands or responsibilities. They may believe that they are incapable of handling the pressures of their responsibilities, that they lack the strength, willpower, skill, intelligence, or emotional stability to cope with some future encounter or task. Their lack of confidence in their abilities is supported by their belief that their world is too demanding or their task too overwhelming. This fearful anticipation can be manifest physically through attacks of extreme anxiety or panic.

Psychological Disorders. Occasionally, severe anxiety is one part of a more complex psychological disorder. Panic attacks can occur in individuals suffering from such problems as depression, agoraphobia, post–traumatic stress syndrome, alcoholism, or obsessive-compulsive disorder.

This book is designed to assist anyone who is suffering from panic attacks, whether they are produced by a fearful response to physical illness, a psychological disorder, some frightening event of the past or future, or the building up of stress from the pressures of daily living.

If you are experiencing some of the symptoms described in this chapter, your first obligation is to go to your family physician for a complete medical examination. (Chapter 2 presents the major symptoms of panic which might be caused by physical illness; under each of these symptom categories you will learn about the types of illnesses involved and any other signs that might indicate a physical problem.) Your doctor will identify any physical causes of your problem, and will suggest a treatment approach or refer you to a specialist for further evaluation.

Once you understand the role—if any—of a physical illness in your symptoms, you can use this book to acquire understanding and skills necessary to overcome anxiety attacks at the moment they are taking place. You will discover how the mind may be triggering this emergency reaction in your body. I will describe and illustrate how altering what you think, what you believe, and what you do brings relief from the terror of panic. Your thoughts, beliefs, and actions will all play powerful roles as you learn to conquer panic.

I will offer relaxation exercises, special breathing patterns, and specific behavioral strategies to use in controlling panic. But change will require more than techniques. You may need to find a new way of looking at old problems. You may discover that your attitudes about life will change as you open your mind to new ideas. And most likely you will know more about the functions of your body, your mind, and your brain; many of my clients report that they began to feel relief as soon as they learned that there is a *reason* for these symptoms.

There are no simple, universal solutions to life's problems, no magic pills. Any real solution to a complex problem will include a broad and stable foundation from which to build greater strength. There is an old Japanese proverb that goes something like this: "You can give a person a fish and feed him for a day. You can teach a person to fish and feed him for a lifetime." This book will give you some specific tools to use during the moment of panic. However, to gain control of panic whenever it arises, you must also understand the complex interactions among your body and your mind, your beliefs and your behavior. In addition, you will find it much easier to conquer these attacks of panic with the support of others, whether they are professionals, friends, or family.

2

Physical Causes of Panic-like Symptoms

Everyone experiences the symptoms of anxiety from time to time, caused by any number of things—changes in our lifestyle, undue stress, tension. These symptoms often reflect a normal response to problems arising in our daily lives. In some cases, however, they may be the symptoms of a psychological or physical illness. The diagnosis of a serious medical problem is not always a simple process.

For instance, a man complains to his physician that this morning he noticed that his heart was racing, he had difficulty catching his breath, and he felt dizzy, with tingling around his mouth and in his hands. He is afraid he is going to die or have a heart attack. These symptoms could be an indication of cardiac arrhythmia, pulmonary embolism, a panic attack, or a hyperventilation episode.

Every day people are rushed into emergency rooms with the distinct symptoms of a heart attack: a crushing pain in the chest, shortness of breath, sweating, rapid heartbeat, and elevated blood pressure. After extensive monitoring and evaluation, for some of these patients the episode is diagnosed as an anxiety attack.

Because these symptoms are so difficult to assess, both patients and professionals can misdiagnose significant physical or emotional problems. Studies in recent years reveal that a number of physical disorders coexist in patients who have psychological disorders, and 5 to 40 percent of psychological illnesses may be caused by some physical problem. In the majority of these cases the physical diagnosis was missed.

Nowhere is this confusion more evident and diagnosis more difficult than with panic attacks. If the symptoms of panic are present, there are three possible diagnoses:

1. A physiological disorder is the sole cause of all the symptoms associated with panic. Treatment of the physical problem removes the symptoms.

2. A minor physical problem produces a few symptoms. The individual then becomes introspective and oversensitive to these physical sensations and uses them as a cue to become anxious. His heightened awareness and unnecessary concern will produce an increase in symptoms. If this continues, he can turn an insignificant physical problem into a major psychological distress.

3. There is no physical basis for the symptoms. Education about the problem, reassurance, counseling, or psychological treatment is needed.

This chapter identifies all the major physical problems that can produce panic-like symptoms. By no means should this chapter (or any other in this book) be used for self-diagnosis. Only a physician has the resources to determine whether any of these disorders is the cause of your discomfort and to advise you of your treatment options.

Through a comprehensive evaluation, your physician can determine which, if any, of these physical problems is associated with your symptoms. In most cases, curing the physical illness or adjusting medication will eliminate the symptoms. In some disorders, the symptoms remain as part of a minor disturbance, and you must learn to cope with them.

When a person suffers from anxiety attacks, one of the greatest obstacles to recovery can be the fear that these attacks are the indication of a major physical illness. And in some rare cases that is true. But predominantly, when a person continually worries about physical illness, that kind of worry intensifies or actually *produces* panic attacks. In other words, the less you worry, the healthier you will become. For that reason, I strongly recommend that you adopt the following guidelines if you are experiencing anxiety attacks:

1. Find a physician whom you *trust*.

2. Explain your symptoms and your worries to him or her.

3. Let your physician conduct any evaluations or examinations necessary to determine the cause of your symptoms.

4. If your primary physician recommends that another medical specialist evaluate your problem, be certain to follow that advice. Make sure that your primary physician receives a report from the specialist.

5. If a physical problem is diagnosed, follow your physician's treatment advice.

6. If no physical cause is found for your anxiety attacks, use the methods presented in this book to take control of your symptoms. If your symptoms persist, consider the possible psychological disorders that can produce panic (see Chapter 3). Ask your physician or some other source for a referral to a licensed mental health professional who specializes in these disorders.

The most destructive thing you can do when faced with panic attacks is to steadfastly believe that your symptoms mean that you have a serious physical illness, despite continued professional reassurance to the contrary. That is why it is essential that you work with a physician whom you can trust until a diagnosis has been reached. No matter how many consultations with other professionals are needed, allow *one* professional to have primary charge of your case and receive all reports. Do not continually jump from doctor to doctor. If you remain fearfully convinced that you have a physical ailment, even when there is a consensus to the contrary among the professionals who have evaluated you, then you can be certain of one thing: your fear is directly contributing to your panic episodes. In Part II you will learn how to control that fear and thereby take control of your symptoms.

Many physiological disorders produce panic-like symptoms; let us look at the symptoms themselves and their possible sources.

PHYSIOLOGICAL DISORDERS WITH PANIC-LIKE SYMPTOMS

Cardiovascular

Arrhythmia	Mitral stenosis
Tachycardia	Mitral valve prolapse
Coronary artery disease	Hypertension
Myocardial infarction (recovery from)	Postural orthostatic hypotension
Heart failure	Stroke

Cardiovascular (*cont.*)

Transient ischemic attack
Pulmonary embolism
Pulmonary edema

Respiratory

Bronchitis
Emphysema
Asthma
Collagen disease
Pulmonary fibrosis

Endocrine/hormonal

Hyperthyroidism
Hypoglycemia
Premenstrual syndrome
Pregnancy
Pheochromocytoma
Carcinoid tumors

Neurological/muscular

Temporal lobe epilepsy
Myasthenia gravis

Guillain-Barré syndrome
Compression neuropathies

Aural

Ménière's disease
Labyrinthitis
Benign positional vertigo
Otitis media
Mastoiditis

Hematic

Anemia

Drug-related

Antidepressant withdrawal
Sedative or tranquilizer withdrawal
Alcohol use or withdrawal
Stimulant use
Side effects of many medications

Miscellaneous

Head injury
Caffeinism

RAPID OR IRREGULAR HEART RATE

Three complaints are common among patients who seek a doctor's advice about their heart: "My heart feels like it's pounding violently in my chest," "My heart is racing," and "My heart feels like it skips a beat." Any irregularity in the heart's rhythm is called *arrhythmia*. If the heart beats more rapidly than normal, this arrhythmia is called *tachycardia*. An unpleasant sensation in the heart, whether rapid or slow, regular or irregular, and of which one is consciously aware, is called a *palpitation*.

Heart palpitation is typically an expected sensation when the force and rate of the heartbeat is considerably elevated. After strenuous exercise we are apt to notice the thumping of our heart against the chest wall. As we begin resting, that sensation may continue briefly until we recover from our exertion.

People who are prone to anxiety may have palpitations more frequently when they find themselves in psychologically uncomfortable situations. In fact, the great majority of complaints about the heart presented to physicians indicate a psychological rather than a physical problem. An anxious person may turn his attention to his physical symptoms instead of learning to cope with the situation causing the symptoms. After several episodes in which he experiences his heart "pounding" or "beating too fast," he fears it is a sign of heart disease or some other physical disorder.

A few minor disturbances of the heart rhythm may be noticed consciously. For instance, some people describe sensations such as a "flop" of the heart, the heart "skipping a beat" or "turning a somersault." This sudden forceful beat of the heart followed by a longer than usual pause is called an *extrasystole*. These premature contractions of the heart are usually of no serious significance and occur in many healthy individuals.

In fact, because of several research findings, we now know that arrhythmias of all kinds are common in normal, healthy individuals. In one recent study published in the *New England Journal of Medicine,* Dr. Harold Kennedy found that healthy subjects with frequent and complex irregular heartbeats seem to be at no more risk of physical problems than is the normal population. In general, researchers are finding that the majority of even the healthiest people have some kind of rhythm disturbance such as skipped beats, palpitations, or pounding in the chest.

Tachycardia, or rapid heartbeat, is the most common complaint associated with the heart and one of the typical reasons that patients seek medical attention. For many normal healthy individuals it is a daily occurrence in response to physical exercise or intense emotion. Any kind of excitement or trauma, even fatigue or exhaustion, can accelerate the action of the heart, especially in overly anxious individuals. Too many cigarettes, too much alcohol, and in particular, excessive amounts of caffeine can cause tachycardia on occasion. Infections such as pneumonia, as well as acute inflammatory diseases such as rheumatic fever, may also produce a rapid heartbeat.

Although most complaints of palpitation reflect a minor cardiac problem or a sign of anxiety, it is possible that some kind of *coronary artery disease* is involved. Such diseases are caused by a narrowing of the arteries to the heart. The predominant complaint of those suffering from coronary artery disease is more likely to be a pain or pressure in the center of the chest. It may also be felt elsewhere in the chest or in the neck, jaw, or left arm.

Recovery and rehabilitation after a heart attack can be a difficult psychological problem. Many people become afraid that too much activity or excitement might produce a second attack. It is no wonder, then, that *post–myocardial infarction patients* become fearfully preoccupied with the sensations of their heart. Many will return to their doctor's office or hospital emergency room with complaints of palpitations. Fourteen percent of cardiac patients later suffer from panic disorder, which is the worried anticipation of having an anxiety attack or heart attack (see Chapter 3). The ways in which panic complicates recovery from a myocardial infarction is described in Chapter 6.

Complaints of a "racing" heart can signal certain kinds of *organic heart disease* and *heart failure*. More often, however, the symptom of these ailments will be breathlessness (see the following section on difficulty breathing). *Infections,* such as pneumonia and rheumatic fever, may also produce a rapid heartbeat.

DIFFICULTY BREATHING

Complaints of difficult, labored, or uncomfortable breathing (called *dyspnea*) can be a signal of a serious emergency or of a mysterious medical puzzle. Immediate professional evaluation and treatment should be sought if this problem has never been diagnosed. Most often a person will describe it as "not being able to catch my breath," or "not getting enough air," even while appearing to breathe normally. Certainly the inability to breathe properly can be alarming, and many persons will immediately react with anxiety, fear, or panic.

Under normal circumstances, difficult breathing comes after any strenuous activity. If the degree of the problem seems out of proportion to the amount of exertion, concern is appropriate. Troubled breathing is sometimes experienced in pregnancy, since the uterus expands upward, reducing the possibility of a full inhalation. Severe obesity can also reduce the capacity of the lungs to inhale fully.

Most physical causes of dyspnea are associated with disorders of the respiratory and cardiac systems. Acute and chronic diseases of the lungs are the most common physical causes. Within the respiratory system, the problem usually stems from an obstruction of air flow (obstructive disorders) or the inability of the chest wall or lungs to expand freely (restrictive disorders). Each of these disorders makes the patient work harder to take each breath and decreases the amount of oxygen that can be absorbed with inhalation. The three major obstructive disorders are bronchitis, emphysema, and asthma. In these problems a second common symptom is "chest tightness" upon awakening, shortly after sitting up, or after physical exertion.

The primary symptom of *bronchitis* is a deep cough that brings up yellowish or grayish phlegm from the lungs. With *emphysema,* the shortness of breath gradually becomes worse over the years. The distinct symptoms of bronchitis and the gradual onset of emphysema will usually prevent these disorders from being misdiagnosed as severe anxiety or panic.

Those suffering from *asthma* will complain of difficult breathing, a painless tightness in the chest, and periodic attacks of wheezing. Severe cases can cause sweating, increased pulse rate, and severe anxiety. The primary trigger of an asthma attack is an allergy to such things as pollen, dust, or the dander of cats or dogs. Attacks can also be caused by infections, exercise, psychological stress, or for no apparent reason. Some asthma sufferers anxiously anticipate the next attack, since an acute attack of asthma can come suddenly "out of the blue" and last for an uncomfortably long time. This fear of an impending attack can actually increase the likelihood of the next attack and can extend the length of each attack. Asthma is a good example of a physical disorder that can increase in severity because of anxiety or panic.

The manner in which panic can contribute to difficulties in patients with chronic obstructive pulmonary disease is described in Chapter 6. Special attention is given to chronic bronchitis, emphysema, and asthma.

There are a number of restrictive disorders of the respiratory system which cause difficult breathing. Some produce a rigidity of the lungs *(pneumoconiosis, collagen disease, pulmonary fibrosis);* others involve the interactions of muscles and nerves *(myasthenia gravis, Guillain-Barré syndrome);* and still others prevent the lungs from expanding to full volume *(pleural effusion, pneumothorax, hemothorax).* A restrictive deficit in pulmonary function can also be caused by *pulmonary edema,* which usually stems from heart failure or occasionally from toxic inhalants.

Dyspnea may occur in any of the various diseases of the heart and lungs, but it is more prominent in those associated with lung congestion. For example, *mitral stenosis* occurs when a small valve between the left upper chamber and the left lower chamber of the heart (the left atrium and left ventricle) becomes abnormally narrow. As blood is forced through the heart, pressure backs up into the lungs and produces congestion. It is this congestion which causes breathlessness.

Pulmonary embolism occurs when a blood clot detaches from the wall of a deep vein, moves through the bloodstream, and becomes lodged in the pulmonary artery close to or within the lungs. This reduces the volume of fresh blood returning to the left side of the heart and may produce some degree of breathlessness.

Other possible cardiovascular problems which can lead to difficulty breathing include *left ventricular failure, aortic insufficiency, pericardial effusion,* and *cardiac arrhythmia.*

DIZZINESS AND VERTIGO

A broad range of complaints fall under the categories of dizziness and vertigo. Dizziness is a broad term which can include lightheadedness, faintness, wooziness, a "swimming" sensation in the head, a floating feeling, double vision, a feeling of "everything spinning in circles" or of whirling in space. Vertigo implies the more specific sensations of either the body or its surroundings turning or the head swaying or revolving. The physical causes of these two symptoms are numerous: problems of the middle and inner ear, dental problems, infections, head injuries, drug effects, and disorders of the cardiovascular, neurologic, and central nervous systems.

The ear is responsible for our sense of balance as well as hearing. The inner ear includes a structure called the *labyrinth,* which monitors the position and movement of the head and relays that information to the brain. When the action of the labyrinth is disrupted by injury or infection, vertigo may be experienced.

In *Ménière's disease,* a common disorder of the labyrinth in adults, excess fluid builds up and increases the pressure within the inner ear, causing vertigo and occasionally a ringing or other noise in the ear (called "tinnitus"). *Labyrinthitis* is an infection of this same region, often caused by a virus, sometimes associated with an upper respiratory infection. This can produce severe vertigo, occasionally with some nausea and vomiting during the first episode. The individual may also experience a rapid flickering of the eyes (called *nystagmus*). *Benign positional vertigo* is caused by calcium crystals floating within the labyrinth. In this condition, a shifting of position, such as rolling over in bed, can produce vertigo and nystagmus moments later, lasting no more than thirty seconds. Several kinds of *ear infections,* such as otitis media and mastoiditis, can cause vertigo but will additionally cause other distinguishing symptoms, such as drainage of fluid, fever, or redness of the eardrum. *Dental problems,* such as an abscessed tooth, malocclusion, or temporomandibular joint (TMJ) abnormalities, can also produce vertigo since the teeth are so closely aligned with the ear.

Any *head injury* can cause a cerebral concussion or a labyrinthine concussion, which may result in vertigo or a sense of feeling dazed, unsteady, or faint.

A number of cardiovascular and neurovascular diseases may affect a person's sense of balance. *Hypertension,* or high blood pressure, is often a symptomless disease. However, a swimming or woozy sensation may be the initial symptom that brings a patient into a physician's office for evaluation.

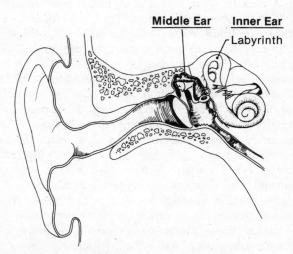

Figure 1. Cross-section of the ear.

If dizziness and lightheadedness are experienced upon rising in the morning or when changing from a lying to upright position, *postural orthostatic hypotension* may be the cause. This is a problem of low blood pressure, producing poor circulation of blood through the body. Typically, when a person shifts positions, the blood vessels reflexively contract to maintain proper blood pressure. In hypotension, this mechanism fails to respond appropriately. Since the needed pressure is not maintained, the flow of blood to the brain is temporarily reduced, causing dizziness and even fainting. Postural hypotension may be caused by diabetes, minor complications in pregnancy, or hardening of the arteries. It can also be a side effect of antidepressant medication, major tranquilizers, and even medications prescribed for high blood pressure (hypertension).

The most serious vascular ailment, requiring immediate medical attention, is *stroke*. A stroke occurs when the blood supply to the brain is significantly altered, causing damage to the brain itself. Three types of vascular problems produce stroke: cerebral *thrombosis,* cerebral *embolism,* and cerebral *hemorrhage*. In thrombosis, some portion of an artery that supplies blood to the brain has reduced in size. A large deposit of fatty tissue in that portion allows blood to clot, causing a partial or complete blockage of the blood flow to the brain. An embolism occurs when a bit of blood clot or arteriosclerotic plaque from the heart or the wall of a large artery breaks off and travels to an artery within the brain, where it lodges and causes the stroke. In a cerebral hemorrhage, the artery actually leaks or bursts, causing blood to seep into the surrounding brain tissues.

A *transient ischemic attack* is usually caused by a small blood clot or piece of fatty tissue (embolus). While passing through the blood vessels in the brain, it briefly becomes lodged and reduces the blood flow through that area. The symptoms resemble those of stroke, but are temporary and do not cause serious harm, since the clot or embolus eventually is disodged. Although emergency medical attention is not necessary, a transient ischemic attack does require medical evaluation and possibly measures to prevent recurrence.

Dizziness alone is insufficient cause to fear stroke. However, if you experience one or more of the following symptoms, you should consult your physician: numbness and/or tingling in any part of the body, blurred vision, confusion, difficulty speaking, loss of movement in the arms or legs. These symptoms can also indicate a panic attack rather than stroke. If you have experienced such a reaction several times and your doctor finds no sign of a physical disorder, you should consider the possibility that some psychological disturbance is precipitating these symptoms.

MULTIPLE SYMPTOMS

Many physical illnesses can produce nervousness in individuals who are not emotionally troubled. Certain other physical disorders—those discussed in this section—can cause a cluster of symptoms which resemble those of panic.

The predominant cardiovascular disorder which can produce multiple symptoms is *hypertension,* caused by a narrowing of the arteries. As your heart pumps blood through your body, it exerts a certain amount of pressure on the arterial walls. If these passageways become constricted for some reason, greater force is required to maintain a steady flow of blood. The entire circulatory system is then under strain, and hypertension is the diagnosis. This, as mentioned earlier, is often a symptomless disease, but symptoms which might be noticed include palpitations, nervousness, dizziness, and fatigue, as well as a general sense of ill health.

Mitral valve prolapse is a common condition found in approximately 5 to 15 percent of the adult population. In this disturbance a valve leaflet within the heart balloons into the left upper chamber (the left atrium) of the heart during contraction. About half of all people with mitral valve prolapse will complain of heart palpitation sometime in their life. Other possible symptoms are rapid heartbeat, shortness of breath, dizziness, and an increased awareness of the heart's action. This rather minor cardiac problem can be erroneously blamed as the sole cause of panic attacks. More often, though, it is the patient's fearful preoccupation with the action of his heart that produces panic. A more extensive discussion of mitral valve prolapse can be found in Chapter 6.

There is growing evidence that hormonal changes can have a dramatic effect on a person's physical disposition and mood. For instance, approximately 50 percent of women experiencing *menopause* report some major physical and/or emotional changes. Another 25 percent have uncomfortable, even distressing, symptoms which can include intense moments of palpitations, sweating, hot flashes, and anxiety. *Premenstrual syndrome* identifies a complex of symptoms, including panic, occurring in the days just prior to menstruation. Premenstrual syndrome is more fully discussed in Chapter 5.

A third hormonal problem is *hyperthyroidism,* the overactivity of the thyroid gland. This gland, located in the lower part of the neck, is controlled by a thyroid-stimulating hormone produced in the pituitary gland. In hyperthyroidism, the normal control mechanisms are disrupted and the thyroid continues to produce an excessive amount of its own hormone, thyroxine. This overproduction causes a general speeding up of all chemical reactions in the body. The person may feel shaky and anxious, with heart palpitations, breathlessness, and increased perspiration—feeling as though he or she is experiencing a constant anxiety attack. Additional symptoms make this disorder easier to diagnose: increased appetite, but with weight loss instead of gain; thinning hair; chronic tension and a sense of needing to keep moving despite fatigue and physical exhaustion. Instead of feeling cold, as the anxious person might, the person suffering from hyperthroidism will feel hot, and his skin will be warm to the touch.

Hyperthyroidism is treated in one of three ways: through antithyroid medication, by surgically removing either a lump in the thyroid or all of the thyroid, or, more commonly, by administration of a radioactive iodine fluid which controls the overactivity of the gland.

Hypoglycemia is the experience of several unpleasant symptoms while there is a lower than normal level of glucose in the bloodstream. This state of low blood sugar generally produces a feeling of being uncomfortable, with cold, clammy skin and profuse sweating. Other symptoms can be dizziness, weakness, trembling, tingling in the lips and hands, palpitations, and fainting. The condition is most often found in diabetics who take insulin. However, many individuals erroneously believe that hypoglycemia is the cause of their panic symptoms and therefore fail to explore other possible diagnoses. For further information on hypoglycemia and panic, see Chapter 5.

The adrenal glands are located on top of each kidney. The adrenal medulla produces two hormones which play an important role in controlling your heart rate and blood pressure: epinephrine (adrenalin) and norepinephrine (noradrenalin). Very rarely a growth, or tumor, develops within or near an adrenal gland and causes an increase in the production of these hormones. Tachycardia, sweating, anxiety, faintness, and pallor—all resembling panic—can occur as a result of slight exercise, exposure to cold temperatures, or minor emotional upset. Typically the blood pressure will become extremely high, and the patient may have the frightening feeling of being about to die. This extremely rare disorder, called *pheochromocytoma,* is cured by surgically removing the tumor.

Anemia is the abnormal decrease of either hemoglobin or red blood cells. Red blood cells carry oxygen from the lungs to all parts of the body. Within each of these blood cells is the protein hemoglobin, which combines with the oxygen while in the lungs and then releases it into the tissues as the blood circulates through the body. Characteristic symptoms of anemia are lightheadedness, rapid heartbeat, difficulty breathing, and faintness. The anemic person may experience palpitations, because the heart is attempting to compensate for the lower levels of oxygen by pumping blood faster than normal. The diagnosis of *iron deficiency anemia* indicates that lower than normal levels of iron in the body limit the production of hemoglobin. *Folic acid anemia* and B_{12} *anemia* indicate that the body has insufficient amounts of these two essential vitamins, which are required for the production of healthy red blood cells. The inherited disease *sickle cell anemia* is found almost exclusively among people of African descent. In this condition, the red blood cells contain an abnormal hemoglobin, called hemoglobin S. This leads to deformation of the shape of each cell so that the smooth flow of blood into smaller vessels is impeded. Premature destruction of red blood cells, and anemia, result. All forms of anemia should be diagnosed and treated by a physician.

Carcinoid tumors are rare; they can form within the digestive tract and elsewhere in the body. Symptoms can include flushing of the face and neck and are often triggered by exertion, intense emotion, or by food or alcohol intake. Other symptoms are tachycardia, hypotension (low blood pressure), and difficulty breathing (caused by bronchoconstriction).

Compression neuropathies, such as carpal tunnel syndrome, are disorders caused by some form of compression to localized nerves. Symptoms may include dysesthesia (a tingling or "pins and needles" feeling), similar to that which occurs during hyperventilation.

The symptoms of *temporal lobe epilepsy* (TLE) are highly variable, but in some cases they are experienced only as a sudden attack of immense fear or panic. In 60 percent of the cases, fear is the primary emotion. The patient may also have a feeling of unreality, as though he is far away from his surroundings, or may feel that his body is strange or dreamlike. Highly charged emotional responses such as these can lead to a misdiagnosis of the problem as one which is psychologically based. A distinguishing feature of TLE can be the presence of an aura, a sudden experience which often takes the form of a strange aroma or taste at the moment of fear.

Caffeinism refers to the uncomfortable side effects that can occur with high intake of caffeine from coffee, tea, cola drinks, cocoa, and over-the-counter medications such as Excedrin and Anacin. Symptoms include anxiety, irritability, agitation, increased respiration, palpitations, rapid heartbeat, and irregular heart rhythm. These side effects can occur with daily consumption over 250 mg to 500 milligrams. Between 20 and 30 percent of Americans consume more than 500 mg of caffeine a day (five cups of drip coffee contain a total of over 500 mg). Some panic-prone persons are highly sensitive to caffeine. If you experience any of these symptoms, you may wish to review your intake of all forms of caffeine.

Amphetamines, whether taken for treatment of depression, for weight control, or illicitly for recreation, can cause severe anxiety to the point of panic. This extreme reaction is also possible with illicit drugs such as *cocaine, phencyclidine* (PCP), and the *hallucinogens* (LSD, mescaline).

Alcohol withdrawal can produce nervousness, rapid heartbeat, confusion, high blood pressure, and panic as well as other symptoms. Too rapid *withdrawal from sedatives or barbiturates,* such as benzodiazepines (Valium, Librium, etc.), can cause anxiety, rapid heartbeat, high blood pressure, and panic, especially after long-term use.

SIDE EFFECTS OF MEDICATIONS

Sometimes a medication may cause unwanted side effects in addition to its needed effects. If these occur, you should check with your doctor. In addition to other possible side effects, each of the medications listed below may produce panic-like symptoms. (All medications are listed by their generic names.)

Atropine is a medication used to dilate the pupil of the eye. It can produce an unusually fast heartbeat. (A number of drugs are atropine-like in their effects. These are usually called anticholinergic medications.)

Digitalis is a medication used to improve the strength and efficiency of the heart, or to control the rate of the heartbeat. It can produce an unusually slow or uneven pulse.

Prednisone is the most commonly used of the corticosteroids and is prescribed to relieve inflammation. Its side effects can include irregular heartbeat, nervousness, muscle weakness, and mood swings. Other corticosteroid medications may cause similar problems.

Isoniazid, an anti-infection medication, may produce rapid heartbeat and lightheadedness.

Cycloserine is an antibiotic medication. Side effects may include anxiety, irritability, confusion, dizziness and restlessness.

Ephedrine is a medication used for lung problems. Side effects can be nervousness, restlessness, dizziness, difficulty breathing, palpitations, and rapid heartbeat.

Epinephrine is a medication used in treatment of the eyes, the lungs, and allergies. Side effects can include faintness, trembling, rapid heartbeat, palpitations, nervousness, and difficulty breathing.

Reserpine is used to treat high blood pressure and certain emotional conditions, as well as a few other problems. Side effects may include dizziness, faintness, anxiety, and palpitations. Some individuals have even developed phobic reactions while taking reserpine.

Antidyskinetics are used in the treatment of Parkinson's disease. Side effects may include dizziness, irregular heartbeat, and anxiety.

Synthetic *thyroid hormones* are used for treating hypothyroidism. Excessive levels of these hormones can cause rapid heartbeat, palpitations, shortness of breath, nervousness, unusual sweating, and anxiety.

Nitrates are used to improve the blood flow to the heart and to relieve angina attacks. Possible side effects are dizziness, lightheadedness, and rapid heartbeat.

Monoamine oxidase (MAO) inhibitors belong within the antidepressant family. In addition to reducing symptoms of depression, they are used in the treatment of panic attacks (see Chapter 19). Possible side effects are dizziness or lightheadedness, especially when getting up from a lying or sitting position, and rapid or pounding heartbeat.

Heterocyclic antidepressants are used to treat depression and, more recently, panic attacks (see Chapter 19 regarding the use of tricyclic antidepressants within the treatment of panic). Possible side effects are dizziness and irregular or rapid heartbeat.

3

Panic Within Psychological Disorders

When the symptoms of panic persist, most sufferers become increasingly alarmed. Even when they can identify what they believe to be the immediate cause of these intense moments of anxiety, they are left with a bewildering array of questions: "Why me? Why now? What does it mean? How serious is it? How do I stop it?"

Only a small minority of panic symptoms persist because of a physical problem. Most difficulties, even if associated with a physical disorder, are sustained through a pattern of thinking which is reinforced by past life experiences (or the lack of them).

For instance, cardiac patients have suffered a physical trauma associated with the heart. A recent study found that up to 14 percent of these patients can also be diagnosed as having the psychological problem called panic disorder. Their episodes of severe anxiety start after their heart trouble but are not caused by it. If the physical trauma was actually the cause, then more people who have heart problems would also suffer from panic attacks. Actually, the problem stems from the way each cardiac patient reacts to his problem. The more fearful he becomes about the prospect of another physical trauma to the heart, the greater his chances of suffering from extreme anxiety or panic.

A number of different patterns have been identified over the years which help us categorize types of panic. Not everyone is so troubled by symptoms that they suffer from one of these psychological disorders. Some people simply pass through a difficult time with symptoms of anxiety, then continue on their way. However, if the symptoms remain over time, they will usually fall within one of six different categories of psychological problems: panic disorder, agoraphobia, generalized anxiety disorder, phobias, obsessive-compulsive disorder, and post–traumatic stress disorder.

PANIC DISORDER

Panic disorder is the only psychological problem whose predominant feature is recurring panic (or anxiety) attacks. Although the first panic attack may take place in a distinct situation, further episodes are unpredictable as to time or place.

The physical symptoms are the same as those described in Chapter 1. One or more of these can be present in a severe form during an actual panic attack or in a milder form at other times: dry mouth; sweating; acute tension in the stomach, back of neck, or shoulders; increased heart rate; dizziness or lightheadedness, feeling faint; increased respiration; trembling hands, legs, or voice; weak, numb, or cold extremities; shortness of breath; body fatigue; difficulty swallowing, a lump in the throat; irritability; blurred vision; inability to concentrate; and confusion.

After a number of panic episodes, the individual can become afraid of being a helpless victim of panic. He or she may hesitate to be alone, to venture far from home, or to be in public places. Even when not experiencing an anxiety attack, the person with panic disorder often becomes increasingly nervous and apprehensive. He or she attempts to remain physically and psychologically tense in preparation for the next attack.

Although the first panic attack may seem to appear "out of the blue," it typically comes during an extended period of stress. This stress is not caused by a few days of tension, but extends over several months. Life transitions, such as moving, job change, marriage, or the birth of a child, often account for much of the psychological pressure.

For some individuals, learning to manage this stressful period or to reduce the pressures will eliminate the panic episodes. For others, it is as though the stress of the life transition or problem situation uncovered a psychological vulnerability. If the panic-prone individual is given increased responsibilities, for instance, through a job promotion or through the birth of a first child, he may begin to doubt his ability to meet the new demands, the expectation of others, and the increased energy required for these responsibilities. Instead of focusing on mastering the task, he becomes more concerned with the possibility of failure. This attention to the threat of failure continually undermines his confidence. Through a series of steps, which will be described in Part II of this book, he translates these fears into panic.

AGORAPHOBIA

Each person diagnosed with agoraphobia, literally "fear of the marketplace," has a unique combination of symptoms. But common to all agoraphobics is a marked fear or avoidance either of being alone or of being in certain public places. It is a response strong enough to significantly limit the individual's normal activities.

For the person who experiences panic attacks, the distinction between agoraphobia and panic disorder is based on the degree of avoidance. In panic disorder, the person remains relatively active, although he may avoid a few uncomfortable situations. If the panic-prone person begins to significantly restrict his normal activities because of his fearful thoughts, agoraphobia is the more appropriate diagnosis.

For some, agoraphobia develops from panic disorder. Repeated panic attacks produce "anticipatory anxiety," a state of physical and emotional tension in anticipation of the next attack. The person then begins to avoid any circumstances which seem associated with past panic attacks, becoming more and more limited in his range of activities.

The fearful thoughts that plague the agoraphobic often center around *loss of control*. The person may fear the development of uncomfortable physical symptoms familiar from past experiences (such as dizziness or rapid heartbeat). He may then worry that these symptoms could become even worse than they were in the past (fainting or heart attack), and/or that he will become trapped or confined in some physical location or social situation (such as a restaurant or party). In the first two situations, the person senses that his body is out of control. In the third, he feels unable to readily control his surroundings.

The following list shows the types of surroundings that can provoke these fears.

Fear of the Surroundings

Public Places or Enclosed Spaces
Streets
Stores
Restaurants
Theaters
Churches

Travel
On trains, buses, planes, subways,
  cars
Over bridges, through tunnels
Being far away from home
Traffic

Open Spaces
Parks
Fields
Wide streets

**Confinement or Restriction of
  Movement**
Barber's, hairdresser's, or
  dentist's chair
Lines in a store
Waiting for appointments
Prolonged conversations in person
  or on the phone
Crowds

Remaining at Home Alone

Conflictual Situations
Arguments, interpersonal
  conflicts, expression of anger

The agoraphobic may avoid one or many of these situations as a way to feel safe. The need to avoid is so strong that some agoraphobics will quit their jobs, stop driving or taking public transportation, stop shopping or eating in restaurants, or, in the worst cases, never venture outside their home for years.

Listed below are the types of fearful thoughts associated with the dreaded situations. These are irrational, unproductive, and anxiety-producing thoughts which last anywhere from a few seconds to more than an hour. At the same time, they are the primary cause of agoraphobic behavior. These thoughts serve to perpetuate the agoraphobic's belief: "If I avoid these situations, I'll be safe."

Fearful Thoughts

Fainting or collapsing in public
Developing severe physical
  symptoms
Losing control: becoming
  confused

Having a heart attack or other
  physical illness
Being unable to get home or to
  another "safe" place
Being trapped or confined

Being unable to cope

Becoming mentally ill

Dying

Being unable to breathe

Causing a scene

Some agoraphobics experience no symptoms of panic. These individuals continue to be controlled by their fearful thoughts, but they have restricted their lifestyle, through avoidance, to such a degree that they no longer become uncomfortable.

When agoraphobics retreat in order to protect themselves, they often have to sacrifice friendships, family responsibilities, and/or career. Their loss of relationships, affections, and accomplishments compounds the problem. It leads to low self-esteem, isolation, loneliness, and depression. In addition, the agoraphobic may become dependent on alcohol or drugs in an unsuccessful attempt to cope. A further discussion of this complex disorder is found in Chapter 4; the problem of alcoholism is presented in Chapter 5. Part II addresses the specific ways in which agoraphobics can take control of their fears and their anxiety attacks.

GENERALIZED ANXIETY DISORDER

With generalized anxiety disorder, panic is not the predominant feature. However, many of the panic symptoms are present to a lesser degree. Instead of brief moments of intense anxiety, the person feels symptoms throughout most of the day.

Although the specific manifestations of anxiety vary for each person, this chronic state of tension can affect six major systems of the body.

In the cardiovascular system, anxiety increases blood pressure, which causes tachycardia (rapid heartbeat), constriction of the blood vessels in the arms and legs, and dilation of the vessels surrounding the skeletal muscles. These changes produce symptoms of palpitations (an awareness of the heart rate), headaches, and cold fingers.

In the gastrointestinal system, anxiety leads to reduced salivary secretions, spasms within the esophagus (the hollow muscular tube leading from the nose and mouth to the stomach), and alterations in the stomach, the intestines, and the anal sphincter. These systemic changes result in symptoms of dry mouth, difficulty swallowing, "butterflies in the stomach," the gurgling sounds of gas in the intestines, and mucous colitis (an inflammation of the colon, causing spasms, diarrhea and/or constipation, and cramp-like pains in the upper stomach).

In the respiratory system, anxiety leads to hyperventilation, or overbreathing, which reduces the carbon dioxide in the blood, with symptoms of "air hunger," deep sighs, and pins-and-needles sensations.

In the genitourinary system, the anxious person may experience the need for frequent urination. Men may have difficulty maintaining an erection during intercourse; women may have difficulty becoming sexually aroused or achieving orgasm.

In the musculoskeletal system, the muscles become tense. Involuntary trembling of the body, tension headaches, and other aches and pains may develop.

Through changes in the central nervous system, the anxious person is generally more apprehensive, aroused, and vigilant, feeling "on edge," impatient, or irritable. He may complain of poor concentration, insomnia, and fatigue.

As you can see, there is often a fine line between the diagnosis of panic disorder or agoraphobia and that of generalized anxiety disorder. Three features distinguish them. First, the symptoms themselves: if an individual is chronically anxious (as he would be with generalized anxiety disorder) and also experiences episodes of panic, then panic disorder or agoraphobia will be the more likely diagnosis.

The second distinction is the kind of fearful thoughts associated with the problem. Most people with generalized anxiety disorder will worry about the kinds of interactions they will have with others: "Will I fail in this work setting?" "Are they going to accept me?" "I'm afraid he's going to leave me." "What if they discover how little I know?" "I'll never perform up to their expectations."

With panic disorder and agoraphobia, the imagined response of others is secondary to the fear of personal catastrophe or loss of control, and the person's internal statements and questions will reflect this apprehension: "What if I faint/become hysterical/have a heart attack/cause a scene . . . and people see me?" The panic-prone person focuses more on his inability to be in 100 percent control of all his physical and mental capacities. The anxious person focuses more on his inability to cope with the expectations and responses of those around him.

The third difference has to do with the person's response to his fears. The anxious person thinks about withdrawing from situations which increase his anxiety and may procrastinate on performance tasks. The person with panic disorder or agoraphobia, on the other hand, is very quick to use avoidance as a way to diminish discomfort. In a matter of days he will begin to identify the situations that are associated with the symptoms and determine how he can steer clear of them. With panic, avoidance is immediately viewed as the single best solution to the problem.

SOCIAL PHOBIAS

A social phobia is an excessive, unreasonable fear that some particular action will be noticed by others in public. The person with a social phobia becomes anxious even at the thought of this activity, for fear that he will be humiliated or embarrassed. Avoidance is his primary defense, which he feels compelled to use.

The types of social phobias range from those that seem to be an exaggeration of common fears to those that seem bizarre to others. The most prevalent are the fears of speaking or performing in public. Most people understand and have experienced the normal anxiety associated with public speaking: trembling hands and legs, increased perspiration, "butterflies," worries about performing poorly. The social phobic not only tends to panic if he is forced to approach such a situation but will do all in his power to avoid it.

Any situation in which others may observe the person's behavior can become a phobic preoccupation: urinating in a public bathroom; signing one's name while being watched; being watched while eating. One client became anxious in almost every public situation because she feared people would begin watching her eyes. This belief was so real and so overwhelming that she was in a constant state of anxiety when not in her own home.

Anxiety, potential for panic, and avoidance behavior link the social phobias with panic disorder and agoraphobia. The distinguishing feature is, again, what the person fears. The social phobic becomes extremely anxious about people's reaction to a seemingly normal behavior such as eating lunch or walking on the beach. The agoraphobic has an irrational fear that his body will not perform normally.

The person with generalized anxiety disorder is usually in the midst of some change in his life which diminishes his self-confidence. Social phobics, on the other hand, may have never mastered some basic social skills. They often report being shy and isolated as children and adolescents, long before this problem began. The phobia might be viewed as an extreme manifestation of a long-standing sensitivity to the opinions of others.

SPECIFIC PHOBIAS

Most people have met someone with a significant fear of a particular object or situation, such as closed spaces (claustrophobia), heights (acrophobia), water (aquaphobia), snakes (ophidiphobia), or lightning (astraphobia). When a person has a persistent, irrational fear of an object or situation and a strong urge to avoid that object or situation, he is sometimes said to have a "simple phobia"—an inappropriately intense reaction triggered by a *single* stimulus. The most prevalent phobias are of specific animals and insects, of the natural elements, such as storms or water, of heights and of closed-in spaces.

The person with a specific phobia may react with mild anxiety or even with panic when confronted with the prospect of facing the fearful situation. However, his fear is not of his symptoms (as in panic disorder or agoraphobia) but of the situation itself, which he believes to be a dangerous one.

Some may fear that they will lose their senses and do something foolish. The person with a height phobia, for instance, might fear that he will forget what he is doing and accidentally leap off the cliff on which he is standing. Others with phobias fear that something will go wrong with their circumstances. The individual with a flying phobia might vividly imagine the tail falling off the plane, or the pilot losing consciousness with no one to take over, or the oxygen running out in mid-flight.

Such fears defy rational thinking. Most phobics know that they are being excessive and unreasonable in their thoughts, but this knowledge is of no use to them. The fearful thoughts come automatically in spite of rational thought and thus the phobic may believe his only recourse is to avoid the problematic area.

Specific phobias may develop rapidly, such as after a traumatic event, or gradually over the years, as in childhood learning and the examples set by parents and others. Usually we find that the phobic has not gained enough of the knowledge and experience necessary to face new, frightening life experiences, whether real or imaginary. Instead of gaining some perspective during fearful times, the phobic becomes a passive victim to his fear. The only action he takes is to back away.

Diagnosing the true fear is an essential part of the cure. For instance, the person with a flying phobia may be afraid of heights or, instead, might actually be afraid of being contained.

When a person has several specific phobias, the relationship between them may not seem evident at first. One agoraphobic client also developed an intense fear of knives and of children. While discussing the problem during a treatment session, she reported that one day several months earlier she had found her seven-year-old son threatening his sister with a kitchen knife. After admonishing her son, she found herself dwelling on the many dangers of knives. Within a day, she began to question her own ability to control a knife. She then developed a spontaneous mental image of herself hurting a child with a knife. In a brief few days she began avoiding knives as well as becoming anxious whenever she looked at young children. The internal belief which was driving her fear was: "I don't have enough self-control [to handle knives/be with children]."

This case illustrates another pattern present in some phobias. The phobia can develop from a current internal conflict and/or a real life fear. With this client, the real life fear was of her young son hurting someone by poor self-control with a knife. But this legitimate fear was coupled with her own internal conflict. She was considering having a third child. At the same time, her marriage was unstable. Her husband was consumed with his business, and she felt unsupported and unloved. As we talked I realized that she was not consciously aware of the degree of her conflict.

Notice, though, how her phobia was, in a sense, helping her solve a problem while at the same time causing her distress. By unconsciously developing these fearful thoughts about her personal inability to control her aggression, she could now say, "Obviously I'm not capable enough to have another child." This irrational fear resolves her internal conflict. It also prevents her from confronting the pain in her marriage.

For instance, if she maintained her desire to have a third child, she might be inclined to rquest that her husband offer her more emotional support. What if he refused? What if he decided their marriage was no longer "workable" for him and suggested that they get divorced? Her fear of abandonment probably played a major role in the development of her new phobia. By increasing her self-doubt, she no longer had the ego strength to risk making demands on her husband. Instead, she became more dependent and less likely to speak up for her needs.

Phobias, therefore, are often more complex than they at first seem. And their "irrational" nature may actually be based on an attempt to solve a real life problem. After a period of time the irrational fear takes on a life of its own, just like a habit, regardless of its initial unconscious purpose.

OBSESSIVE-COMPULSIVE DISORDER

Obsessions are repetitive, unproductive thoughts which almost all of us have experienced from time to time. We can be driving down the road, ten minutes from home, heading for a week's vacation. Suddenly the thought enters our mind, "Did I unplug the iron after I finished with that shirt?" And then we think, "I must have . . . but I don't know, I was rushing around so at the last minute. Did I reach down and pull the cord out of the socket? I can't remember. Was the iron light still on as I walked out the door? No, it was off. Was it? I can't leave it on all week, the house will burn down. This is ridiculous!" Eventually we either turn around and head home to check as the only way to feel relieved, or we convince ourselves that we did indeed take care of the task.

This is an example of what can take place inside the mind of any of us when worrying about a particular problem. But in the mind of the person with obsessive-compulsive disorder, this pattern of thought is exaggerated and persistent. The second form of the problem is compulsions: repetitive, unproductive behaviors which are ritualistically followed. As with obsessive thoughts, there are a few compulsive behaviors in which the average person might engage. As children, we played with supersititions, such as never stepping on a sidewalk crack or turning away when a black cat crossed our path. Some of these persist as we become adults: many of us still never walk under a ladder.

Obsessive-compulsive disorder, however, is much more serious.

The obsessive person is driven by persistent negative thoughts which are involuntary, uncontrollable, and consuming. He is filled with self-doubt, ambivalence, indecision, and impulses. These thoughts are a defense against making any mistake. His internal belief often is, "If I keep worrying, I will prevent anything tragic from happening." At the same time, the person knows that these thoughts are irrational and tries to resist them. But the more he resists, the stronger they become.

The obsessive thoughts which are most common are those of violence (poisoning one's spouse or stabbing a child), committing an immoral act, doubting whether one has performed some action (turning off the kitchen stove), and contamination (catching germs by picking up objects or touching someone).

Compulsions also seem to be motivated by a need to relieve anxiety through rules or required rituals. Common compulsions are hand-washing, as often as ten times an hour throughout the day, ritualistic touching of specific objects, and checking behavior. Anorexics, for example, often have rituals involving how they eat, such as not allowing food on the fork to touch their lips. One compulsive client felt compelled to check if she had left the stove on each time she left her house for an errand. She would lock the front door as she was leaving, then feel a strong urge to return to the kitchen and touch each burner control knob as she checked it. As soon as she was back outside she would again feel a strong compulsion to repeat the process. After twelve or so times, she usually felt free enough to leave the house. Sometimes, however, this fear forced her to cancel her plans.

Panic comes whenever the person attempts to stop the ritual. The tension and anxiety build to such an intense degree that he surrenders once again to the thoughts or behaviors. Unlike an alcoholic, who feels compelled to drink but also enjoys the drinking experience, the obsessive-compulsive person achieves relief through the ritual, but no pleasure.

Obsessions can sometimes intrude into the life of the agoraphobic, as was exemplified earlier in this chapter by the woman who feared she would stab a child with a knife. Such obsessions can lead to a phobic avoidance of the objects. You might think of it as a two-stage defense system. The obsessions are used as a way to control some problem ("As long as I keep worrying, I won't make a mistake"). If the individual begins to lose faith that those worries are enough to stop the feared response, then another "solution" must be found, and phobias provide the answer: "If my thinking won't keep me safe, then the sure way to prevent a mistake is to avoid the situation altogether."

POST-TRAUMATIC STRESS DISORDER

Post-traumatic stress disorder (PTSD) identifies a specific emotional distress which can follow a major psychologically traumatic event. This uncommon event would typically produce fear and anxiety in anyone who experienced it. Examples are rape or assault, a natural disaster, being part of or observing a serious accident, major surgery, and wartime combat duty. Symptoms may begin immediately or not surface for six months, a year, or even longer.

Severe anxiety and panic may be only two of several symptoms. The person will have recurring images of the traumatic event, often with the same degree of anxiety as during the event itself. Or he will suddenly feel as though the event is occurring in the present. Recurring nightmares of the trauma are dramatic and disturbing. Sleep can be disturbed by dreams, anxiety, or depression. The person may remain tense and anxious throughout the day, and may startle easily.

As they become more physically involved with these experiences, the traumatized individuals begin to withdraw from the world, show less emotion, and become disinterested in people and activities which were once important. They avoid any situations which might stimulate memories of the traumatic event. Guilt, depression, and sudden outbursts of aggressive behavior may also surface. Drug and alcohol abuse develop in some as they attempt to manage these responses.

The largest subgroup to experience this problem is the combat veteran. And in the United States, the Vietnam War has produced the largest percentage of PTSD cases. In fact, it was after studies of Vietnam veterans were added to studies of civilian post-trauma sufferers that the American Psychiatric Association created, in 1980, the diagnostic category: post-traumatic stress disorder (acute, chronic, and/or delayed).

The major task in overcoming this problem is to incorporate the traumatic event into one's sense of the world and understanding of one's personal life. It is possible that the nightmares and spontaneous reliving of the trauma are unconscious attempts to heal the psychic wounds.

The singular experience of Vietnam combat veterans illustrates how traumatic changes can be difficult for the mind to incorporate and how this "working through" process is essential. The Vietnam War was like no other in American history. The average age of the combat soldier was nineteen, not twenty-six as in World War II. Soldiers were often flown into duty as individuals, not as teams. Once there, nothing seemed straightforward. Arriving soldiers were not readily accepted by those already fighting. The enemy was not easily identifiable or necessarily in uniform; women and children could kill you in the streets. And women and children civilians were therefore sometimes killed by U.S. soldiers. There was no "front line," and the same territory had to be won over and over again. Leadership was young and inexperienced. The object was to kill as many people as possible and survive.

The coming home process of the Vietnam soldier failed to account for the mind's need to assimilate this experience in a slow-paced manner. After twelve to thirteen months of combat duty, soldiers were flown back to the States in a matter of hours and, again, as isolated individuals rather than as teams. This is in stark contrast to the weeks or sometimes months that World War II veterans spent on ships returning to the U.S., while sharing time with other soldiers close to them. In forty-eight hours the Vietnam combat soldier could go from a unit assault in which he killed four North Vietnamese soldiers with an M-16 to sitting on the front steps of his house in the U.S. While in Southeast Asia, soldiers would dream of that day. But when it arrived they weren't prepared. The American people, for the first time in its history, turned against its war and the returning soldiers. Ticker-tape parades were replaced by anti-war marches. A soldier in uniform on the streets of our country might be spat on. The heroes were now the villains.

It is no wonder that some Vietnam veterans have continued to experience chronic post–traumatic stress disorder, since the primary cause of the disorder is an inability to assimilate the experience into current life. Time and the support and understanding of other people are needed for one to assimilate a trauma of this significance. The person with post–traumatic stress disorder must have an opportunity to talk about the traumatic experience and, eventually, to feel the emotions associated with it. As he works through these feelings, he can begin to connect the trauma with the rest of his life. Part of that

4

Agoraphobia and the Panic-Prone Personality

The nature of agoraphobia is so complex that it must be viewed as different from all other phobias. It is not the moment of panic that distinguishes agoraphobia, nor is it simply that a broader group of fears is involved. The physiological reactions of a claustrophobic who is facing an open elevator can be as severe as those of an agoraphobic, and the claustrophobic may avoid just as many situations for fear of being trapped.

The primary difference is in the beliefs that sustain the fear within the individual. These beliefs are established by the past life experiences of each agoraphobic and are supported by current relationships and by memories of the past.

If you are agoraphobic, you must do more than learn to master the moment of panic. You will need to take every opportunity to learn more about yourself, your relationship with the significant people in your current life, and your childhood development. The issues in agoraphobia include not only how you feel about frightening situations, but what you think about yourself, how you compare yourself with others, how you treat others, and how you let them treat you.

Learning how to handle your thoughts and your physical sensations as you approach a feared situation is an essential skill, just as it is for other people who are experiencing panic from any other source. At the same time, you must learn about your self-perception and any limitations you feel as a human being. You will need all the strength you can muster to conquer this problem. In this chapter I will show you how self-perception, current relationships, and past relationships or events can set the stage for panic and weaken your stand against fear. In Chapter 3 you read that the major fear of the agoraphobic is loss of control. As you read this chapter, keep that in mind. I will be illustrating a number of ways that people learn to feel out of control, not only in the panic-provoking situation but in their entire lives. The loss of control during panic is only one reflection of the belief system within each agoraphobic's personality.

Since approximately 85 percent of agoraphobics are women, I will focus primarily on the difficulties of the female agoraphobic and I will use the female pronoun in this chapter.

Researchers have not yet established why agoraphobia is found so disproportionately in women. In the years to come we will most likely find that there are a number of influencing factors. Here are several hypotheses that have been suggested but have not been validated by scientific method:

1. Traditionally, parents and our culture have focused little attention on preparing young women to manage independently after leaving their parents' home. The fairy tale fantasies of the delicate female protected by the dominant, caring male can be shattered by the actual pressures of marriage and parenthood. If they believe that their skills are no match for the tasks they face, these women can become vulnerable to anxiety, self-doubt, and overdependence.

2. Agoraphobia develops within the person who succumbs to the fear of panic by avoiding situations. The stereotypical image of the macho male may pressure men to tolerate anxious symptoms and face fearful situations. By continually confronting anxiety you desensitize yourself to those symptoms. In this way, some men learn coping mechanisms that prevent anxieties from building into panic.

3. In this same vein, those who work at home are at a disadvantage compared with those who must travel to work each day in order to maintain their jobs. For instance, consider a married couple with a new infant, the husband with a full-time job and the wife as the primary caretaker. If the husband begins to feel panicky as he gets up in the morning, he also feels a strong, competing pressure to tolerate his symptoms and make it to work on time. He feels the responsibility to provide his family with that weekly paycheck; he cannot easily avoid facing work. If the wife begins to feel anxious about going grocery shopping this morning, her schedule often permits her to postpone the trip until tomorrow. If driving to the park with her child might be

anxiety-provoking, they can play at home today. So the spouse with a flexible schedule runs the greater risk of using avoidance to control panic instead of using the more successful methods of direct confrontation. Soon, the need to avoid can become predominant, and agoraphobia develops.

4. There are biological differences that may play a role in increasing a woman's susceptibility to panic. Changes in the endocrine system are considered the strongest influencing factors. For instance, a large number of agoraphobic women develop their first symptoms after the birth of a child. This is the same period of time in which there are great changes in hormonal levels. Other agoraphobic women report increased anxiety symptoms or increased frequency of panic during their premenstrual week. This is the same time in which estrogen and progesterone levels temporarily drop. These hormonal factors are also considered influential in premenstrual syndrome, discussed in Chapter 5.

Although these biological factors may prove to be significant to agoraphobia, psychological influences may play an equally important role during postpartum or premenstrual times. For example, agoraphobia usually develops during a prolonged period of stress. Every mother knows of the surprisingly large number of adjustments that are faced physically, psychologically, interpersonally, and economically as a new baby enters your life. Stress stems from the degree of change in one's life regardless of whether that change is viewed as positive or negative. The stress of new parenthood can take its toll. Regarding premenstrual influences, if a woman regularly experiences physical and emotional discomfort during a certain week each month, then she will inevitably begin to anticipate that week. And if she hasn't found any successful way to manage her symptoms, she will most likely anticipate with anxiety. In other words, the actual discomfort caused by biological factors is intensified by fearful expectation. This soon leads to a conditioned response: the woman unconsciously begins to brace in preparation for discomfort. Such bracing increases tension levels and makes her more susceptible to panic.

Another biological factor is the difference between males and females in the levels of testosterone. This hormone, which is found in much higher levels in men, is linked with dominance behavior. Thus men may be somewhat less likely to experience fear and might confront fearful situations more aggressively than women.

5. It is possible that the disproportionate ratio of female to male agoraphobics reflects an underestimating of male agoraphobia. One argument for this hypothesis is the suggestion that men mask their panic symptoms through abuse of alcohol (see Chapter 5). While women more readily admit to psychological causes of problems and are more likely to seek out mental health professionals, that macho male image may stop men from admitting problems or asking for appropriate help. Abuse of alcohol is a convenient self-treatment that offers short-term relief. However, once alcoholic agoraphobic men do seek help, they more likely end up at Alcoholics Anonymous meetings or alcohol treatment centers. While addressing the substance-abuse problems, these programs only indirectly help with agoraphobic issues.

Since such a small percentage of men have been identified as agoraphobic, our understanding of their difficulties is less developed. As a group, men who are agoraphobic seem more extraverted, aggressive, and ambitious than some of the women discussed in this chapter. Their greatest difficulty is in expressing their emotions directly, especially in intimate relationships. For this reason, the first symptoms may develop soon after conflicts arise within a marriage. Learning self-confidence within an intimate relationship, and learning to accept some of the changing roles of women today, may be an important factor in helping some agoraphobic men.

Each of the psychological themes within this chapter will be illustrated through the reflections and insights of five women who have suffered from agoraphobia. Before you meet each of them, there are several things you should know. First, these women generously agreed to permit an audio recording of our interviews. All names and biographical information have been altered to protect the confidentiality of our relationship. Second, their childhood experiences are typical of those suffering from severe forms of this disorder. Their long-term struggle with agoraphobia—from twelve to forty-nine years—is common for those who do not receive appropriate professional treatment. With our new treatment approaches designed specifically for agoraphobia, people no longer need to remain trapped by panic for so many years. However, the accounts of these women provide an understanding of the workings of agoraphobia, and it could not be so clearly and briefly illustrated by less dramatic cases. Third, it is not within the scope of this book to outline the complex treatment of all aspects of agoraphobia. Instead, I will describe each of these women as they appear at the initial stage of treatment and will summarize the therapeutic tasks ahead of them as they learn to control panic attacks.

And, fourth, I am limiting the details about these women's lives to that which helps support the themes of this chapter. Many issues come to bear on complex psychophysiological problems, and those issues are distinct for each individual.

As each woman shares her story, reflect on whether your experiences or feelings are similar. Take this opportunity to learn about yourself. Each theme which is not a problem for you is a positive sign of strength. When you do relate to an issue, consider it an area in which you will need to find strength. Make use of this important guideline: *Every time you gain strength in your personal life, you will be laying a solid foundation for mastering panic.*

Karen L. is a thirty-four-year-old mother of two who began experiencing anxiety at the age of seven. She can remember at that age running home from friends' houses because of overwhelming feelings of fear. Once back in her own room she felt momentary relief from those strange tensions but would cry alone on her bed. After several years of psychological treatment, she became free of symptoms. Then, during her senior year in high school, her father died. For the next twelve months she withdrew into depression and rarely ventured outside of her bedroom. The following year her family moved to another city. Within a few months, Karen began to have panic attacks, first in restaurants, then at the movies and on trips.

Now, thirteen years later, Karen continues to experience panic, especially when traveling anywhere alone. Her symptoms include rapid heartbeat, blurred vision, clenched jaws, weakness, numbness, shooting headache pains, chest pain, and physical imbalance. Although she can comfortably travel with a companion, she rarely makes commitments for activities with others for fear that she will have to cancel plans.

Undoubtedly there were many experiences in Karen's childhood that contributed to her susceptibility to panic. But more relevant to this chapter is how Karen's symptoms are supported by her current self-image. In the following pages you will hear how she feels inferior to her peers, how she constantly criticizes her own actions, how she seeks approval from others yet refuses to accept their compliments. She believes that she is socially inept, that she is not capable of carrying on a normal conversation with her women friends. And she is so afraid of her husband's anger that she placates him through concession after concession.

When we place Karen's symptoms within the context of her current life we can see how they reflect a basic self-distrust. She doesn't believe she has what it takes within her to handle the adult world. Therefore, whenever life places a challenge in front of her, she naturally becomes afraid. Although quite uncomfortable and distressing, her panic symptoms are only one part of her fear of being forced into adult responsibility.

As she recovers from agoraphobia, Karen will learn to face travels alone. But she will also learn that she is a unique and important member of our world, deserving of respect from others and deserving of her own self-respect. She will find that if her marriage is a good one, her husband won't leave her just because she sticks up for her needs. And she will learn that she can survive losses, that she can tolerate mistakes, and that she doesn't need the approval of others in order to feel OK about herself.

Sheryll W. is a forty-five-year-old housewife who has experienced the symptoms of agoraphobia for twenty-two years. Her greatest difficulties come when she begins to plan for some event, large or small. As she contemplates going shopping, entering a crowded place, or driving to the beach, she begins to feel smothered, as if she can't breathe. She feels dizzy and nauseous, her heart rate increases, and her legs become weak. At the same time, her mind races through a series of fearful thoughts about the activity. If she decides to venture out, all she can think about is getting back home. After several hours of this anxious anticipation, Sheryll becomes physically and emotionally depleted and withdrawn within her house for several days.

The symptoms started when her oldest child, Susan, was born. Sheryll became pregnant on her honeymoon. After the child was born, Sheryll's husband worked seven days and nights a week while she remained home. Thus, her life was dramatically altered: From enjoying a carefree, single life, she became isolated at home alone every night. Then, three months later, the family was evicted when their rental house was sold. This was "the straw that broke the camel's back." Sheryll became depressed and anxious. One day, while trying to locate an apartment, she started having chest pains and thought she was dying of a heart attack. Her mother rushed her to the hospital, where the doctor diagnosed the problem as anxiety and prescribed tranquilizers. From that time on her symptoms became progressively worse. She began having difficulty attending church. Before long she became fearful at the supermarket. Within a year she was housebound, too afraid to even step outside of her front door. During the past seventeen years she has gone through phases of improvement followed by dramatic setbacks. As is true with many agoraphobics, Sheryll was evaluated again and again by physicians. She spent several years in psychotherapy, tried a number of medications, and was in and out of the hospital for two years. In addition to her agoraphobia symptoms she has suffered several bouts of severe depression.

But agoraphobia is more than being afraid of powerful physical symptoms. It is also the way each person views herself and her role in this world. In this chapter you will hear Sheryll describe herself as the "worrier" in her family. She is always preparing for the worst, always on guard. Her biggest daily fear is that her husband will abandon her, even though she has no information that supports this dread. In general, her life revolves around her anxious bracing for some loss. Her fear of losing control in the grocery store is symbolic of a deeper belief about her life: If I let go and enjoy myself, something bad will happen.

You will also hear Sheryll talk about her childhood, about how she lived in fear, confusion, and secret emotional pain, always worried that her alcoholic father would seriously injure her mother during his frequent Saturday night beatings. She will also tell you how her mother dominated her life; how, as a teenager, her mother took away her independence, made decisions for her, and attempted to control her thinking.

Such experiences in childhood leave a young woman unprepared for the responsibilities of adulthood. As she overcomes agoraphobia, Sheryll will master many new skills. But in addition she will develop a special sense of independence. As a child she had little choice but to be afraid of her father's violence and to follow the overprotective directives of her mother. Today, however, she will learn a new self-trust that gives her a sense of freedom, choice, and independence.

Donna B. is a forty-seven-year-old married woman with three children. She has been agoraphobic for twenty-one years. For many of those years her agoraphobia symptoms were overshadowed by prolonged episodes of severe depression. She has been hospitalized several times for treatment of her depression and her thoughts of suicide. Her treatment, however, never involved extended psychotherapy. Instead, it was limited to medications, such as antidepressants, tranquilizers, and electroconvulsive therapy (ECT), a neurological treatment for severe depression. (Such extended use of ECT is no longer practiced. When used with discretion, as it is today, ECT can produce spectacular changes in some severe depressions within three to four sessions. However, Donna was given over 100 ECT treatments during a seven-year period. Because of this she now suffers long-term memory loss.)

Her first anxiety attack came three months after the birth of her oldest child. Over the past ten years she has become completely housebound for about two months each year. During her worst episodes she is unable even to leave her bedroom without panicking.

Donna is most susceptible to panic during the two-week period surrounding her monthly menstruation. In her panic attack she becomes dizzy and has blurred vision, poor concentration, weak leg muscles, clammy hands and cold feet, nausea, and tight jaw muscles. At the same time, she experiences depersonalization: the feeling that her mind and body are separated, as though she is in a dream. Her thoughts turn to the fear of losing control, and she wants to run. "If I stay here, I'll faint . . . I'll humiliate myself . . . I'll be overwhelmed by these feelings." Even more frightening is the fearful question, "Am I about to become housebound again?"

In this chapter Donna will speak of childhood experiences that I believe are relevant to her struggle with agoraphobia. She was the youngest of five children; the next youngest sibling was eight years old when she was born. When she was seven her father died in a car accident. Her mother then became reclusive; she stopped socializing, never dated, and never remarried. Donna withdrew as well. For the next five years she went to school, came home, and helped prepare supper while her mother was at work, then spent the rest of the evening in her bedroom.

During her teenage years Donna allowed her mother to dominate her life. She never argued, never said "no." In her eyes, her mother had made great sacrifices, so if she ever thought about opposing her, Donna's sense of guilt would stop her assertive actions. Her most important task was to please her mother, and the easiest way to do that was to give up her own decision-making power. Donna will explain how this relationship generalized to others later in her life, how she learned to hide her own needs while trying to do what others want.

There are several reasons that Donna puts on this façade. One is her long-standing fear of abandonment. Remember that after her father died, Donna's only relationship for years was with her mother. It is possible that her thinking was this: "As long as I'm good, she won't leave me." And how does someone figure out how to be "good"? You ignore your own needs while you focus your attention on what would make others happy. And that is what Donna does to this day.

The best way to ignore our needs is to ignore our feelings, since our emotions guide a great many of our decisions. As a young girl Donna put a high price on her desire to keep her mother's love: she stopped paying attention to her own feelings. After years of practice, she is no longer able to distinguish and manage each of her feelings.

Donna's struggle with panic is closely related to her fear of abandonment, her depression, her need to please others, and her supression of her own desires and feelings. She will not win over panic without also facing these lifelong issues. Over time she will learn that adults live interdependently. Each of us has the right, even the responsibility, to express our emotions directly and to strive for our personal goals in life without fearing the repercussion of isolation and abandonment. Close, caring friends and relatives want to know our feelings, even if different from their own. It is only through openly and honestly sharing our authentic feelings and needs that we establish ourselves as unique, special human beings. As Donna learns to trust this sharing process, she will not allow trapped emotions to express themselves through the vehicle of panic.

Ann C. is a thirty-nine-year-old married woman with one child. She began to experience panic attacks at twenty, just one month before her wedding day. After returning to work from her honeymoon, she remained highly anxious throughout her day, with headaches and episodes of panic. With the encouragement of her family she finally began treatment with a psychiatrist, who also placed her on a tranquilizer. After several months of weekly sessions without improvement, Ann stopped all treatment.

When her son was born four years later, Ann began to avoid more and more situations as a self-treatment for panic. This solution helped reduce her anxious episodes but at the same time greatly diminished her freedom of travel. Today, twelve years later, Ann is city-bound: She never drives outside of her town. Whenever she drives within town, she must first devise an "escape route" back to some "safe" location, such as a friend's house. She is able to travel alone, but usually enlists the companionship of her son, her husband, or her mother. Her greatest difficulties are staying at home alone at night, grocery shopping, and standing in lines.

But what about the rest of Ann's life? We will see how these difficulties relate to her attitude about herself, to her ability to handle conflict, her relationships with those close to her. Her rigid perfectionism keeps her from enjoying her achievements. She also has difficulty sorting out her emotional responses to events. Expressing anger or experiencing the anger of others is to be avoided at all costs. She fears that if she truly lets herself feel angry, she will become explosive. And she will go to great lengths of prevent anyone from becoming mad at her.

Ann's need to please others and her fear of rejection are partly responsible for her overdependence on her husband and her mother. She will tell you how they fight her battles for her, that they "have always bailed me out whenever I've had to do something that makes me anxious." Within this protective system that Ann has created, she can always run away from conflict. But every time she runs away she reinforces her belief that she is incapable of handling life as an independent adult.

In addition to taking control of anxiety attacks, Ann will learn how to take charge of her self-esteem and pride. Her belief in her own self-worth will be based on something other than perfection or the opinions of others. She will find, through experience, that she can handle her own emotions and can manage her conflicts with others. Some of her changes will come easily, like learning to say thank you when someone compliments her instead of rejecting the compliment with some self-depreciating comment. Other changes will take more time, since they are part of the deeper fear of abandonment. As Ann recovers she will be less and less troubled by her profound sense that to think, feel, and act for herself will cause her to lose everyone and everything she values in this world.

Dorothy P. is seventy-two years old. She has experienced agoraphobia for almost fifty years now, but hasn't had an anxiety attack in over thirty years. Long ago she learned that if she avoided all uncomfortable situations she could avoid panic, and that is just what she has done. For instance, she never travels outside her city limits, she never drives a car, she never stays home alone or goes out alone. She sits in the aisle seat at the movie theater, walks out into the lobby several times during the show, and always leaves before the end of the movie. If she goes to a restaurant she sits next to the door and watches the door throughout the meal. In other words, she never challenges her fears; she stays away from all things that might produce a sense of being trapped.

A brief review of Dorothy's early life shows how one's past can have a direct bearing on one's current susceptibility to the fear of panic. Her father died during World War I, when she was a young child. A few years later her mother remarried. In this chapter you will hear Dorothy explain how her mother rarely left the house (and was probably agoraphobic), while her stepfather did all the shopping. She will also tell you how her stepfather continually ridiculed her and her sisters, how he controlled and physically abused their mother, and how her loving, caring mother eventually broke under the pressure. Dorothy developed the traits of a perfectionist at an early age so as not to give her stepfather any justifiable reason to verbally attack her. By fourteen their family doctor placed her on tranquilizers because of her anxiety symptoms.

At seventeen she married in order to escape from her home life. Her new husband was as strong as her stepfather. To Dorothy this was an important trait, because while growing up she never learned how to think independently about her own needs. It was important to marry someone who would also take care of her.

But soon this relationship turned on her as well. After the birth of their second child, her husband's alcoholism flared. As he drank he became violent. When their new daughter was only three months old, he came home one night in a drunken rage. Dorothy ended up in the hospital with a fractured jaw and a concussion. With the help of the courts she pressed charges, became legally separated, and then divorced.

But her problems didn't end. Her ex-husband began to appear at her house randomly during day or night, sometimes breaking down a door or window to demand "visitation rights." Dorothy lived in constant, anxious fear of being violently surprised.

It was during this traumatic period in her life that Dorothy's panic symptoms began to surface. Returning home on the train after a day at the beach with her two children, she suddenly became over-whelmed with fear and the need to escape. Within a matter of two weeks she restricted her travels to within her home town.

You will hear Dorothy explain how she married the second time not for love but for security, how she never wanted to "cause trouble" by making demands of her children or her second husband. She kept herself from expressing angry feelings by thinking "they're going to lock me up." In her mind she believed she could never be in control of her anger; she'd be angry every day if she allowed it. Then in Chapter 7, Dorothy will say that she never attempts to drive a car for fear of completely losing control: "If there was a detour, or if traffic backed up, I'd have to either get out and run, or jam on the brakes, knock everyone down, knock the policeman down, go through red lights . . ."

Dorothy's recovery from agoraphobia will depend on her willingness to face fears she has avoided for almost fifty years. Her central fear, however, is not driving a car or being alone at home. It is the fear of her own emotions. She has a number of legitimate emotions that she has held inside year after year. She keeps them in check by scaring herself with exaggerated images of losing control.

Dorothy will not resolve this problem by herself. She will do it with the help of new friends and a supportive professional who will help her express her authentic emotions a little at a time. As she does, she will learn how her emotions express her personal values and her self-esteem. She will begin to reassess her priorities with regard to personal relationships. Being protected by a strong individual will have less and less importance as she learns to manage her own life. And the desire to be close to loving, active friends will slowly increase in value. While these changes are taking place, she will begin to face panic by gradually expanding her restricted limits.

Her very first task, however, will be to stop verbally degrading herself. Dorothy's stepfather was wrong; she is not stupid, incapable, or worthless. The sooner she changes these personal beliefs the sooner she can start taking control of panic.

"I've always felt inferior"

When the agoraphobic is a person with low self-esteem, she places others above her in life. She usually "talks down" about herself and is self-critical. She may not attempt to take on a new challenge because she doubts her ability or competence. And when looking back into her past, she sees only a series of failures.

What's more, a person with low self-esteem will tend to think that other people see her in a similar light. "Who could possibly like me?" is the question in the back of her mind. Since she doubts people could like her for just being who she is, she will try to "make" people like her through her generosity and self-sacrifice.

The major problem with this approach is that she attempts to get others to like her before she learns to like herself. If it really were true that other people needed to be persuaded to like her, the problem would not be so difficult. But truly she is her own worst critic; when someone says, "Good job!" she says in her mind, "No, it wasn't."

This is quite a painful process. So much time is spent seeking the approval of others, so much thinking, worrying, physical and emotional energy is spent in the wrong direction, that the woman is actually out of control. She allows other people to have control over her self-esteem. How *they* act determines how *she* feels.

KAREN: We lose our self-confidence. That's what agoraphobia does to us. We just don't deserve it. We're not good enough. We overcompensate because we're just not worthy.

   I probably spend all my waking hours looking for approval, recognition, and attention. I think I've always felt inferior, thinking that everyone else can do better than me. I need someone to build me up constantly, which is bad because no one's going to do that.

   Acceptance. That's my biggest issue. I am so critical of myself. I'm never content with my performance. Even when I am complimented on something, I think, "That's just not my best." It's strange, but I think deep inside I hate myself—I really do.

In the next segment, Donna discusses her current relationship with her mother. As I listen, I notice her eyes beginning to water and her face flushing with color.

DR. W.: There's that sadness again.
DONNA: No, it's resentment. Resentment that I've let myself be pushed around all my life. I've allowed it to happen. I never said "no" to my mother. Never. If I thought about it, I felt guilty. And

the guilt was difficult to deal with. Even today, she will constantly try to lay guilt on me—that she's all alone, I should spend more time with her, that other mothers and daughters are so close. Well, I can't tolerate much of her.

DR. W.: This inability to say "no" to your mother—does that generalize into other relationships?

DONNA: Yes. I have always been a people pleaser. If you wanted to go to a restaurant, you'd decide the restaurant and I would say, "Fine." I could hate the place, but I would say, "Wonderful."

Karen speaks of needing acceptance and approval. Although this is a natural need for all of us, Karen allows her entire life to revolve around a fear of disapproval. At the same time she says, "I'm never content with my performance." Before she can believe that other people accept her, she must learn to accept herself.

She explains that she continues to give and give because she wants to make up for being "not good enough." Where did that standard come from? What are her criteria for "good enough"? For some reason, Karen has set standards for herself that she can't meet; because she doesn't meet the standards, she is not "worthy." Belief in one's self-worth is essential to conquering panic.

Donna presents another dimension of low self-esteem. She doesn't deserve to say "yes" to herself. She will say "yes" to everyone else in her life; she reserves "no" for her own needs.

Here is one typical belief system of a person who won't say "no" to others:

A. I am not worth much as a human being.

B. Therefore, I'm lucky this person has stayed with me for so long.

C. Since I don't deserve all that this person has generously given to such an unworthy person as myself,

D. I owe him or her a great deal.

E. Therefore, I would feel guilty if I refused this request.

This faulty line of reasoning is often supported by a second set of beliefs:

A. Besides, I must not forget that I am not worth much as a human being.

B. If this person left me because I didn't keep pleasing him or her, then most likely I would end up alone in the world.

C. Not only would I be isolated and lonely, but I would not be capable of managing my life.

D. Therefore, I must forget myself and think of others at all times.

"I can't stand making a mistake"

The strongly self-critical person will often demand perfection, but only in herself.

DR. W.: Do you feel as if you have to be perfect at everything you do?

DONNA: Oh, yes. In the sense that either I do it up to my expectations or I don't do it at all. I have a real problem being a perfectionist.

I don't demand perfection of other people, only of myself. I'll always say to someone else, "That's fine! You did the best you could do," but I can't seem to apply that to myself. And I can't stand making a mistake. Doing paperwork, even if nobody knows that I make the mistake, and even if I correct it on the next line, I get this really frustrated feeling—it's just unacceptable to me.

DR. W.: Is there any other time that it gets in your way?

DONNA: Yes, in my hesitation to try things. I don't venture to try certain things for fear of making a mistake or not being perfect. I'd rather not do them at all.

Notice the significance of Donna's last statements. She is not speaking of hesitating about going shopping or moving into a crowd. She is speaking of not attempting *any* new, creative tasks which might be pleasurable or rewarding, such as painting a picture or writing a poem. Some agoraphobics, if they take time to notice, can see that they don't just avoid phobic situations, they avoid any chance of making a mistake—because to make a mistake is one more way for them to feel out of control. If they can't guarantee that an undertaking will be done perfectly, they will not even begin the task.

ANN: I can't say, "Well, that's good enough." It might be a question of one little detail that nobody will notice. But anything that I do that reflects me, that I'll get praise for, I have to do perfectly.

Somebody might see it and say, "Oh, isn't that beautiful! Oh, you're so talented. Isn't that nice!" But while they're telling me that, I don't believe them. I just kind of laugh it off. I say, "Oh, it's silly, you can do it. Anybody can do it." I always put it down. Or if I make something, and there's something about it that bothers me, I'll always point it out. I'll say, "See, I didn't do so well right there."

Ann works compulsively at any task which might bring praise from others. After tremendous effort, she finally receives her deserved acknowledgment and praise. Even at the exact moment the person is speaking, Ann is discounting the compliment in her own mind. And as if that weren't enough, she then explains to her friend that the praise was undeserved, since there was a flaw in the workmanship.

Can you imagine a carpenter spending all weekend remodeling his kitchen, then on Sunday night taking a sledgehammer to his handiwork? Can you imagine a secretary spending all day typing a thirty-page report, then at five o'clock placing it in the shredder? Think of the carpenter or secretary repeating that same procedure every week, and now you are getting the picture of an agoraphobic's life. People like Donna and Ann make a career out of earning self-worth, then never accepting it. It is an exhausting cycle.

Strong self-esteem is important as you begin to control panic. If you believe in your own worth, then you can believe that these symptoms of panic are standing in the way of an important person. You will feel more energy to push through setbacks and tough times. You will devote more energy to yourself and less to having to please others.

Here are some questions on which to reflect:

- Do I think I am a lovable person?
- What do I have to do to be loved?
- What are my good qualities in each of my roles (spouse, friend, parent, employee)?
- What are my weaknesses in these same roles?
- How do I describe myself? What kind of language do I use to describe my weaknesses? Do I call myself derogatory names (lazy, childish, stupid, chicken, worthless, etc.)?
- Am I "devastated" by others' criticisms?

- Do I tend to point out all my mistakes to myself and others?
- Do I accept compliments? Do I really believe people when they speak well of me or my accomplishments?
- Do I need to do everything perfectly? Can I accept my mistakes?
- If I can't do something perfectly, do I avoid it?
- Do I have trouble setting limits on how much I give to others?
- Do I have trouble setting limits on any projects I undertake?
- Do I hesitate to try new tasks for fear I will fail?
- Do I consider mistakes to mean the same thing as "failure"?
- Am I constantly watching and monitoring myself? Do I evaluate my every move?
- Do I consider everything that I do to be of great significance? Or, do I use good judgment to determine the difference between small and large tasks, significant and insignificant projects?
- How many times have I said "yes" to myself this week? This year?

No one has to earn the right to be loved; we are already lovable. Your answers to the above questions will indicate how much you withhold love from yourself and how hard you work at gaining the love of those around you.

If your self-esteem could use some strengthening, you must first learn how to love yourself, including all your weaknesses. Then, look around to find people who are willing and able to love you just the way you are. Once you truly love and appreciate yourself every day, you will begin to notice what kinds of people will love and appreciate you. You will also notice the many people who have been appreciating you all along.

Here are a few guidelines to help you on your way:

- Praise yourself every time you accomplish something, no matter how small.
- When you make a mistake, give yourself a helpful suggestion for your next try, or find someone who can.
- Refrain from calling yourself names or putting yourself down for your mistakes. Life is hard enough. No one deserves to be humiliated, even silently by themselves.
- Consider the idea that you deserve to be loved, not solely for how much you give to others, but simply for being a unique human being.

- If you are failing to meet your goals, change them.
- If you are failing to live up to your standards, lower them.
- Never stop setting goals and standards for yourself, only bring them within reach. Success breeds success.
- Set a small enough goal, work to reach it, praise yourself for your accomplishment, then set your new reachable goal.
- When someone compliments you, be a sponge; absorb the compliment, believe it, feel it.
- When someone criticizes you, don't swallow it whole. Chew on it to see if you can learn anything for next time. Spit out the name-calling and hostility. Digest only what you believe is beneficial.
- Re-evaluate your self-expectations. Make certain that your expectations are based on your own belief system, what you think is good and right today. Do not allow beliefs taught years ago to rule your life without questioning them. Take control of your expectations and you will have control of your self-esteem.
- Find ways to say "yes" to yourself every day of your life. If *you* are unwilling to say "yes" to yourself, why should anyone else?

"But if I didn't have him . . ."

Self-doubt can have a major impact on all parts of your life. In the context of your panic symptoms, self-doubt can produce a multitude of questions. At a party, for example: "Will I be able to stay the whole time? Will I embarrass myself? Will it get worse? Will anybody see me?" Those same types of doubting questions can be found elsewhere in an individual's life, and nowhere will self-doubt have a more dramatic effect than in the realm of personal relationships.

Consider, for example, a woman who has an underlying belief that she is inherently a weak person. If I honestly believe that I am incapable of caring for myself, then I have to find someone in my life who will protect me. I might hate being dependent, I might detest my subservience to another human being, but those feelings will never be stronger than my fear of going it alone. When I believe I will be helpless if left alone, then my basic survival is at stake. All other considerations take on lesser importance. I must survive. Therefore, I must keep people around me, at whatever cost.

This is a crucial issue in the understanding of panic. Our basic belief systems will always overpower any other thoughts or emotions. Many of these beliefs were adopted years ago and are outside our conscious awareness. This is what is so confusing for agoraphobics. They really would love to not have to depend on others; they want independence more than almost anything else in the world. But their belief systems tell them that they won't survive without a strong person next to them. Keeping this significant conflict in mind, listen to how it has caused so much pain in these women's lives.

DOROTHY: When I met my second husband, something should have gone off in my head, I should have known that he was not going to be a friend. We had no common interests, we had nothing to talk about. Something told me—I don't know what it was—that I was going to be sick and unable to work; I was going to need a roof over my head. I had had it up to here trying to make ends meet. I was really wanting security. I didn't love him, not at all.

Dorothy made a major life decision based on fear. In order to gain security, she surrendered love, happiness, and companionship.

KAREN: I think I don't want to grow up—that's what I really feel. I just don't want to admit it. I don't want to be thirty-four, with two children; I don't want my responsibilities. I know that I can get rid of agoraphobia tomorrow, but then where do I go? I'm not ready for the adult world. I don't know how to act. I mean, I don't know how to pull up in people's driveways and talk to them.
ELIZABETH (to Karen, in a group therapy session): One night when we came out of here, you were rushing to go to your husband, and I wanted to talk to you for a minute. Your husband was outside, and you said, "If I keep him waiting for too long, he'll get mad. If he sees me crying, he'll get mad and say, 'You can't come here anymore.' " And I say, "The hell with him, the hell with him!" You can use us, the hell with him. Lean on us, that's what a support group is for.
KAREN: You're right, you're right. I know that. It's a nightmare the way it is now. But I don't know how much of a nightmare it would be if I didn't have him.

ELIZABETH (still angry): So therefore you would rather do everything his way?

KAREN: I get up in the morning and I say, "How low do you have to lay? I mean, how low does someone like me have to go? How long will I let him treat me this way?" But to turn around and say, "Knock it off, I want to be my own person"—I can't say that to my husband. I need him too badly.

Karen says that she doesn't want to grow up. That is probably based on her belief that she is not capable of handling her responsibilities. She worried so much about failing as a mother that she gave her entire attention to her children. She monitored her every move and left no time for her own pleasures. She now believes that the world has passed her by, that she no longer knows how to communicate with her peers.

Her belief that she is incapable is so strong that she allows herself to be completely dominated by her husband. She hates what she is doing to herself. And I am sure some of her friends have said, "If you hate it so much, why don't you change it?" But, as Karen says, she believes she "can't," that she is not capable of independence. Therefore, her actions continue to lower her self-esteem. She fears the loss of her husband's support because she believes she cannot survive without him.

KAREN: When I need to get my daughter to the doctor for a checkup, or I need to shop for new clothes, I have to say to my husband, "Three weeks from Saturday, would you take me to the mall?" And I have to build him up. I think, "No, I'd better not antagonize him because he'll say, 'OK, we're not going.'" What a way to live! I have no control over my own life.

ANN: My mother will still do my fighting for me, and I'm thirty-nine years old. My husband does a lot for me, too. He's the "take charge" kind of person. So I have these two people that have always bailed me out when I've had to do something that makes me anxious.

Even now, if I go to a group meeting my husband will say, "What time are you going to be home?" And if I'm a little bit late, he gets upset. I always say I'm his oldest child, because he treats me like a child in a lot of ways. But I let him treat me like a child,

I don't assert myself with him. It doesn't seem worth it. I'm just happy to go along like this.

My husband and my mother are always around to help me with this, to help me with that. I don't want to lose them but, deep down inside, I know that it's wrong. Still, I fear what will happen if I start to get really independent. . . .

As you may be starting to sense, if a person feels as though she is incapable of managing the demands of the world, she will search out someone who can manage them for her. Perhaps she is skilled at giving to others, being kind and sensitive, but feels unable to stand up for herself when necessary. Within the logic of that belief system, she believes that she would be smart to marry a man who is powerful, dominant, and controlling. Together they make a whole person, one who can be kind, compassionate, and giving, and also strong and forceful if need be.

Unfortunately, they are *two* people, not one. This has caused many a painful marriage. They may stay together because they satisfy certain basic needs (simply put, he remains dominant and receives nurturing while she feels protected). But other needs go unmet or get stifled, because each of them behaves completely differently. He controls and dominates, she surrenders and submits. They don't have a common, shared relationship between two equals. It is very difficult for them to have fun together, to solve problems together, to plan the future together.

"If I stop worrying, something bad will happen"

Over time, our roles and self-perceptions begin to solidify within our relationships. Ann, in the above example, sees herself as always the child, both with her mother and with her husband. Sheryll sees herself as the worrier.

SHERYLL: Nothing ever bothers my husband. And my kids take after him. Nothing ever gets on their nerves. Everything's very easy for them.
DR. W.: So what role does that leave you?
SHERYLL: I do all the worrying. Somebody's got to worry in my family! [Laughs]

DR. W.: Or what would happen?

SHERYLL: I've never thought of the consequences. Nothing would get
    done. All my husband cares about is his tennis.

DR. W.: "I have to keep worrying about the kids, because if I
    don't . . ."? Fill in the blank, Sheryll.

SHERYLL: Well, I'm afraid something will happen if I stop worrying
    about this, that, and the other thing. If I relax and take it easy, if I
    stop worrying, something bad will happen. Does that make sense?
        I'm always prepared. I've been married twenty-three years.
    And still, every night when my husband walks through the door, I
    wait for him to say, "Sheryll, I've found somebody else." This is
    how I live.

DR. W.: "I'm always on guard . . ."

SHERYLL: I'm always on guard, you'd better believe it.

Sheryll first states that she must worry or nothing would get done
in her home. But with just a little prodding, she reveals a deeper, more
significant concern. Sheryll expresses a basic fear of something bad
happening to her, especially the fear of being abandoned. It is not a
minor fear; she thinks about it every day. But it is an irrational fear,
one based on an internal belief system rather than any real evidence.
She tells me that her husband has given her no reason to doubt his
commitment to the marriage.

But she does give us a very important piece of information, something that I doubt she understood at the time she said it. It is as though
she has a magical strategy to prevent anything bad from happening.
Her belief is: "As long as I keep worrying, as long as I remain tense
and on guard, nothing bad will happen. If I relax and take it easy, if I
stop worrying . . ."

This is exactly the same feeling that a person has about panic
attacks. You remain tense in anticipation of a negative experience (at
a store, in a car, or in a crowd). You remain on guard, expecting the
worst. For Sheryll and other panic-prone people, that fear epitomizes
of the way they think about their life in general.

Looking back over Sheryll's therapy we were able to see this
thought pattern more clearly. The interview you just read took place
during our tenth session. Prior to that I had taught Sheryll a relaxation
process (which you will find in Chapter 12). She was petrified at the
thought of listening to the exercise on an audio tape. "I *can't* relax,"

she said. I instructed her to do some household chore, like her ironing, while playing the tape on low volume in the background, just as a way to get used to the sound. She was so afraid of the concept of relaxation that she would not take the risk. "Relaxation," at that point, meant "loss of control."

After this tenth session, I learned that her unconscious fear was long-standing and of a much stronger nature. She feared great harm or loss if she let go of her tension and worry. Her tension was her protection. Unfortunately, this belief was causing her great discomfort in her current life. But in her mind, her worry and tension seemed to be working, because she had averted any trouble. Since she always remained tense, she assumed her method of self-protection was successful. You may remember the old joke of the man who constantly paces around the outside of his house to keep away the tigers. "There aren't any tigers loose around here," exclaims his neighbor. "See how well it works," responds the man. The agoraphobic's use of physical as well as psychological tension to guard against mistakes or harm takes this same strategy. Even to experiment with relaxing holds too many risks.

"I am deathly afraid of that anger"

There are few people who could say that they enjoy conflicts. Most people feel somewhat uncomfortable before, during, or after an argument. For many agoraphobics, though, conflicts are to be avoided like the plague.

ANN: Last winter I was hemmed in in a parking space downtown. Someone parked illegally behind me, and I became livid. It was very cold and I had one child with me. Just driving into town with my children was a big step, because I was really feeling housebound at the time. Well, I came out and said, "How am I going to get out of this space? Look at that jerk parked there."

It started welling up in me—the anger. I thought that I should stay and give him a piece of my mind, that I should call the cops because he'd parked illegally. Then all I could think about was getting out of there, getting the heck out of there and getting home. I didn't want to confront this; I didn't want this person to come out because I would have had to get mad and I wasn't sure what that would do to me.

DR. W.: So you'd start to have those feelings about getting mad, and you even had the image of getting angry at the person. At the same time you'd be thinking, "Let me get away from it."

ANN: Yes, but not all the time, because I can get mad, too. But that happened to be a particularly sensitive week, when I was feeling a lot of panic; I was highly sensitized.

Women such as Ann will expend much energy to avoid a confrontation. They may also attach themselves to a husband who will fight their battles for them. Ann expresses not only a fear of conflict but also a fear of her own anger. From my observations, such comments by agoraphobics reflect two types of fears. First is the fear of conflict and the repercussions it might bring, such as a separation or loss of relationship. Second is the fear of one's own intense emotions. Ann did not want to confront the driver of that car, "because I would have had to get mad and I wasn't sure what that would do to me."

Earlier in this chapter you heard Donna talk about being a "people pleaser": she never expresses her own desires if she believes that they conflict with yours. Notice how that same pattern continues with regard to her feelings.

DONNA: I've had an awfully hard time with anger. I have trouble sorting out my emotions. Sometimes I think my feelings get tangled into a big ball. I don't know if I'm mad, or what.

I really don't get mad at all. And if I do, I keep it all in. I mean, I don't direct it at anything. I suppose I'm directing it at myself and just running away from it.

My husband never knows what I'm feeling. I never share negative feelings. I'm one of these people who talks positively and feels negatively. And I always play that game. I tell people what they want to hear or what I judge they want to hear. If I feel angry, they never hear about it—I never show it. I don't even think I give nonverbal cues for anger. A person would have to be very in tune to me to see a nonverbal. I just suppress a lot of stuff. And I think the reason isn't so much that I don't want to show I am angry as that I never really feel just anger, I feel rage. And I am deathly afraid of losing control of that anger, of hurting somebody. Consequently, it is unusual for me to even raise my voice in the house. When I yell at the kids, they move, because I so seldom do it.

DR. W.: So your anger has to evolve to a bigger level before you even begin to notice it yourself.

DONNA: Yes, I have to feel it to an extreme. And then I sometimes don't know exactly what I'm feeling. When I feel anger and rage it's usually mixed with self-pity. When I feel fear, it's more terror than fear.

DOROTHY: I was too lenient with the kids, and I'm still too lenient with my husband. If he says something, I think to myself, "Why cause trouble? Why have an argument? I'll just let it go." But once in a blue moon, I hit the roof.

DR. W.: And what would happen if you did that more often?

DOROTHY: Well, I'd be doing it every day of the week. Why bother getting upset over something that's not going to change? My fear is that they're going to lock me up.

Donna and Dorothy speak of holding in their emotions. Whenever we hold on to something tightly, we feel tension. Try physically holding your fist in a tight squeeze for one minute, and you'll be experiencing the amount of psychic energy we must use to hold in our secret emotions. It is exhausting physically and emotionally.

In order to incorporate our emotions into our lives in a beneficial way, it is important to do these three things:

1. *Notice* what emotion you are feeling.

2. *Respect* that emotion as a legitimate expression of who you are and what you value as a human being.

3. *Take care* of that emotion in some manner. Simply acknowledging the presence of a feeling inside you and permitting it to exist can sometimes be enough. If the emotion is in response to another person, you may need to express it directly to the person who stimulated your reaction. In still other situations it may be more beneficial for you to express your emotion to another, more objective and supportive listener instead of the person to whom you are reacting.

Your values and your emotions are the two essential ingredients that distinguish you as a unique individual. When you cut other people off from knowing your values and emotions, or if you only present the values and emotions you think they want to see, then you do yourself and them a disservice. You don't give people a chance to treat your true self with respect. You do the same thing when you cut yourself off from knowing your feelings. You don't respect your rights and your values as a human being.

In addition, when you refuse to pay attention to your milder emotions, they tend to grow stronger in order to be heard. Everyone knows what it's like to be in a noisy environment calling out someone's name. "John?" (in a normal tone). No answer. "John?" (a little louder). Not even a turn of the head. "JOHN?!" you yell with force, finally grabbing his attention. John will probably jump, startled.

Your emotions work the same way. As you ignore them, they grow and grow. Once they are so big that you can't ignore them, they scare you instead. This is how Donna's fear turns into "terror."

Dorothy is afraid that if she expresses her anger:

1. It will never end. She will be angry forever.
2. It will fail to change anything.
3. She will go crazy and be locked up.

Here are my answers to those fears:

1. *I'm afraid that if I let myself feel this emotion, I will be unable to stop feeling it.* Anything that is fully experienced will disappear. As soon as you begin to express an emotion, you begin to change it. Of course, if you remain within a situation which stimulates new anger inside you every day (such as your boss treating you with disrespect), you will have a new sensation of anger each day. If you never face your old anger, that new one just gets piled on top.

2. *What good will it do? It won't make the other person change.* Expressing anger rarely changes the person you are angry at; it changes you! Don't think of anger as a weapon, something you use to fix the other person. Those of us who are parents know how poorly it works on our kids. For starters, expressing anger can keep it from balling up inside you. Left inside you unattended, it can do much damage. It can turn into self-hatred and self-pity. It can contribute to such physical problems as headaches, muscle tension, ulcers, colitis, and high blood pressure. And it can grow into anxiety, emotional tension, or depression. And, second, noticing your angry feelings over some incident helps you learn about your personal values, what is important to you, how you need to be treated by those around you, and how you need to respect yourself. These lessons are invaluable.

3. *If I really feel my emotions, I'll totally lose control.* Expressing an authentic, honest feeling has never driven anyone "crazy."

"And he never came back"

Thus far I have presented several traits which are sometimes present in the panic-prone personality: low self-esteem, self-criticism and self-doubt, worrying, the need to do every task perfectly, the need to please others, and the fear of anger or conflicts. These characteristics do not develop after symptoms of panic begin in the agoraphobic's life; they are part of the individual's makeup, part of her personality.

Most of our behavior patterns are shaped between birth and our teenage years, so our personal histories can tell us a great deal about our current lives. The primary decisions we make about our future, most of the beliefs we hold, and the ways we view ourselves and our world come from what we learned long ago. And we act on that learning with little, if any, conscious thought.

When we are first born into this world, we are completely helpless and vulnerable. We are dependent on our parents for our every need, our very survival. The process of development from birth to late adolescence is a progressive maturing—physically, emotionally, intellectually, and socially. Critical to that maturing is learning independence—thinking for ourselves, trusting our instincts, setting personal goals, having confidence in our own abilities, and being capable of independent living.

In normal development, by the time a child is two years old she has begun to strike out on her own by opposing her parents (through a broad range of "terrible twos" maneuvers) and by learning to feed herself. By age six, she has learned that it is okay to disagree, to speak up, and to ask questions.

Once the normally developed child is eleven years old, her interactions with her peer group have evolved to a sophisticated level. She is skilled at arguing, competing, achieving, and negotiating. By sixteen, the teenager is in the process of adopting a comfortable sexual identity and self-image. She has learned to be assertive and to initiate activities while taking adult responsibility for many of her actions. By young adulthood, the woman has acquired a sense of self-worth. She can take risks and take time for her own activities, even if they conflict with the activities of others.

As you can see, achieving a sense of independence is a gradual,

step-by-step developmental process, equal in intensity and importance to our physical growth during those same eighteen years. If we
miss the achievement of certain developmental tasks when we are
young, then our ability to experience independence as adults will be
restricted. None of us had perfect parents, nor could any of us *be*
perfect as parents. It is not beneficial to blame anyone for what happened in the past. Every parent does the best that he or she can. Very
few parents purposely hurt their children.

All of us have the ability to overcome any developmental limitations. We have the power now, as adults, to identify the strengths we
are missing and to train ourselves in independent thinking, feeling,
and living. Childhood experiences are not excuses for our adult difficulties.

I look to the past with my clients for one primary reason: to identify what new learning is needed. For the client, however, this looking
back helps her to understand certain of her current beliefs in light of
past experiences. And it guides her in seeing what changes need to
take place today in how she thinks, feels, and acts. Studying the past
does not in itself change anything. Only positive action today changes
how we think, feel, or act, and only thinking, feeling, or doing something new today produces change.

Some of my agoraphobic clients are women who had quite traumatic experiences in their pasts. I share their particular stories with
you because they can best illustrate how some unconscious learning
takes place. I do not intend to imply that all agoraphobics have had
unhappy childhoods, because I don't believe this to be true. I do want
to suggest that some of the agoraphobic's beliefs may be irrational,
acquired unconsciously. Many of the lessons we receive during our
lifetimes are quite subtle. But nonetheless they shape our belief systems, and what we believe strongly determines how we act.

DONNA: My father died when I was seven. And I don't really remember the next five years of my life. I spent a lot of time in my
bedroom during those five years. I would go to school, come
home, help out around the house, and then I would go upstairs and
listen to the radio.

I was one of five kids, but when I was born, my brothers and
sisters were much older than me. They were already in junior high
school. So it was really just my mother and I. She never socialized

or dated any other men, and never remarried. She worked very hard, was very loving and giving.

DOROTHY: My father joined the service during the war. And he never came back—he was killed. I can remember the day we heard of his death.

I think maybe that's when it started. From that point on my mother gave up her life for us.

Each of these women experienced a significant loss during her childhood. Both Donna and Dorothy have a traumatic scene etched in their minds, one in which their fathers disappeared and never returned. At seven years old, Donna was given no explanation of death or of how to manage her feelings in response to death. She became depressed and remained that way for many years, withdrawing from the world and feeling a "void." She now has no memories of those years, but we can presume that she had great difficulty understanding or expressing her emotions, in part because of this early childhood experience.

While we are children, our parents serve as our models of how to act in life. Dorothy's mother withdrew from the world after Dorothy's father died. She watched her mother become isolated, stop taking care of herself, and rarely leave the home. Donna's mother made the same decision. Both girls watched their mothers surrender their personal lives while continuing to give to their children.

Four issues are significant to our understanding of childhood learnings. First, the experience of loss of a significant person in the child's life is highly traumatic. If a person disappears from a child's life, she becomes confused as to why the person left. Death, separation, and divorce can cause the child to wonder, "Did I cause that?" The child may become fearful of her actions, not being sure which of her behaviors was "wrong." According to a child's logic, if you can be abandoned once, you can be abandoned again. That is a terribly frightening thought. There are a variety of decisions the child might make in order to protect herself from another loss or separation. One is to resolve not to get close to anyone else, to prevent any further hurt. Another is to be very good, not to make waves, because if you are bad, people might leave you.

These are examples of unconscious decisions which can be made by a child and can remain in place into adulthood. Such behaviors are based on a belief system and logical framework which is not part of our conscious thought. They have been "implanted" into the brain without our awareness. But this store of beliefs influences many decisions in adulthood. It can lead the agoraphobic to resolve, "I'd better keep pleasing the people around me, or I'll be left alone."

Second, when one parent leaves or dies, the child can develop a strong attachment to the remaining parent. That attachment can become a powerful unconscious force which plays havoc with the person's life in the future. As adults we have responsibilities which require us to think, feel, and act independently. Adults with unresolved attachments can suffer great internal conflict. Many of my agoraphobic clients speak of their resentment of parents who are too close to them emotionally, or who attempt to run their lives. At the same time, they feel incapable of setting limits on the relationship and are unable to bring about a separation as adults. They make statements such as, "I'm angry about how my mother treats me, and yet she is my closest friend. I don't know what I would do without her." This same kind of relationship can be found with an agoraphobic's spouse instead of the parent.

The third issue is that experiencing a loss produces a great many emotions inside us. For a child, it can be the first time she has felt so many feelings so intensely: sadness, fear, surprise, shock, even anger. She will probably feel confused and overwhelmed by these new sensations. Unless special care is taken, it is possible she will never sort out those feelings. I believe that Donna, for example, remained swallowed up by that confusion for years. Agoraphobics like Donna, beginning treatment some thirty years later, may still be unable to manage any extreme emotions.

The fourth issue is the concept of "modeling." When we are young, our parents or guardians constitute our entire world. They probably model 90 percent of all our learned behaviors. As we grow up with them, we learn, by observing their actions, how to share our feelings of love and affection, how to solve our problems, how to communicate with others, how to respect ourselves, how to face the world. Most of these lessons are absorbed unconsciously. We begin, automatically, to imitate the actions of those close to us. Both Donna and Dorothy watched their mothers become socially isolated and withdrawn. What they did *not* see was a woman who had self-pride and self-esteem, who looked on life as a challenge. At the same time, though, both received a great deal of love and affection from their mothers. This, I am sure, was a positive, nourishing experience which they remember and appreciate to this day. No one's childhood is all bad or all good.

DONNA: My mother went out to work after my father died, though she had never worked before in her life. I felt I was a burden, so I never made waves. I never gave her any aggravation. I always did what I could do around the house to help out. I was very grateful that we were able to keep the house that I grew up in, that we didn't have to move, change our environment.

DR. W.: What makes you think she thought you were a burden?

DONNA: The fact that she had to go out to work in order to maintain that house, that she had never worked, and so forth.

DR. W.: So this was something that you decided on your own, as opposed to any cues that she was giving you?

DONNA: I think so. I don't really remember any particular cues.

Here Donna describes her belief (that she was a burden) and her decision (not to make waves) based on that belief. Notice that her belief was not based on anything that her mother did or said. She also felt grateful that nothing else was taken from her after her father died. She was careful to be good, so that her mother wouldn't leave her also. Now as an adult, Donna has incorporated these early childhood decisions into all of her relationships. She hides her needs if they might conflict with yours and works hard to please those around her. Even with her closest friends, she smiles on the outside when she is actually feeling sad or hurt. It is as though the same childhood fears continue to plague her: "If I express my needs, I'll be too much of a burden and others will abandon me."

"I lived in fear that something would happen"

DR. W.: Tell me more about what it was like in your home.

SHERYLL: Oh, Saturday nights I'd wake up and my father would be beating my mother up, and . . . oh, I don't know . . . [voice trails off. She looks down at the floor.]

DR. W.: You don't want to talk about it.

SHERYLL: It was tension. What else can I tell you? It just stunk. I used to be mad because other families seemed so intact, and I had to put up with this. There was always this fear. I guess I lived in fear that my father would do something to my mother. Don't get me wrong, it was weekends that he was really frightening. Other than that, he'd put up with a lot of garbage from her. She was an aggressive woman in her own way.

I didn't feel secure in the house. I always felt that something bad would happen, that one Saturday night, something was going to happen. The situation was at its worst during my teens. Maybe going to school and being a cheerleader and being in clubs was my way of blocking all this out. I don't know.

Long before Sheryll ever developed agoraphobia, she lived in fear. She had no control over her environment. She had reason to be afraid that "something bad was going to happen," since her father physically abused her mother. But it was not something that she could prevent as a young girl. Her only option was to avoid the situation, to be outside of the home as much as possible.

Again, notice how this is similar to the response an agoraphobic has toward fearful situations: to worry about something bad happening over which one has no control, and to avoid the situation as much as possible. This early life experience provided Sheryll's first lesson in such behavior.

SHERYLL: I was very confused as a child. Sometimes I wished that my father would leave or my mother would pull herself together. It was very difficult. But on the outside, I always acted as if everything was fine. People on the outside would never know there was anything going on in the house.

Sheryll made a generous, unselfish decision to protect her family's secret. She hid her feelings from all her friends so that they wouldn't discover the problems within her household. But she did this to her own personal detriment. She pretended to be a happy-go-lucky, active child on the outside, while on the inside she was sad, confused, tense, and scared. Since no one knew of her emotional pain, no one could respond to it in a caring manner.

Sheryll decided at a young age to withhold her emotions. This decision and all its repercussions served as the foundation of many personal difficulties later in life.

KAREN: I have suffered from anxiety since the age of eight. I can remember actually having to run home because of overwhelming feelings that I had, but couldn't logically understand at the age and mentality of five. And from that point on, I was labeled an emotionally disturbed child. I was also asthmatic. I coped with it as best I could. I just accepted it, and if I didn't feel well while over at a friend's house (this is at the age of eight), I'd just go home. I always knew what I had to do. And then when I got home, I'd feel relief. But I'd go in my room and cry; I'd have deep depression.

In grammar school and in junior high school, I always had a lot going for me. Then, when I was a teenager, I went to an analyst at some type of clinic because my mother thought I was depressed.

DR. W.: Why?

KAREN: As I look back on it I can remember that I spent a lot of time in my room—one whole year, in fact. And I had no goals, no achievements, no ambition.

DR. W.: When was that?

KAREN: Right at the time that my father died. I was a senior in high school. During that year after my father died I'd shut myself in my room. I just wanted time out, wanted my own time. And I caused my own depression, I'm sure. In fact, when I was depressed, I had no anxiety, I just secluded myself from everybody.

I remember that my first anxiety attack came when we were moving. I left the place where I had grown up. My mother had remarried, and we were moving to another state. And I had to leave my boyfriend. All this was happening at once. Important things—my house, my security . . .

DR. W.: How old were you then?

KAREN: Eighteen. And shortly after that I started having my spells. In restaurants, movies, theaters, on ski trips.

In this brief exchange, Karen describes three patterns that are common in some agoraphobics.

1. She had a long-standing tendency toward anxiety.
2. She also suffered bouts of depression. In fact, her year of being housebound was more likely a depressive reaction to her father's death than it was a sign of agoraphobia.
3. Her panic attacks began during the time when her mother remarried and she had to move away from many important people and things in her life. This fits the pattern we have seen so far: agoraphobia tends to manifest itself during a stressful period in the person's life.

A new and significant psychological issue is supported by Karen's history. Many women who suffer from agoraphobia have difficulty coping with separation, not just in childhood but throughout their lives. Developing an independence from their parents as adults or choosing to separate from an unhealthy marriage can produce feelings of overwhelming anxiety. Even though they may intellectually believe that a change is needed in the relationship, psychologically the task is untenable. As a psychologist I can frequently identify experiences agoraphobic clients have had during their childhood and adolescence which reflect this difficulty in coping with separation.

Karen's extreme reactions to her father's death and to the family's cross-country move are examples. This single issue can place a powerful roadblock in the way of recovery.

"So I allowed her to dominate me"

DONNA: When I got married, I had absolutely nothing to do with the wedding. I didn't pick out the gown, I didn't pick out my maid of honor. My mother wanted a particular girl and that was it. I was always trying to please her, because I felt that she had sacrificed for me. And so I allowed her to dominate.

SHERYLL: My mother had always been a very domineering woman. She wants to control the world. She's go to be in control at all times. When I was a teenager I was never allowed to do anything, she used to do everything for me. I never had any independence. She tells me that this is because she was the youngest of nine and had to do everything in her family. Well, she shouldn't take it out on me!

In just those brief excerpts we observe that neither Donna nor Sheryll developed independent thinking and behavior during their teens. Regardless of the reason, they left their developmental years lacking an essential skill. Each of them has suffered greatly from that deficit.

In order to conquer panic, each of them must learn now what they should have learned then. If they fail to develop independence of thought, feeling, and action, they will remain trapped by their symptoms, because those symptoms are controlled by fear, hesitation to act, and self-doubt.

DOROTHY: My stepfather, no matter what we did, always bossed us. We never could do anything on our own. If we did one thing we were "stupid," if we did another we were "wrong." My mother was phobic, I guess, because he took charge of everything. He did the food shopping, my mother stayed home. He bossed my mother, he bossed me. He meant well, I'm sure he did, because we had a very good life, materially. But as I got older, I used to hear her crying a lot in bed.

My stepfather had to be right. She did try to fight him; as a child I remember them arguing about different things. But if they didn't go his way, he'd hit her. My mother was once lovely and strong. She ended up having a nervous breakdown. She's a nothing now, she just takes pills.

My mother would allow him to boss us. She'd say, "Just do it. Make him happy." In other words, we never had our own minds. We couldn't say, "I'm doing this because I want to do it."

After a while, I think it was ingrained in me. I was a perfectionist even as a child. I wanted everything just so. And I worried about everything. They called me "anxious." I was more of an emotional type. At fourteen the doctor put me on a tranquilizer.

I married my husband at seventeen to get away from the place. He was as strong as my stepfather, he also had control. So it's as if I never got the chance to find my own way.

These passages from Dorothy's session contain a wealth of information about her limitations today. First, Dorothy learned from her mother's modeling. It appears that her mother, too, was agoraphobic. Her world was no larger than the walls of her house. Remember that simply *observing* the significant people and events around us in childhood provides us with a great many of our beliefs. Dorothy also watched her mother attempt to stand up to her stepfather— and fail. Standing up for what she thought was right produced not only physical pain but humiliation as well. Independent thinking or acting became associated with discomfort, over and over again. In that setting it was natural, even smart, for Dorothy to become passive and dependent.

Dorothy made two other decisions in attempting to cope at home. She became a perfectionist, and she worried about everything. Could this have been her belief?: "Maybe if I do things perfectly, he'll stop criticizing me." Did she become anxious because she never knew what bad thing would happen next? "Will he get angry about this?" "How will he react if I do this?" No matter what she did, her step-father would never let her have control. In that setting, attempting to avoid his criticism may have been her best move.

The problem is that Dorothy's coping strategies as a child (to be passive, dependent, worried, and perfectionistic) became un-conscious patterns which she continues to use today, even though the situation that made these strategies necessary is no longer pres-ent. In order to change, she will have to experience a new trust in the benefits of activity, independence, and an acceptance of mis-takes.

The lessons we learn need not come from major, traumatic expe-riences; they can come from subtle influences, as illustrated by these comments from Helen, another agoraphobic client: "I was an only child, and I always wanted to please my father, I think. If I was doing anything wrong, he never hit or scolded me, or yelled. But he'd give me a look—that was all it took. My mother was a very passive person. She'd hold the peace at all costs, and I think I always wanted that, too—peace at all costs." Regardless of what actually took place in the home, it is what the child learned and decided to believe in re-sponse to what took place that determines her current behavior. We are not run by our past, we are run by our learned beliefs. Helen watched her mother "hold the peace at all costs" by being a quiet, undemanding wife who would never argue. She also experienced a loving family and observed a happy marriage between her father and mother. One belief Helen adopted was that "keeping the peace" would produce a happy marriage, and she decided to follow that rule in her adult life.

COPING IN THE PRESENT

Panic never rises "out of the blue" into someone's life. For some people, the causes are more obvious. The phobic, for example, has learned to become fearful based on past traumas or modeling from others. The post–myocardial infarction patient fears a second heart attack. However, the experience of panic in an agoraphobic is the physical manifestation of a complex constellation within the personality.

Certainly a great many people in the world suffer through traumatic events, perhaps the death of a parent or physical brutality. Even more people have experienced stressful periods during their lives which have produced brief episodes of anxiety and panic. All of us go through times of self-doubt and self-criticism, of wanting to please others and of avoiding conflicts.

So, what "makes" an agoraphobic? Just as with most other psychological problems, we are not certain, and probably never will be. The understanding of personality cannot be an absolute science. However, the patterns illustrated in this chapter reflect some of the common experiences of the present and the past which shape and support the panic-prone personality of the agoraphobic.

There is no going back to fix the past. There is no way to get today the things you failed to receive when you were younger. What is done is done. But, fortunately, knowing the causes of agoraphobia is a different issue than knowing how to cure it. Panic is maintained by our current beliefs and attitudes, our current emotions, and our current behaviors. These three parts of us *are* changeable, regardless of our past.

One difference between an agoraphobic with panic and other panic-prone persons is that the agoraphobic may feel more "stuck" and have a sense that "I'll never change." So many variables come into play during the treatment of this disorder. With the agoraphobic, you might say that the moment of panic is much like the head of a pin with a freight train behind it. For this reason it is the general agreement of experts in this field that agoraphobics require the assistance of a specially trained mental health professional to master panic.

Part II of this book takes into account the many issues facing the agoraphobic with panic. Most important, it reflects my firm conviction that by attending to current beliefs, emotions, and actions one can overcome any obstacles in one's way.

5

Four Complicating Problems

There are four specific problems which can complicate the diagnosis and treatment of panic. The symptoms of panic closely resemble those of premenstrual syndrome and those of hypoglycemia. This can cause some difficulties in diagnosis. A missed diagnosis can delay appropriate treatment for some sufferers. Depression and alcoholism greatly disrupt the treatment process by lowering motivation and by contributing additional serious problems to an already complex picture. In most cases, the depression or alcoholism must be treated before significant progress is made toward controlling panic.

PREMENSTRUAL SYNDROME

Premenstrual syndrome (PMS) is the occurrence of a wide variety of physical and psychological symptoms in women during the days or weeks prior to menstruation. Studies have found that 30 to 95 percent of all healthy females may experience a premenstrual increase in depression, irritability, and anxiety in addition to physical discomfort. Central to diagnosis of this disorder are both the type of symptoms present and the time in which they occur.

In PMS, a woman will experience moderate to severe emotional and/or physical symptoms which begin up to fourteen days before menstruation, but usually start five to seven days prior. The discomfort comes in almost every monthly cycle and only during the premenstrual phase. The symptoms disappear during the week after menstruation begins.

The menstrual cycle is one of the most complex of the body's functions. Despite fifty years of research, we do not fully understand its process. There is no known cause of PMS that has been substantiated by large-scale research findings. No one treatment has achieved solid support, either. We can now say, however, that this is a physical, not psychological, disorder.

Since the possible kinds of symptoms are so numerous and can vary dramatically among women, I will present here only the psychological and behavioral symptoms that frequently occur during the premenstrual phase. If your symptoms are so severe that they seriously disrupt your life and if you have four or more of these symptoms, then you should discuss this with your physician:

1. Irritability, hostility, anger, "short fuse"
2. Tenseness, restlessness, jitters, upset, nervousness, inability to relax
3. Decreased efficiency, fatigue
4. Depression, crying, spontaneous mood swings
5. Poor coordination, clumsiness, proneness to accidents
6. Distractibility, confusion, forgetfulness, difficulty with concentration
7. Change in eating habits, usually cravings and overeating
8. Increase or decrease in sexual desire

Although most women with PMS suffer both physical and psychological symptoms, the psychological can be the more devastating.

PMS is one of several problems described in this book which often go undiagnosed; since so many of its symptoms are psychological, the women, their families, and health professionals can dismiss it as "all in her head." Failure to receive a proper and early diagnosis can greatly complicate the problem.

We know that stress has a direct effect on the menstrual cycle. It can cause a delayed period or a missed period. When troubles and tensions increase in a PMS sufferer's life, they also take their toll by increasing her symptoms, such as irritability and depression.

Panic can be one symptom of PMS, and the stresses of life as well as the stress of having undiagnosed symptoms only serve to increase the possibility of panic. In fact, professionals who fail to consider this syndrome may misdiagnose the problem as panic disorder. The best way to distinguish the two is to keep a daily chart of your symptoms for two or more months. By matching your discomfort with your menstrual cycle, a clear pattern should emerge if you have PMS.

Treatment for PMS must be individualized, since medical science is still exploring the exact causes. Several approaches are considered to have potential benefit. The broadest recommendation is an attention to food, vitamins, exercise, and emotions. Foods to avoid are those high in sugar, salt, or fat, highly processed foods and those containing chemicals. Controlling eating binges and weight gain can also lower risk. Foods which may be beneficial in reducing symptoms are those high in protein and those from whole grains, the legume family, seeds and nuts, vegetables, fruits, and unsaturated vegetable oils. The B-complex vitamins, especially B_6, and vitamin A may be needed. Increased physical exercise will promote an increase in metabolism. And finally, counseling to help in coping with stress is important.

Other treatments are still in the exploratory stage, with either mixed findings or too few research studies completed to adequately support their wide use. These include progesterone suppositories (if a hormone imbalance is found) and medications such as diuretics (to reduce water in the body), oral contraceptives, and biomocriptine or danazol (for breast symptoms).

You may find that, even though your symptoms are not identifiable as PMS, they become stronger prior to menstruation. A number of my clients have remarked that they are more likely to panic during this time. Their comments support my belief that hormonal changes can influence susceptibility to anxiety attacks. Specifically, the female hormone progesterone has been found to increase the sensitivity of certain chemical receptors in the body. Progesterone is secreted during the premenstrual phase of a woman's cycle. It is possible then that these alarm systems become too sensitive, causing the brain to respond to a misinterpreted signal. This may account, in part, for the far greater frequency of panic in women than men, as well as the increase in anxiety and irritability during the premenstrual phase.

The symptom of panic in a PMS sufferer can begin to take on a life of its own, causing many complications. In Part II of this book you will learn to "desensitize" this alarm system so that your symptoms remain under your control. You will learn how to manage panic and eventually eliminate it from your lfe as you find the best treatment for your other PMS symptoms. While some anxiety may persist, no one needs to feel swallowed up by the fear of unexpected, uncontrollable attacks of panic.

HYPOGLYCEMIA

As mentioned in Chapter 2, hypoglycemia (meaning "low blood sugar") is the experience of uncomfortable physical symptoms during times when there is a lower than normal level of glucose in the bloodstream. This condition is quite rare and is found predominantly in people with diabetes mellitus. Other causes of "functional" or "reactive" hypoglycemia include high fevers, liver disease, pregnancy, stomach surgery, some kinds of cancers, a reaction to certain foods or drugs, and anorexia nervosa.

In diabetes mellitus, the pancreas produces insufficient amounts of insulin, a hormone used to break down and store sugar in the body. One result is a higher than normal amount of glucose in the bloodstream. The disease is controlled by daily insulin injections and/or a controlled diet. If the diabetic takes too much insulin, or does not keep to the prescribed diet, or is engaged in extended strenuous physical activity on a particular day, he may experience a drop in the blood glucose level, leading to symptoms of hypoglycemia.

When the symptoms of hypoglycemia are severe, they are indistinguishable from those of a panic attack: trembling, lightheadedness, perspiration, anxiety, irritability, tachycardia, unsteadiness and weakness. The similarity in symptoms is not coincidental. To combat low blood sugar, the medulla of the adrenal glands secretes the hormone epinephrine, which helps release extra sugar from its storage in the liver and dump it rapidly into the bloodstream. But epinephrine does more than that. It is a stimulant of the sympathetic branch of the autonomic nervous system. During times of emergency, fear, anger, or threat, epinephrine prepares the body by increasing the heart rate, raising blood pressure, increasing respiration, tensing muscles, and causing a number of other rapid changes (this process is fully described in Chapter 8). During a panic attack, the individual believes he is threatened in some way. That belief is enough to signal the brain to secrete epinephrine.

Since hypoglycemia and panic attacks are so closely related, misdiagnosis is a serious problem. In the past hypoglycemia has been diagnosed by physicians through a five-hour glucose tolerance test preceded by three days of a high-carbohydrate diet. Even such a rigorous evaluation is insufficient, since 23 to 48 percent of normal individuals will experience random periods of low serum glucose levels. An accurate diagnosis requires that the patient experience *symptoms* during those times of low blood sugar and a *relief of symptoms* as the blood sugar rises.

Evaluating the patterns of your panic episodes, however, can provide important information:

1. *Do you wake up with panic attacks?* Blood sugar levels are lowest in the morning, since the body has experienced its longest period of time without a meal. If symptoms occur every morning, not just every few mornings, hypoglycemia might be present.

2. *Are there regular patterns to your panic attacks?* Blood glucose levels are lowest just before lunch, just before dinner, and two to three hours after lunch and dinner. If your panics consistently coincide with one or more of these periods, low blood sugar may be contributing to the problem.

3. *Does sugar in some form completely remove the symptoms?* If you are prone to panic during these times, experiment with consuming sugar in some form (a sweet roll, fruit juice, candy, or pure sugar) when you begin to panic. If your symptoms consistently diminish within ten to thirty minutes, you should check with your doctor to consider hypoglycemia.

A number of popular books have proclaimed hypoglycemia to be the undiagnosed culprit behind a vast number of physical and psychological problems. In fact, the exact opposite may be true. Poor diagnostic procedures by professionals and self-diagnosis by lay people account for the inordinately large number of false cases of hypoglycemia. For instance, in a recent study of 135 patients claiming to have or suspected of having hypoglycemia, only 4 could be confirmed with the diagnosis. Eighty percent of the other patients manifested some kind of psychiatric condition, especially depression and somatization (continual focus on multiple physical complaints).

The misdiagnosing of hypoglycemia is a dangerous affair, since a false confirmation of this illness prevents the true diagnosis from being identified and treated. Serious physical problems such as hypertension and hyperthyroidism (both are described in Chapter 2) may be present, as may treatable psychological problems.

For the panic-prone person, the diagnoses which may be missed, in addition to depression, are panic disorder and agoraphobia. There are several reasons for this. First, of course, is the fact that panic symptoms can be present in hypoglycemia. There is also a relationship with the times in which panic might occur. If a person has panic attacks routinely while standing in line at the grocery story or waiting for a meal in a restaurant, is it panic disorder or hypoglycemia? If the person hasn't eaten in a few hours, he may feel the same jitteriness and other symptoms which any of us might get when our body reacts to a low blood sugar level.

The panic-prone person will not only notice his symptoms while in the store or restaurant, but will react fearfully to them. Consuming some form of sugar to diminish the physical symptoms will not relieve his worry, but leaving the scene will.

Many people with panic disorder cling to the belief that they have hypoglycemia instead. This provides them with a number of benefits which all fall under the category of avoidance. By deciding that they have a physical disorder they avoid facing the psychological and stress-related problems in their life. Psychological problems continue to carry a stigma for many in our culture. Their treatment also requires dedicated effort on the individual's part. Hypoglycemia provides relief by placing a clear label on some perplexing and ambiguous symptoms. And it offers an easier solution, since the sufferers simply pay special attention to their diet. But some patients not only limit what they eat but begin to restrict their social functioning. This can be a clue that the individual may be keeping a firm hold on the label of hypoglycemia as a way to avoid facing more fearful possibilities.

As mentioned earlier, to make the diagnosis of reactive hypoglycemia, the physician must determine that the patient's symptoms are present when the blood sugar levels are at their lowest and are relieved when the blood sugar rises. Merely performing a glucose tolerance test on patients who experience spontaneous panic attacks is insufficient, since a large minority of normal subjects can show random low glucose levels.

If a positive diagnosis of hypoglycemia is made, the panic-prone person may still have to work at managing his emotional reaction to those times of low blood sugar. Here are a few suggestions. Carry sugar in some form with you at all times. When you notice the early signs of an attack, you can calmly eat some until you begin to feel normal again. Explain to friends how to help you if you become disoriented. Instruct them to give you fruit juice or other sweets until you are able to help yourself. A general maintenance diet and any necessary precautions will be explained to you by your physician. Part II of this book will help you control the physiological reactions of your body during a hypoglycemia attack and will assist you in remaining emotionally calm so that your symptoms can be kept to a minimum.

DEPRESSION

It is not surprising that some people who experience anxiety attacks become depressed. When we begin to feel our world closing in around us, when we are unable to face situations that previously caused us no anxiety, when we experience physical symptoms that seem to have no clear cause, then self-doubt, discouragement, and sadness are understandable side effects.

Many people who experience panic also complain of symptoms related to depression: a low energy level, feelings of hopelessness, low self-esteem, crying spells, irritability, difficulty concentrating, lack of interest in normal activities, a decrease in sexual desire, difficulty with sleep, and fluctuations in weight.

The relationship between panic disorder and depression has been well established through numerous controlled studies. At the same time, this research indicates that panic disorder (and agoraphobia) and depression are distinct and separate problems which happen to coexist within the same individual. A large majority of patients with panic disorder or agoraphobia have had episodes of serious depression. One study found that half the panic disorder and agoraphobia patients entering treatment with a history of depression had experienced at least one major depressive period prior to developing panic disorder or separate from periods of panic. In other words, depression doesn't develop simply in reaction to prolonged struggles with panic. And your depression can lift even though a problem with panic continues.

For the person suffering from panic, the most important issue regarding depression is the way it complicates and slows the recovery process. Consider for a moment the thoughts of an anxious person who experiences panic attacks. He looks to a specific future event and worries, "Can I handle it?" He considers the possibility of failure and says, "It's possible I'll fail." He desires to take some action but says, "I'm too afraid." The panic-prone person wishes to actively engage his world, but is doubtful he can manage specific tasks. As panic lingers in a person's life, his outlook and his self-evaluation may take on depressive qualities. The person who is primarily anxious will look to the future with uncertainty. He is not sure how difficult his future tasks will be; he doesn't know whether or not he will perform up to par or if he will be able to control the situation. He doubtfully questions the future.

If he begins to adopt a more depressed attitude, this uncertainty is transformed into fatalistic expectations. He looks to a specific future event and says, "I won't be able to handle it." He considers the possibility of failure and says, "I'll fail." The internal struggle, between wishing to take action and feeling too afraid, shifts. Instead of doubting the future he becomes more certain of what will happen: "I will not succeed." An even more self-destructive attitude may arise: "I don't really care that much."

These negative predictions and lack of drive are supported by a pervasive sense of personal worthlessness, as though he is missing the essential traits to be a complete, competent human being. Instead of thinking, "I'm not prepared for *that job*," or "I doubt I can enter *that building*," he begins to think, "I'm inadequate. I don't have what it takes. I don't fit in." As he looks to his past, he finds justification for this feeling. "Things are no different than they've ever been. Nothing has ever made that much difference. My limitations are unchangeable."

Helping someone face panic when he or she has adopted a depressed attitude is a difficult task, for obvious reasons: If I believe that I am basically inadequate, that nothing ever really changes in my life, that tomorrow will be about the same as yesterday, then why should I bother considering alternatives to my present state of affairs? Through my eyes, there seems to be no point.

If you are feeling this kind of depression, you must confront and shift your entrenched attitude in order to face the challenges presented by panic. Through some means, you must move your attitude from a position of certainty ("Nothing is going to change things") to one of uncertainty. Even an anxious attitude ("I don't know whether or not I can manage this") is an improvement. In fact, this is the position I want and expect my clients to take as they begin facing panic. It is not necessary to embrace some false sense of confidence and assurance, because uncertainty is a major component of adult life. By saying "I'm not sure," you are opening your mind up to the possibility of change ("Maybe I won't handle this particular challenge, and maybe I will.")

There are two ways to begin changing this depressive attitude; both are addressed in Part II of this book. The first is to directly wrestle with your negative beliefs: to listen to how you state those beliefs in your mind, to learn how those statements influence your actions, and then to explore other possible attitudes which might support your goals.

The second way is to begin to change your activities even before you change your attitude. Try some specific, small activities, without needing to believe they will help you. Change your patterns of behavior during the day, alter your routine, do some things that you imagine someone else might consider "good for you." There is no requirement that you engage in these new activities with the belief that they will help you. At first, just do them. Don't predict how you are "supposed" to feel during or after them—that will usually be a setup to prove, once again, that "nothing will change." Simply change your patterns as a way of giving yourself experiences that might challenge your beliefs in a small way.

Let me illustrate the purpose of this process by describing its use with another kind of problem. In my practice as a clinical psychologist I specialize in the treatment of anxiety disorders and also in the management of chronic pain syndromes. Years ago I worked as a therapist at the Boston Pain Center, a medical in-patient unit for chronic pain patients. The facility is designed to help those who have tried every known medical treatment and yet remain in significant physical discomfort because of a physical injury or illness.

The chronic pain patient and the person suffering from panic disorder share the predominance of depression. Consider the patient who enters the treatment unit with chronic low-back pain. He describes himself as "vegetating in front of the 'boob-tube' all day for the past five years." He perceives himself as useless, since he hasn't been able to work in five years and his wife supports the family. He can't even mow the lawn or take out the garbage because of his back pain, much less figure out how to return to productive, paid employment. And "all of the doctors have given up hope" on him, so how could the future be anything else but just like the past, or worse?

The in-patient program takes him out of the normal routine of his home and provides a broad range of activities which are designed to challenge this attitude. He lives for four to six weeks among twenty other patients with similar pain problems. He is required to rise first thing in the morning, make his own bed, eat in a group dining room, attend four support/therapy group meetings a week plus medical sessions, community meetings, and special outings. To manage his physical pain he attends individual and group physical therapy sessions, receives massages and ice massages, hot packs, ice packs, and whirlpools. He is taught biofeedback and relaxation techniques. His pain medications are slowly diminished and eventually discontinued, as he learns alternative ways to successfully manage his pain.

This is the typical design of a "therapeutic community," where the medical staff and patients work together to find the best treatment for each individual. We don't expect every approach to work for every patient. Instead, we provide as many options as possible in order to discover which combination will be most effective.

But one of the first things that must change is the patient's attitude, since a depressive outlook can prevent any learning. How does that attitude shift? Most frequently it changes because the patient begins to have experiences that don't fit into his negative expectations.

For instance, a low-back pain patient may complain of an inability to stand or sit for more than twenty or thirty minutes at a time (he then must lie down to relieve his discomfort). By altering his pattern of activities, the therapeutic community offers him a chance to have new experiences which change his belief. On day five of the program he discovers that he just sat through an hour-and-a-half group therapy session without having to stand or lie down. Then he remembers that this is the third time in two days that he has sat for over one hour. It is this kind of awareness that can lead him to say, "Maybe I can do something to help myself. Maybe things can change."

This is usually the turning point for patients on the Pain Unit. Once they decide that change is possible, they tend to look at any new treatment with a ray of hope. They stop being so certain of failure and begin thinking of their options. Trying each new technique now involves curiosity. "How might I benefit from learning biofeedback?" "I wonder what results I'll get if I do these physical therapy exercises every day for a couple of months?"

If you are suffering from depression, this is the kind of curiosity you must strive for. Part II of this book will suggest a number of new techniques and activities for you to practice. It will also directly address your depressive attitude, giving you alternative ways of thinking about yourself and your future. As you proceed, keep in mind the need to confront your negative view. For a while you may have to try the suggestions even though your mind is saying, "What's the use?" Above all, you must take action. No matter how low you feel, some part of you believes that you can help yourself. Even if it is a small ember of hope deep within you, let that supportive self give you the gift of curiosity.

ALCOHOLISM

Alcohol can have a dramatic effect on the body. It is primarily a central nervous system depressant, similar to major and minor tranquilizers, barbiturates, narcotics, and nonbarbiturate sleeping pills. It is just as addicting as these drugs in that there is a specific physical and psychological withdrawal process necessary after prolonged use.

As a central nervous system depressant, alcohol slows down and numbs the higher and lower brain and spinal cord centers. The first centers affected are the inhibitory ones, so alcohol's first effect is usually the removal of tensions and inhibitions. This is the primary reason why people with anxiety, fears, or panic might turn to drinking. With alcohol, they typically experience warmth, relaxation, and a general feeling of well-being.

As larger amounts of alcohol are consumed, however, the entire central nervous system becomes depressed, leading to impairment in judgment, motor coordination, speech, vision, and balance. And, of course, since judgment is distorted, the person who has been drinking in excess is unable to judge the negative changes in his behavior.

Heavy drinking can lead to a hypoglycemic reaction, usually occurring twelve to sixteen hours after a drinking bout. As the liver metabolizes alcohol, it stops manufacturing glycogen (the precursor to glucose). Blood sugar levels are then maintained by using previously stored glycogen. Once that supply is used up, blood sugar levels drop, producing a hypoglycemic reaction. As mentioned in the earlier discussion of hypoglycemia, this reaction can be indistinguishable from panic. Some panic-prone persons are more susceptible than others to low blood sugar levels. For instance, drinking may diminish their anxiety level during an evening out. Twelve or so hours later, as the next morning begins, they experience panic symptoms "out of the blue." This, of course, reinforces their sense of being out of control and may encourage another drink to "calm the nerves."

Several studies have explored alcoholism and phobias, bringing interesting patterns to light. It has been estimated that between 5 and 10 percent of all phobic people are dependent on some chemical such as alcohol. Studies of alcoholics indicate a high correlation between the degree of the person's dependence and the presence of a phobia.

For example, a study of 102 alcoholics admitted into an alcohol treatment unit in England found that one-third of them also had agoraphobia or a social phobia. Another one-third had phobic symptoms of a less disabling degree. A second study by the same investigators found that, in a group of 44 alcoholics who were phobics, the majority had developed their phobic symptoms prior to their alcohol dependency.

It appears, then, that not only do some panic-prone persons drink to relieve their anxiety but their crutch may end up causing them more serious problems. Often the drinking pattern will become autonomous: the person still has the same fears and still avoids uncomfortable situations but is now also consumed by alcoholism.

I predict that in the years to come, research will continue to confirm this significant relationship: for one subgroup of alcoholics, anxieties regarding their abilities to handle themselves in specific situations draw them to drink. For the short term they perceive the drinking to be helping them by diminishing their sense of fear. Yet, as time passes, the alcohol takes on a stronger, independent role in their lives. They increase their alcohol consumption, which actually increases their work-related problems, their emotional instability, and their isolation from family members and friends.

Because of the serious problems caused by alcoholism, the phobic symptoms in the patient tend to go unnoticed, even within a professional treatment program. Since the symptoms of detoxification are similar to those of anxiety, both the patient and the alcoholism treatment staff may not consider any phobic or panic disorder as an additional diagnosis. When the anxious fears return, though, that patient may once again reach for the only relief he or she knows. The more skilled the staff can become in identifying anxiety-related drinking problems, and the more the patients can wrestle directly with these issues, the less that revolving door in the detoxification unit will spin.

Dependency on alcohol reinforces the panic-prone person's negative belief system. The person sees alcohol as a form of self-medication, but at the same time, his dependency reinforces the belief he is not in control. He feels safe only after he has had a few drinks. Any difficult situation becomes the cue to reach for a drink. In time, self-assurance, confidence, and pride are replaced by this numbing process.

As you might imagine, depression in the panic-prone person is another problem which is supported by alcohol. The scenario may unfold in dozens of ways. Here is a hypothetical example: One day, to my great surprise, I have an anxiety attack just before making a presentation at a business meeting. Over the next several weeks I worry about "losing control" like that again. I'm feeling tense in general these days because of expanded job responsibilities and competition from some others in the company. Before my next presentation I down a shot of whiskey, "just to take the edge off." It actually works: I'm calmer just before my talk and during it. But I continue to remain on edge during the week.

Before a dinner party next week I again become panicky. Out comes the whiskey, in order to turn the evening into a pleasant time. I am discovering that I can manage the tensions with this little helper, even though I notice an unusual increase in my anxiety level the next morning.

Time passes. It is four months later—four months of swings of tension followed by relief. Four months of doubt about my ability to handle the pressures of work. Four months of distortions in my normal thinking about my job, my life, my capabilities. My anxiety begins to change. Now, instead of thinking, "Oh, no, how will I handle these responsibilities," I begin to think, "I don't really care that much." The persistent drinking to ease the anxiety takes its toll as my anxious feelings become wrapped in a blanket of depressive indifference. "The job's not that important" might be my conscious thought. But underneath this is a growing sense that I am no longer the man I thought I was, I don't have what it takes to control my life, I am stuck and might as well surrender. Nothing will fix the problem, so I can only learn to cope with it.

Through the powerful combination of alcohol and depression, the symptoms of panic have led to a serious and complex syndrome involving denial, self-defeating behaviors, avoidance, loss of self-esteem, and physical deterioration.

If alcohol has become your crutch you must remain alert to its seductiveness. Facing your fears without it may seem tougher, but your successes without this drug will provide your only avenue to long-lasting change. If you suspect that you may be dependent on alcohol, or if people close to you all agree that you have a problem, seek out professional help or the help of Alcoholics Anonymous. A panic-prone person with alcohol dependency should treat his alcoholism first, then begin managing his fear responses.

6

Panic Within Heart and Lung Disorders

It is easy to take the human body for granted. Its complex functioning is so phenomenal that we can scarcely imagine the process, much less appreciate it. With nourishment and upkeep, it runs without any major complaints for decades. All systems work together for one single objective: to maintain equilibrium throughout the body and between the body and its environment.

The cardiovascular system and the respiratory system work together as the primary forces behind this process. Through its smooth, rhythmic action, the respiratory system ensures that adequate levels of oxygen are available instantly for any circumstance and maintains the delicate acid-base balance in the blood. The cardiovascular system makes certain that every cell in the body is fed nutrients and oxygen and is cleansed of its waste products. The heart circulates five quarts of blood through the body every minute, which also helps it maintain a constant, comfortable temperature.

Because these two major systems are so vital to our moment-by-moment life, the body and mind will react faster than the speed of light if they are threatened. This automatic alarm, evolved over hundreds of thousands of years, directs all our human capabilities with two instructions: "Find any way to breathe, and keep the heart beating."

Only two months ago I was reminded of this in a dramatic moment. I am standing on the porch of my parents' farm in the mountains of North Carolina. My father is holding our twelve-month-old daughter as we talk casually about one thing or another. I glance at Joanna at the same moment her eyes bulge and she stops breathing. I lunge forward and slap her on the back while three other options to free her passageway instantly appear in my mind. Within five seconds from start to finish, the piece of ice that had lodged in her throat had melted and cleared through the esophagus.

As an infant, Joanna hardly knew anything had happened. I, on the other hand, experienced the remarkable speed and skill of my unconscious life-saving instinct. And my body and mind were left with the aftereffects of this psychophysiological response. As soon as I saw that Joanna was breathing again I also noticed that my head was pounding from all the blood that had rushed there. And I mean "rushed": my circulatory system pushed an abundant supply of blood to the vessels of my brain within my first two heartbeats.

This, of course, was only a minor crisis, because no harm was done. But the body doesn't wait around for some panel of experts to vote on the degree of the crisis. If the brain signals "crisis," the body responds. It is this instinct that saves our lives.

The person with a chronic heart or lung problem faces many new challenges. One of these is how to adjust the signals from the brain so that the minor symptoms of the problem are not interpreted as life-threatening. If the patient with heart disease reacts fearfully to every pressure in his chest, he places unnecessary strain on his healing heart. If a patient with emphysema becomes anxious about every new activity, he directly aggravates his safe, comfortable breathing pattern. And yet, the brain has been trained for hundreds of centuries to shift the body into crisis gear when the heart or lungs seem to be threatened. Therefore, learning to cope with these chronic conditions can be quite challenging.

In disorders of the heart and lungs, panic arises when the body and mind respond to a relatively minor symptom with the weapons typically reserved to combat a life-threatening situation. This chapter addresses five of these conditions: mitral valve prolapse, recovery from myocardial infarction, emphysema, bronchitis, and asthma.

MITRAL VALVE PROLAPSE

The mitral valve is a structure within the heart which controls the opening between the left atrium and the left ventricle. In mitral valve prolapse (MVP), this valve leaflet balloons slightly into the left atrium during contractions. (Figure 2 shows the location of the mitral valve

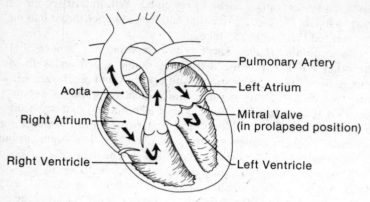

Figure 2. Location of mitral valve and change in appearance after ballooning.

and the change in its appearance after ballooning.) This minor cardiac abnormality is found in approximately 5 to 15 percent of all adults and is especially prevalent among young women. Most people are never aware that they have this problem, since 50 percent of those with MVP experience no symptoms. On average, even if MVP is identified, no medical treatment is needed.

Of the 50 percent who do notice symptoms, the predominant one is palpitations, the conscious awareness of some unpleasant sensation of the heart. They may be aware of premature contractions of the heart chambers, called extrasystoles, or of a rapid heartbeat (tachycardia). Other possible symptoms are shortness of breath or difficulty breathing (dyspnea), dizziness, chest pain, fatigue, fainting, and panic attacks.

Given these symptoms, what is the relationship between panic disorder and mitral valve prolapse? Demographically, they appear to be related. Both are found with the same frequency: in 5 to 15 percent of the population. Both are predominant among women, with symptoms beginning in early adulthood. Research findings indicate that some people with MVP may have inherited the condition. Thus, there may be a genetic link which associates these two problems for some individuals, but that question remains unanswered.

Growing evidence indicates that MVP does not cause panic disorder. Instead, panic-prone persons become overly attentive to their physical sensations. It is this worried observing of the heart's activity that invites anxiety. The more anxiously preoccupied the person becomes, the stronger his symptoms, until panic erupts. Consider the fact that half of MVP patients have no symptoms at all. Others develop symptoms but experience them only as a minor nuisance. They continue in their normal activities without turning their attention inward.

It seems that between 10 and 20 percent of MVP patients experience panic. Research indicates that MVP is found in sufferers of panic disorder as infrequently as it is in the normal population. And treatment of panic disorder in individuals with MVP is no different than for those without MVP.

The pivotal aspect of the relationship of these two conditions is in how the person responds to his awareness of symptoms. In order to panic, a person must not only notice some new sensation of the heart but must also become fearful of what that sensation means. The autonomic nervous system will then respond to the person's fearful thoughts, not to the heart palpitation itself. This process, fully described in Chapters 7 and 8, will produce more dramatic symptoms, such as a racing heart, dizziness, shortness of breath, and even a panic attack.

Since mitral valve prolapse can produce palpitations at random, it contributes to the panic-prone person's belief that he must remain "on guard" at all times to defend against mysterious "out-of-the-blue" attacks of panic. One advantage of receiving a clear physical diagnosis of MVP is that it can reassure the panic-prone person that these symptoms are not a sign of danger. By diminishing worry and anxiety you automatically diminish the potential for symptoms.

Diagnosis of mitral valve prolapse is made by a cardiologist through echocardiography (recording the position and motion of the valve by echoes of ultrasonic waves transmitted through the chest wall) and through listening to the sounds of the heart during contraction. Evaluation by a physician is recommended if a person experiences a sudden occurrence of physical symptoms, such as true vertigo (room spinning), fainting, or chest pains or palpitations.

If you are diagnosed with MVP, Part II of this book will help you learn to manage your symptoms. It is important to understand a few points. First, changes in the rhythm of the heart are a frequent occurrence in most people, and are rarely harmful. By learning to accept, tolerate, even ignore them, you will diminish your anxiety. Second, don't let those symptoms frighten you into avoiding activities. By avoiding, you feed a negative pattern which unnecessarily restricts your life. Third, you can actually reduce your symptoms to a few annoying but not distressing sensations by learning to accept the normal process of mitral valve prolapse and by preventing panic.

RECOVERY FROM MYOCARDIAL INFARCTION

A heart attack is certainly cause for reflection. It is a traumatic blow to the ego which jerks us out of our mundane patterns and calls our attention to the vulnerability of life. Physically, the return to health is slow and steady for those with uncomplicated problems. Psychologically, the recovery almost universally includes a struggle with two stressors: depression and anxiety. The patient feeling depressed wrestles with thoughts and feelings of resignation: "My life is no longer worth fighting for." The anxious patient continually faces the fearful question, "When will I die?"

Time and the skilled maneuvering of the mind heal these psychological blows for most recovering myocardial infarction patients (post-MI patients). For instance, two or three days after a heart attack, many will begin to deny the significance of the problem. They become increasingly animated and cheerful with the staff of the coronary care unit. Although the customary hospital stay is two weeks, they talk of their readiness to go home and get back to work immediately.

To concerned family members, such talk seems inappropriate, as though the patient is not facing up to the seriousness of the situation. Actually, this denial seems to be the mind's clever way of giving the body some rest during the early stages of recovery. To allow the person to experience the full blunt reality overstresses the cardiovascular system and slows the healing process. Eventually, though, this denial must gradually give way to acceptance of the true picture, or the patient will not take necessary precautions and follow the medical advice and guidelines. As he faces reality his primary question will be, "How cautious should I be?" After a heart attack this becomes a complicated question, since its answer affects hundreds of small daily decisions for years to come. It is no wonder that many of these patients continue to restrict their lifestyle and feel uncertain about activities for months and even years beyond the acute phase of the illness. "Will I die at the same age as my father died? Should I ever risk having sex again? Will I die in my sleep tonight? I shouldn't be getting excited like this. Is that a pain in my chest as I inhale?"

There are three basic life-choices a post-MI patient can make:

The Healthy Stance. Knowing my limits and my options, I work within them in order to expand them. There is an old expression that says, "Freedom is what you do with what's given to you." In order to experience freedom, this post-MI patient works with his physician and other medical professionals to understand his current physical state and capacity. He then learns what activities are possible given this stage in his healing process. He acts on his desire to live his life to the fullest within those limits, while simultaneously adopting a medical plan which can help expand those limits. This is the only life-choice which will successfully control panic.

The Panic-Prone Stance. I must remain constantly on guard since the slightest provocation could cause my death. Panic arises because the post-MI patient is unclear about his limits or his options. He notices a symptom or potential symptom and has no specific plan for monitoring or controlling it. This lack of preparation turns his body against him. Without the proper signal of reassurance from the brain, the body reacts by shifting into crisis gear, which causes an increase in symptoms. This life-choice encourages chronic anxiety and panic attacks, which seriously strain the heart.

The Depressive Stance. There is no point in continuing to try, since my course is now charted. This patient surrenders his power to heal himself. Because of his willingness to become dependent on others, helpless, and restricted in his activities, he has been labeled a "cardiac invalid." Often, he withdraws from friends and retires from work. This life-choice dissolves the person's spirit to live. And by becoming physically passive he worsens his medical status by weakening the cardiovascular and respiratory systems, since regular exercise helps maintain all organs and systems of the body.

Sometimes the panic-prone stance leads to the depressive stance, in this way: If I continue to face situations which I believe might stress my heart and do not develop a plan to manage those situations, eventually I must alter my course. My only solution, then, is to avoid those situations. Soon avoidance is my first choice. Since preventing another heart attack is more important than some brief pleasure, I also stop partaking in the activities I enjoy. I am now less anxious, but I've lost my pleasures too. Depression steps in to fill the void.

If you are recovering from a heart attack, your physician will help you understand your physical limits and will design a rehabilitation course so you can return to your highest level of functioning. He or she will also help you understand and respond appropriately to any unusual symptoms you might experience. Before reading Part II of this book, you should discuss with your doctor the appropriate response to various symptoms.

Part II of this book will offer information and a number of skills for you to use within the context of your medical treatment. You will learn how to think clearly in case of any medical emergency, how your attitude toward your health affects your reaction to symptoms, and how to calm yourself if you become anxious or if you panic. We know from research and numerous clinical reports that the simple mastering of a few basic calming skills is one of the key ingredients to recovery from any of the cardiovascular illnesses, including hypertension and coronary artery disease. Most important, you will learn how to return safely to the physical and social activities that give your life meaning and pleasure.

CHRONIC OBSTRUCTIVE PULMONARY DISEASE

"I'll never breathe again." That is the statement that screamed out in my mind. And for that instant, I believed it with all my heart, soul, and mind. There was not the tiniest sliver of belief that I would live. You don't live without air. I cannot inhale, and I have no air in my lungs at this moment. I'm dying. Good-bye.

That moment occurred during the second half of a soccer match this past summer. As a defensive fullback, I stepped in front of the offensive forward just as he followed through on a forceful kick toward the goal. The ball slammed into my chest at "point-blank" range. The power behind the blow knocked all the air from my lungs, leaving me, literally, breathless. The game continued as I stood there, frozen, leaning halfway forward, incapable of inhaling and incapable of speaking. This marked the moment of panic for me: I believed, based on my physical experience, that I did not have the control to save my own life.

In this situation, my panic lasted about twenty seconds. Within thirty seconds, action had stopped in the match, two teammates had helped me to lie down on the ground, and I had had my first taste of that ever-so-precious-but-lost-forever air.

I can look back now and laugh a bit at my extreme reaction to such a benign occurrence. On the other hand, this was the second time in three months that I had lost my breath on the playing field. And during both moments I thought, "I'll never breathe again." The panic associated with heart or lung problems is special. You don't experience it as a passing moment, you experience it as your *last* moment.

Panic plays its most damaging role in patients suffering from chronic obstructive pulmonary diseases. The illnesses themselves interfere with the natural breathing process and diminish vitality and endurance. For some the symptoms become more severe over the years. If the illness progresses, the patient becomes less and less able to work or to enjoy social and recreational activities, since any kind of exertion or emotional shift could trigger a breathing problem. Thus, the patient with a chronic lung problem learns to brace himself for any sign of discomfort and often chooses to avoid activities in order to feel safe. This is the fearful stance which is most vulnerable to panic.

The essential feature in many respiratory disorders is a narrowing of the bronchial tubes. In chronic bronchitis, the mucous membrane that lines the main air passages (or bronchi) of the lungs becomes inflamed. This leads to breathlessness, coughing that brings up phlegm, and an increased risk of infection. In chronic asthma, the muscles of the bronchial walls contract, causing a partial obstruction of the bronchi and the bronchioles (the smaller air passages in the lungs). The patient experiences attacks of wheezing and difficulty breathing, triggered by allergy-provoking substances, physical activity, or psychological stress. With chronic emphysema, the air sacs (alveoli) at the ends of the bronchioles are damaged. Since these are the site of oxygen and carbon dioxide exchange, the lungs become less and less efficient at their job. The primary symptom is difficulty breathing, which worsens over the years. Figure 3 identifies the parts of the respiratory system affected by these diseases.

Since breathing is one of the two most prominent life-supporting processes (along with the pumping of your heart), patients with chronic obstructive pulmonary disease (COPD) are likely to develop

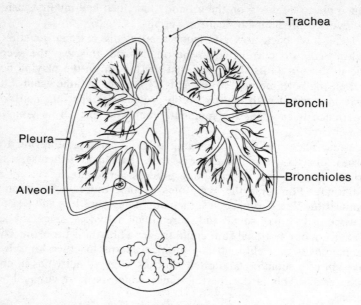

Figure 3. Parts of respiratory system affected by chronic obstructive
     pulmonary disease.

anxiety, panic, and depression because of their inability to control
this vital function. Their most-feared problem is having difficulty in
breathing. When an episode of difficult breathing begins, they may
respond with panic, believing that they will die from suffocation as
they are gasping for breath. This brief period of panic becomes etched
in their minds. The aftereffects of this trauma are maintained by vivid
recollections of the attack, by nightmares of being unable to inhale,
and by thoughts that the next attack could come anytime, anywhere.
The results of one study illustrate the outcome of such recurring experiences: the researchers found that 96 percent of the subjects with
COPD developed "disabling" anxiety.

    As they withdraw from their world to protect themselves from
anything that might cause breathlessness, the patients' general level
of anxiety may diminish. But they then become susceptible to depression. If a person is socially isolated, cuts himself off from pleasurable

activities, and avoids conflicts, strong emotions, or any new experiences, he sets himself up to become a victim of depression.

Dr. Donald Dudley of the University of Washington has aptly stated that many severely disabled COPD patients live in "emotional straightjackets." It is no wonder, since any shift in emotion, whether toward anxiety, joy, or depression, can trigger a physiological reaction. If the patient becomes preoccupied with the problem, he may complain of nervousness, faintness, rapid breathing, and poor concentration. His impending sense of doom can translate into obsessions, compulsions, phobias, and ritualistic behaviors. Some will even become fearful of visits to their physician. Depression, fueled by low self-esteem and hopelessness, can lower the patient's motivation to carry out important treatment programs.

I want to emphasize the degree to which emotions have a direct mechanical effect on the respiratory system. Since a COPD patient has limited pulmonary reserves, his ability to supply oxygen throughout the body and his ability to remove carbon dioxide is compromised. Each emotional state has a corresponding breathing pattern. For most people these changes are easily accommodated. However, the patient with a severe COPD problem becomes incapable of managing even minimal changes in respiration.

For instance, as we become angry, afraid, or anxious, these more active emotional responses require an increase in metabolism. This need cues the respiratory system to increase breathing, to increase the oxygen supply and remove excess carbon dioxide. The COPD patient may be physically incapable of accomplishing this increase in breathing. Instead of taking in more air, he begins to have difficulty taking in enough air. The oxygen level in his body drops while the amount of carbon dioxide increases. As the difficulty persists he, of course, becomes anxious or panics, causing more symptoms, in a vicious circle of symptoms-producing-anxiety-producing-symptoms.

A similar process can take place if the patient experiences episodes of sadness, depression, or apathy. These emotional states will lower the respiration rate, which leads to low levels of oxygen and high levels of carbon dioxide in the body.

Even if the COPD patient is able to inhale sufficiently, he may still become anxious in his awareness of the increased demand placed on his lungs by an emotional state. In normal circumstances the breathing pattern matches the demands placed on the body. If I am involved in a vigorous physical activity, the increased oxygen my lungs are supplying is utilized efficiently during metabolism. During anxious moments, however, the body often cannot use the oxygen as rapidly as it is put into the bloodstream. At the same time, the lungs remove more carbon dioxide from the body than is useful. This is hyperventilation, which causes a number of uncomfortable symptoms in addition to those caused by the illness. A complete study of breathing processes and hyperventilation is presented in Chapter 11.

If you suffer from a serious chronic obstructive pulmonary disease, managing your daily living presents a great challenge. Often your predicament seems hopeless. But there is a beneficial attitude and set of skills that can be brought to this challenge. I believe that those suffering the discomforts of COPD can begin to feel safe and more involved in their life and community by considering the suggestions and by practicing the skills described in this book. Here are several guidelines which may help you along the way as you read Part II:

- Your central goal should be to find as many ways as possible to keep physically active and maintain your interests in life without harming yourself. Setting realistic goals and working progressively and safely toward them will improve your spirits, strengthen your respiratory system, and decrease any unrealistic fears you may have.
- As you socialize, find ways to make yourself comfortable. Some people become easily fatigued and must end an evening earlier than expected. Those with chronic bronchitis may have to tolerate a severe coughing spell and dispose of sputum while in public. In order to remain active you will need to find ways to handle these situations without withdrawing in embarrassment.
- If you are taking medications, discuss with your physician whether any of them might cause increased nervousness or irritability. For instance, certain drugs help open up the bronchi by activating the sympathetic nervous system. In doing so they may make you feel a little more jumpy. Knowing this can help you prepare for any mild symptoms.

There are three classes of medications used for COPD patients that are most likely to cause unpleasant side effects. The oral medications used for bronchospasm—aminophylline and the beta-Z adenergic agents—can cause general anxiety and a rapid heart rate. The inhaler form of the beta-Z adenergic agents, such as Isoproterenol and Metaproterenol, can produce general anxiety and shaky hands. The corticosteroids, such as Prednisone, may briefly elevate the patient's mood, then cause a swing into depressed feelings.

- The problems of your life will not disappear just because you avoid them. Your best approach will be to learn ways of facing and coping with any stressful changes. If you don't respond to the curves that life throws at you, then you will eventually surrender control of your life.

- If you suffer from a severe lung disease, you may find it necessary to avoid any situation which causes anxiety or can lead to any rapid change in your emotional state. It is sometimes a tricky balancing act to remain an interested participant in your world and at the same time not become too caught up in the dramas of life.

- When nervousness, worry, and depression do come, learn how to diminish them by applying skills such as those found in Part II. The less worried you are, the fewer severe breathing episodes you will have, and the less you will need to use emergency care.

- Most important, learn the best ways to think, feel, and act during an acute episode. You can learn specific techniques that minimize symptoms and support your return to comfortable breathing. The breathing problems that confront COPD patients are quite unique. Our bodies and minds do not instinctually respond to these attacks in a supportive way. In fact, it appears that some of our instinctual reactions cause increased symptoms. It is necessary, therefore, to study your individual patterns and adjust them, in order to diminish your anxiety and increase your sense of well-being. You must develop the ability to notice your symptoms without reacting emotionally to them. By adopting a set of response skills, by creating a plan for when and how to use these skills, and then by repeatedly practicing these skills, you will begin to take control of the symptoms of your illness. Anyone would react with anxiety to the thought of not being able to breathe. Your task is to reduce your anxiety once you notice it, then begin steps to improve your breathing pattern.

PART II

TAKING CONTROL
OF ANXIETY ATTACKS

7

The Anatomy of Panic

The battleground of panic is not isolated to the few seconds or few minutes of an anxiety attack. The more panic attacks you experience without gaining mastery over them, the more they seem to invade other territories. Imagine for a moment that panic is an enemy which has chosen to wrest control of your life away from you. The cleverest of invaders will overcome their victims by undermining their foundations, withholding their nourishment, destroying their confidence. And that's just what panic will do, given the chance.

One panic attack can be a surprise, later dismissed as "a fluke." Two panic attacks might be viewed as coincidence; you rationalize that "too much stress" caused the problem. You tell yourself to "slow down, take it easy, don't get uptight." However, if the episodes continue, panic makes its first inroads into your life. You begin to question yourself, to doubt your strength, to wonder if you are coping. This is panic's most powerful weapon. This is what begins to loosen the bricks in your foundation. By creating self-doubt, panic gains its first stronghold in your life. After a while, the panic attack itself plays a role in the ongoing battle. With all the cleverness of a magician, panic appears in your life; and with all the swiftness and power of a judo master, panic takes your mental energy and turns it against you. Before you know it, you've reversed the tables on yourself. Just as with any of the martial arts, the more you fight panic, the more you seem to lose.

Am I overstating the case? I don't think so. People who call my office for a first appointment usually have been experiencing panic attacks for anywhere from six months to dozens of years. Here are some of the many ways panic, over a period of time, can use your thoughts, feelings, and beliefs as weapons against you.

- Some reminder causes you to hesitate before venturing back into the arena of that last attack.
- The need to avoid becoming "trapped" is given high priority each time you consider certain activities.
- You anxiously wonder when the next attack will come. "Will it be here, now?" Simply asking the question seems to bring on symptoms.
- You nervously think about the last panic attack, and then you doubt your control over your body.
- You worry that some unknown physical illness or an emotional breakdown is causing your attacks.
- If you have a diagnosed physical illness, you fear any undue stress or aggravation.
- You begin to avoid certain people or places as your only defense against attack.
- You become more socially isolated and secretive, perhaps feeling trapped by appointments, roles, expectations.
- You brood, you worry, you criticize yourself and become discouraged.
- You may stop trusting yourself and turn to alcohol, drugs, or doctors to carry you through your days.

To portray the anatomy of panic, then, requires a broader brush than you might at first imagine. Since every individual is unique, the ways in which panic affects each of us will be different. There are no absolutes here; this is not a black-and-white picture of straight lines and curves. There are many gray areas and a number of frightening shadows. For each person the intensity, duration, and depth of the specific problem areas will differ. To present all the possible ways in which panic can affect a person's life, I will often describe serious problems encountered by my clients. In no way do I mean to suggest that you will also face these same difficulties. Please read these passages with a curious mind. Ask yourself whether that particular aspect relates to your experience. For instance, the inability to understand why you are experiencing an anxiety attack at a particular moment can dramatically increase your anxious symptoms. I address this problem and ways to handle it in a number of sections of this book. On the other hand, readers who suffer from chronic bronchitis, emphysema, or asthma *know* why they panic: they become afraid that they won't be able to get enough air. These readers will not need to focus on this issue. Therefore, in order to help yourself you must first paint an accurate picture of your unique situation. Only then can you decide how you must change that picture to regain control.

The first change you achieve will probably be a greater understanding of how panic affects you as an individual. But knowledge alone will never be enough. You must then evaluate your way of thinking about yourself and the world you have created around you), your beliefs (about yourself and your roles), your emotions (especially the feelings you are afraid of), and your actions (the things you do and don't do). Panic invades all four arenas; therefore, you must gain control of each territory in order to regain control of your life. To challenge your attitude about your present-day life, to explore the roots of your many beliefs, to learn from your emotional responses, and to experiment with new actions—these together are the keys to long-lasting change.

One of your strongest resources for overcoming panic will be knowledge, since panic uses doubt, uncertainty, and fear of the unknown as its powerful allies. At this point you should know whether your problem with panic is serious enough to merit a diagnostic evaluation by a physician or a mental health professional. If a physical or psychological disorder is diagnosed, learn as much as you can about it: What is its cause? What are the other problems associated with it? What professional help will you need? How can you help yourself? A broad understanding of your situation will serve as the foundation to your success.

Don't Panic is designed to address all the issues central to panic attacks. Let's begin by separating panic into its component parts. How does it disrupt your confidence? How does it leave you victim to its surprise attacks?

The central element of panic, of course, is its symptoms, which I described in Chapter 1. Needless to say, if this book is going to help you, it must advise you on how to manage those symptoms. In Chapter 8 you will learn about the physiology of panic, and in later chapters you will gain the tools necessary to become master of your body again. Now, however, I want you to think about the ways brief episodes of anxiety can play havoc by disrupting your thoughts.

WINNING THROUGH INTIMIDATION

The only way panic gains control over you is through psychological intimidation. The actual panic attacks last only an infinitesimal amount of time—even if you had one panic episode every day and that episode lasted five minutes, you would be experiencing panic only *one-third of one percent* of your life—and yet some people can become completely dominated by the repercussions of those moments of panic.

Consider the concept of "losing control." What does that mean to you? For most people it means losing security, safety, protection. If we have a sense that we are out of control, we immediately, almost instinctively, begin searching for some small way to regain our equilibrium, whether we have lost control of that burst water pipe, or slippery roads have caused a momentary loss of steering, or our young child has disappeared from sight in a shopping mall.

And after you have lost control once, what do you do? You probably start checking *all* the pipes in the basement to make sure there aren't other potential breaks. A few hours later you might go back down those stairs "just to check if everything's OK." After momentarily losing control on the highway you may grip the steering wheel a little tighter, even chastise yourself for being "overconfident" by driving with one hand. Once you find your missing child in the mall you probably keep a constant vigil over her whereabouts. *When the mind fears loss of control, it begins to think more intensely about how to keep control in the future.*

Panic attacks—especially spontaneous attacks—stimulate the sense of being out of control. All of a sudden, you are not the one who is in charge of your body; heart, lungs, throat, head, legs—all seem to have minds of their own. That is very frightening. Just the thought of it can make you anxious.

And that is how it begins, how panic starts to invade your life. You fear that those uncomfortable physical symptoms might return yet again. And how bad will they get? Worse than before? You don't know. It is that "not knowing" which proves to be a devastating weapon against you: "Since I didn't manage the last attack, how can I possibly handle this one?"

THE SURPRISE ATTACK

To add to your confusion, the attacks are not always consistent. You might get hit with symptoms at a restaurant one evening, have no problems the next three times you go out for dinner, then on your fifth time out you begin to feel that same trapped sensation. It is like spinning the chambers of the pistol in Russian roulette. Mentally, and even physically, you begin to brace yourself in anticipation. You become constantly on guard. For some, these fears translate into a desperate need not to feel "trapped," because being trapped implies surrendering control. "Staying in control" is the primary objective.

Katherine M. is a twenty-nine-year-old single woman who works as an editor for a computer software company. She had been experiencing anxiety attacks for about nine months when I first saw her.

Her first moment of panic occurred out of the blue, as she was walking to work from the subway station. But as is often the case, this morning was preceded by several months of stress: her boyfriend had broken off their relationship, her boss was transferred, a close friend was diagnosed with a terminal illness, and Katherine was seriously considering moving from her hometown of Philadelphia to California.

During the past nine months since that first panic attack, her fears and her self-imposed limits have gradually restricted Katherine's world.

Here is how she described some of her concerns when I first interviewed her: "I work downtown, but I won't walk around outside when I'm there. I'm afraid I'm going to pass out. If I went out to lunch I would be afraid I wouldn't make it back. I also have trouble driving. I get afraid I'll be trapped if I get into the outside lane or if I'm not near an exit. Restaurants bother me. Again it's that trapped feeling: once the order is taken, I can't leave."

Katherine and millions like her suffer from panic disorder. They experience unexpected anxiety attacks and seek a safe asylum from that sense of being trapped. Before venturing out of their place of security they mentally evaluate each new environment. If they can imagine any chance of being trapped, they will avoid that situation.

When such avoidance behavior dominates their lives, the diagnosis of agoraphobia is considered.

The fears are not only of being trapped but of any experience that might produce a sense of being out of control. In Chapter 4 you were introduced to Ann C., a thirty-two-year-old woman who has experienced agoraphobia for twelve years. Listen to her concern in this brief anecdote.

> When I had surgery for a biopsy, they were going to put me to sleep. The scariest part of the ordeal to me was being put to sleep. I asked the doctor to give me a local anesthetic instead of a "general." He said, "You know, you're so brave. Many people say, 'Knock me out, knock me out.' " I said to myself, "Little does he know that my fear *is* of being knocked out, of just *letting go.*"

Why does Ann fear general anesthesia? Because she believes that the way to remain in control of her life is to always be on guard, to monitor her every action, to always watch for potential threats. This belief is actually causing her physical and psychological harm. The mind and body cannot tolerate the pressure of constantly bracing for an emergency. It is no wonder that she also reports feeling tense, anxious, and physically and emotionally exhausted.

Panic plays on the imagination. It gains its greatest power through the thoughts and images that you create in your mind. A person who fears elevators doesn't simply get anxious while standing in front of an elevator. When he thinks of calling his physician for an appointment, he remembers the doctor's office is on the fifteenth floor. He reminds himself immediately of his fear. And now, weeks before the appointment, he feels afraid. While sitting in his living room he imagines himself standing in front of the elevator. Then he begins to feel the butterflies in his stomach, his fists tighten and turn white, he feels a little lightheaded, and he changes his mind about calling his doctor. Most likely he will rationalize his decision, attributing it to more than just fear ("I don't *need* an appointment, yet. I'll just wait a while").

Dorothy P. is another agoraphobic whom I described in Chapter 4. In the following comments, notice how she anticipates losing control. She imagines the worst possible scenario, and it is this mental image that scares her away from driving.

> I don't want to lose my license, so I just don't drive. If I had
> a panic situation driving somewhere—if there was a detour or if
> traffic backed up—I'd either have to get out and run, or jam on
> the brakes, knock everybody down, knock the policeman down,
> go through red lights . . . I would have to escape. I can't seem to
> say, "Well now, calm down. You know you can. It's only going
> to be a short time." I can't rationalize it. I don't think at all.

Dorothy is right: she *doesn't* think rationally about her driving skills.
The fact is that she has never had an auto accident and has never
responded with such hysteria while driving. But she imagines the
possibility, and that image is enough to keep her out of the driver's
seat.

CONTROLLING THE MIND

For the victim of panic, panic controls more than just those brief
moments of physical anxiety. It connects physical sensations directly
with your thoughts, so that simply by entertaining an idea, you stimulate a physical reaction.

For example, the *thought* of biting into a lemon can cause the lips
to purse. The *thought* of a violent crime can make the muscles tense
with anger. The *thought* of sinking into a nice long, deep, warm,
soothing, quiet, peacefully restful bath . . . can begin to relax those
same tense muscles.

With panic, the body responds to the mind in a similar fashion.
For instance, I asked Katherine what happens after she has ordered
in a restaurant and then thinks of being trapped.

> I get terribly anxious and panicky. I'll sit there and eat, so no
> one will notice. But I become very uncomfortable physically,
> even dizzy. It's the same when I stand in line at the bank. Once
> I get to the teller's window and hand my business through, I get
> very nervous. Because I think, "I can't leave until she gives me
> my receipt. I'm stuck!" I start thinking that I'm going to pass
> out.

Katherine remains under control while she is in line only because she
tells herself, "I can just get out of the line and leave." But once she

has begun her transaction, she imagines that she cannot leave without "causing a scene."

Another client, Michelle R., was a regional manager of a national corporation and had been experiencing panic episodes for six years.

Her first spontaneous panic was while driving her car: She became dizzy and lightheaded and felt as if she was going to faint. After her second attack four months later, she visited her family physician, who diagnosed the problem as "nerves." During the months prior to the onset of her symptoms, Michelle had become involved in an extramarital relationship. Within one month, she and her husband separated. Even with the episodes of panic and her physician's diagnosis, Michelle remained calm and unemotional regarding the separation process and saw no relationship between her symptoms and her marital conflict. During those next six years she managed her panic disorder without any professional help. She divorced her husband and two years later she married the man with whom she had become involved.

By the time of her first appointment with me, she had stopped driving. She never took a walk, or stayed home alone, or shopped alone. In her business she continually found excuses to refuse out-of-town meetings. In addition, I suspected that she was subtly sabotaging her chances for further promotion.

In one of our sessions Michelle described how she had gained some insight into the ways panic plays havoc with the mind. During her previous appointment I had asked her to listen for the silent statements she makes just prior to a panic episode. She entered this session with a satisfied smile on her face.

> Now I know what you mean. I produced my own anxiety attack! I was sitting at a staff meeting this morning—and I did it to myself without knowing it. I thought, "What happens if you feel overwhelmed, or you get that panicky feeling?" And I started feeling it! I could sense my heart racing. I became intensely nervous.

Michelle had always described her panic attacks as coming out of the clear blue. In fact, that was one of the worst parts of her experience: she never had a clue as to when or why they would appear. Once she learned that particular ways of thinking can influence physical symptoms, she started paying attention to some of her thoughts. In this way she was able to discover one typical pattern: first, she would simply question the possibility of experiencing symptoms, then the symptoms seemed to begin. In the past she had not been aware of those thoughts going on in her mind, so the only thing she noticed was her physical reaction. As soon as she discovered that she could produce negative symptoms by the way she was thinking, her improvement was rapid. She realized that if thoughts could bring on panic, controlling thoughts could also get rid of panic.

FORECASTING THE FUTURE

Sheryll W., whom you met in Chapter 4, became agoraphobic after the birth of her oldest child twenty-two years ago. She began to feel uncomfortable in church and in grocery stores. Then the anxiety attacks started.

> When I panic, my heart rate increases, I hyperventilate, feel dizzy, my legs get weak, especially if I'm experiencing a lot of stress. If I even *think* about going to the beach or another crowded place, I get that smothering feeling and I can't catch my breath. That brings on all the other feelings.

Her comments illustrate the same process that Katherine and Michelle speak of. As soon as they begin to think negatively about the future, they fall into the panic trap.

It is as though panic has implanted a small voice in your mind. Let's say that you have had some anxious feelings driving long distances on the highway. Today you decide to drive to your sister's house, fifteen miles away. As the time to leave approaches, that little voice begins. "Now, can you get there without having an anxiety attack? Really, honestly, and truly get all the way there?" That's all it needs to say, because that question alone plants a seed of doubt in your mind. "Are you 100 percent certain you can get there? And what if you start to panic . . . then what?" These kinds of questions imply that you *can't* get there without being anxious, and that you can't handle the anxiety.

How does panic reach the body through the mind?

First: you contemplate venturing into a type of situation that has caused problems in the past. ("I think I'll go grocery shopping today.")

Second: you remind yourself that this situation has the *potential* to stimulate your physical symptoms. ("Oh, no, last week when I went with the kids I got so dizzy I thought I'd pass out.")

Third: you doubt your ability to handle those symptoms. ("Who knows what would happen if I went alone? I'd be so humiliated if I had to run out of there. I'm already feeling queasy just thinking about it.")

Your fears may be completely irrational. A part of you may even say, "I know I'll be fine. I've never fainted. Even if I do faint, I'll survive." But despite that voice of logic, the fearful doubts remain. You gradually become plagued by the *concept* of losing control, and that plaguing fear seems to defy logic.

You can now see what a powerful ally panic has if it can instill in your mind a fear of losing control. Add to that fear the uncertainty about when the symptoms will strike and how long the attack will last, and you can see why so many sufferers of panic become physically and emotionally exhausted. They must be on twenty-four-hour sentry duty.

THE PLANNED RETREAT

Only one defensive move seems to bring relief from panic: avoidance. "If I can just keep from having to give that speech [or do any exercise, take an airplane, confront my boss, use an elevator], then I'll be fine." And so you retreat back to some safe ground. Remaining safe becomes the highest priority.

For certain fears, avoidance can be an acceptable solution. City dwellers needn't be comfortable confronting snakes. Nor does everyone have to be comfortable crossing suspension bridges. But for too many people, avoidance has made a significant impact on the quality of their lives. I have worked with clients who have given up driving, who have stopped entering stores or taking buses, who have refused promotions or quit work altogether, who haven't been in a restaurant or to a party in years. I have had to visit some agoraphobics in their homes because they refused to venture outside.

In reaction to an actual physical illness some people will dramatically alter their lives. For instance, I worked with a twenty-four-year-old woman who had suffered from asthma since she was twelve. As you probably know, the symptoms of an asthma attack include wheezing, tightness in the chest, and difficulty breathing. Even though she had not had an asthma attack in over a year, Cynthia was profoundly fearful of having a spontaneous attack. She rarely traveled beyond her hometown. When she did drive outside the city limits, she would mark on her map the location of each hospital along her route. If she did not think she could reach a hospital emergency room for oxygen within five minutes' time, she would not venture that route. In addition, she remained afraid of ever becoming "too" excited, which might trigger a bout of asthma.

Dorothy P. had not traveled outside a two-mile radius of her house in over forty years, nor had she ever been alone during that time.

> I don't actually go someplace and panic, because I just tell myself I can't go. I never leave Chapel Hill. Any time I travel in Chapel Hill I have someone with me. If I go into a restaurant I have to watch the door, even sit near the door. I very seldom go to movies, and when I do go I take the aisle seat. I have to walk out to the lobby from time to time, and I always leave before the end of the show. I hate to say this, but I haven't had any anxiety symptoms in years, because I never push myself. I stay away from all things that might produce this trapped feeling.

Few people go to such extreme measures to protect themselves, but many people begin to hesitate in their everyday life. They start to delude themselves about what they want and need out of life. Actually, they begin talking in terms of what they *don't* want or need: "I don't really need to go out, I'm happy just staying home with you." "I don't really want to get all dressed up tonight. Why don't we skip that party?" "Who needs the added pressure of that promotion?" "I'd love to meet with you next week, but I don't want to make commitments so far in advance. I never know what might come up."

Some cardiac patients, frightened of overexertion or overexcitement, can become socially isolated and physically inactive. Their fear of triggering a heart attack becomes masked behind indifference and depression. "I'm too old to start taking walks around the block" really means "What if that walk is all that it takes to produce another attack? I don't want to die." Such a fear is understandable, but when it begins to take primary control over most of your daily activities, you are being run by panic.

Sam S. was a sixty-three-year-old plumber referred to me by his family physician. He had developed the common signs of agoraphobia: He was afraid to ride the subway, take a bus, or drive. He remained home most of the time. And he had developed a peculiar fear of his plumber's tools, which prevented him from returning to work.

After our first interview I had a strong sense that I understood the cause of his problems. After four sessions, my hunch was confirmed. With my encouragement and a few simple suggestions, Sam was able again to take the subway and drive his own car. But his tool phobia was immovable. He said his fears were so great that he couldn't even consider the idea of touching the tools without starting to feel tense and anxious. In fact, he said, his fears were so great that he didn't wish to continue treatment. I never saw him again, but I learned from his physician that six months later he still remained out of work.

What did I believe was behind Sam's phobia? Three months before he first saw me, Sam had had his second heart attack. This brush with death triggered his fears of travel and activity. But most important, he feared causing his own death by bringing on a third heart attack. Sam had unconsciously found a way to prolong his life. By developing a phobia of his tools, he would not have to pick them up again. He would no longer have to crawl under a person's house, lift a 22-pound plumber's wrench, strain to tighten down a joint, place his weakened heart under that kind of stress.

At his age and after two heart attacks, perhaps Sam should have considered retiring his tools. But panic took that decision away from him. Consciously, he did not feel that he had any choice in the matter. Even explaining my sense of the problem to him had no effect. Panic won, and last I heard, Sam was applying for 100 percent disability based on his phobia.

This case illustrates how panic can even disrupt the healing process after a physical illness. Regardless of what produces the initial worries or anxieties—whether the cause is emotional or physical—panic can take on an identity of its own and continue to play havoc with a person's life.

WHY ME?

If you are suffering from unexpected panic attacks that defy all methods of self-control, you want desperately to know *why*. You will typically consider one or both of these two answers: there is something physically wrong with you, or there is something psychologically wrong with you.

If you are convinced the problem is physical despite objective findings to the contrary, you will begin a long and frustrating pilgrimage from doctor to doctor. You might take that same route if you consider the problem to be psychological in nature. Or you may feel so humiliated by the possibility of being "mentally disturbed" that you hide behind the cloak of secrecy. Some of my clients have never told a single person about their years of silent anxiety. Adding to the pain of social isolation is the destructive force of self-doubt and criticism. You begin to blame yourself for your "weakness": "Why am I so afraid? Why don't I just *do it?*"

Panic attacks that defy simple cures can lead a person into a downward, self-destructive spiral. Since you feel that you cannot control your life, you gravitate toward any person or thing which might provide that control for you. Through your physician, you may try tranquilizers, sedatives, muscle relaxants, or antidepressants. Or you begin to self-medicate, using alcohol to "take the edge off." Some adults unconsciously choose to remain very close to their parents, even though consciously they feel ambivalent about that decision. Others gravitate toward strong and dominant friends, or unconsciously choose a spouse who is powerful and controlling, as a means of feeling safe. These choices are the result of a belief system that follows these lines: "Since I know that I am inadequate, I must find someone who will stay close to me and watch over me."

Panic begins to erode your self-confidence by convincing you that you are no longer in control of your life. After a few months, you may face a new set of problems: a loss of drive, diminished motivation, a sense of hopelessness, helplessness, worthlessness. Not only are you feeling out of control of your body, but the people around you seem to be taking control over your life decisions. Thus, depression can complicate an already difficult life.

In other words, panic gains further inroads in your life by its ability to elude cure. It becomes the great unsolvable mystery. You surren-

der to the problem while waiting desperately for something or someone powerful enough to conquer it.

The following paragraphs are excerpts from therapy sessions with
several of my clients (whom you met in Chapter 4). I have taken these
passages out of context, so of course a great deal of information is
missing. Nonetheless, read between the lines to imagine how such
experiences can erode the self-confidence and hope of these women.

ANN: After my honeymoon I returned to work and felt utter tension
all the time, with very bad headaches and several anxiety attacks.
I finally visited the psychiatrist at school. He put me on Valium [a
mild tranquilizer]. I would go to see him each week, but I never
got anywhere because he never did any talking. In the end I said,
"What's wrong with me? Just what is wrong?" And he said,
"Well, you suffer from classic, classic tension." That was his
answer.

DONNA: The doctor put me in the hospital for four weeks. During the
first week I had all kinds of physical tests, and then I went over to
the psychiatric unit for observation for three weeks. That cost us
nearly five thousand dollars. And when they were through, they
said to me, "We don't know what's wrong with you." The psychiatrist said, "You're as sane as I am," and the medical doctor said,
"We can't find anything physically wrong with you." I've tried
Valium, Stelazine, Tofranil, and Elavil. They had absolutely no
effect. So the doctors said to me, "We're taking you off of all
medication and we're discontinuing psychiatric treatment because
there's nothing we can do for you."

KAREN: When I had my second child, I finally was diagnosed as
having "cabin fever." I tried to understand it and tried to rationalize it, saying, "Well, you've got two little babies under the age of
two, and you have cabin fever. It's the middle of February, and
it's a terrible time for people." But deep inside I knew it was
something more than that.

SHERYLL: The symptoms began after Susan was born, my oldest. I
had postpartum depression, but I also kept experiencing anxiety
attacks. One afternoon I was on the phone trying to find an apartment. I started to have chest pains and other symptoms. I called

my mother, and they rushed me to the doctor's. They thought I was having a heart attack. That's how it all started. I found that when I went to church I would have a problem. Before long, it was supermarkets. And then I think it all mushroomed. I went to doctor after doctor, and they all said it was my nerves.

As you can see, the mystery that surrounds panic also feeds the panic. To label anxiety attacks as "nerves" and to offer only medications rarely succeeds. In fact, as those medications fail to eliminate panic attacks, the sufferer will often become more distressed.

Other people are more secretive. Here is how Katherine described her feelings:

> I think I was just ashamed. I thought I was having a nervous breakdown. I mean, I couldn't just go up to my friends and say, "Hi. I'm having a nervous breakdown." I guess I didn't know how to talk to anyone about it. I thought they would laugh at me. Besides, I don't like to bother people with my problems. People have their own problems, they don't need mine. Or they won't take me seriously. They'll say, "Don't worry about it."

So instead of giving her friends a chance to support her and express their care, Katherine became more withdrawn and turned to alcohol for control.

> I didn't know what was happening to me. And I was also drinking a lot. I would get home at night and drink to calm myself down. There were some weeks when I'd go home and I'd drink a half a pint of whiskey at night. I didn't understand what was happening to me, and it seemed to be the only thing that would calm me down. But the alcohol didn't work, because the next day I would feel terrible and the symptoms seemed to be worse.

What accounts for such dramatic physiological changes which defy simple cures? How does panic remain so powerful, yet so mysterious? Part of the answer, discussed in Chapter 8, lies in our inability to trust our bodies' unconscious control. And another part of the answer, examined in Chapter 9, lies in the way we think during times of crisis.

8

Who's in Control?

To me, there is little that brings such peace and serenity as a walk along the beach during the quiet of the early morning. It's as though it's just me and the universe having our private time together, undisturbed. The problems of home seem so far away as I let my mind just drift in its own easy thoughts. The sun slides up from the Atlantic; it seems so big and orange. Everything seems wondrous: the sand crabs swimming deeper, leaving only a small hole for the next wave to wash over; the school of dolphins in the near distance diving one way then the next through the surface of their playground; the seagulls seeming to hang carelessly in the sky. The ocean shore changes my perspective and slows my busy thoughts. Life seems simpler. The natural world surrounding me invites me to join in its rhythm.

There appears to be a balance in this universe of ours, which is maintained by constant change. The tides of the sea are either in the process of rising or in the process of falling. Nothing is still. Everything in nature is in constant flux, but it is not random change. Just as the pendulum swings, the rhythms of this world seem to produce a balance between two poles. Every molecule in the universe expands and contracts.

Our years on earth are balanced between the heat of summer and the cold of winter. Our days move from the brightness of noon to the darkness of midnight. The rhythm of living things brings movement between rest and activity. For many of us, every twenty-four hours bring sixteen hours of activity and eight of rest. We work five days and rest two days. Each year we balance months of work with weeks of play.

But nowhere is this rhythm more profound than in the human body. Consider the heart. It expresses a singular pattern as it beats within the chest: contract, relax, contract, relax, contract, relax. Blood doesn't flow through the body; it pulses. Push, relax, push, relax. Each blood vessel expands and contracts as needed, rhythmically.

When you receive a blood pressure reading, you are given two numbers. The higher number (the systolic pressure) indicates the greatest force exerted by the heart and the highest degree of resistance put forth by the walls of your arteries as blood is pumped. The second, the lower number (the diastolic pressure), identifies the lowest pressure in the arteries, at the time when the heart is most relaxed. Your pulse rate, on the other hand, expresses how often this activity-and-rest cycle of your heart takes place each minute. Physicians are concerned only when this basic life rhythm is not in balance. A good strong heartbeat and pulse of blood through the body is a sign of health to physicians, not a cause for worry.

Consider your breathing. The lungs fill with air as you inhale. When the lungs expand, they stretch the diaphragm, which is a sheet-like muscle above the abdomen. When the diaphragm is stretched, its natural tendency is to relax again. As it moves back to its relaxed position, air is gently pushed out of the lungs—you exhale, and the lungs contract again.

Expanding and contracting. Activity and rest. That is the principle polarity which maintains equilibrium within all the systems of the natural world, whether we speak of the oceans, the seasons, our daily activities, or the organs of the body. This force which sustains life is self-generating. It need not be supervised. It is a force of great tradition, extending back to the beginning of time.

DISTRUSTING THE UNCONSCIOUS

When I speak of this life-sustaining rhythm in the human body, I refer to it as being managed by the "unconscious." Let's establish our own working definition of "unconscious" as *any part of our mind other than that which we are conscious of.*

I needn't consciously remind myself to take my next breath, or to have my next heartbeat. All the important functions of my body and mind are controlled unconsciously. I can certainly control the rhythm of my breathing consciously, but if I tried not to breathe, I wouldn't succeed. Even if I did a great job of holding my breath, I would eventually be forced to exhale or to faint so that my unconscious could regain control.

When I sleep at night my conscious mind relinquishes complete control of my body to my unconscious. If I were injured and feeling severe pain I would probably faint (or "lose consciousness") while my unconscious regulated my essential bodily functions.

So, what am I leading to, you might ask? You are glad I like the ocean, you already know how long you work each day, and, yes, your hearts beats regularly without constant reminders. What's the point?

The point is this: Panic erodes a person's basic trust in his body. Panic wins control over you by convincing you to doubt your body's natural *unconscious* monitoring system. Panic says, "Keep watching, keep listening, keep monitoring." These are the destructive messages of panic.

If you are constantly on guard over your body's sensations, you will need to start thinking about your body in a new way. Answer this question: how do you allow yourself to fall asleep at night? Sure, you are exhausted from the day and you need your sleep. But when you fall asleep, you are no longer going to be able to consciously monitor your vital functions. You can't listen to your heart beat, you can't make certain that you take the next breath of fresh air. What lets you relinquish that conscious control? What is it that you are implicitly trusting?

If you found an answer, it was probably like "trusting that something would make sure my heart kept pumping." Again, for simplicity's sake, let's label that something the unconscious mind. What if, at the time of a panic attack, you could convince yourself to rely on that same unconscious to help you manage your body's sensations? I can guarantee you that when you learn this skill you will be back in the driver's seat. You will no longer be letting panic have control, nor will you be forcing your conscious mind to do all the work. Instead, you will take full advantage of the remarkable control possible through a "team" effort. Your conscious thoughts will do half the work; your natural unconscious processes will do the rest.

As you may know, the "unconscious" has been viewed in the past as implying some dark and deep part of the psyche, full of painful

traumas and repressed emotions from childhood. Psychoanalysis was
seen as a decade-long process of dredging up these hidden memories
through studying the patient's dreams and free associations. Its goal
was to gain conscious insight and control over negative unconscious
impulses.

This, I believe, is the wrong approach for coping with panic. The
unconscious is 99 percent brilliant in its ability to constantly direct the
body toward health. Perhaps 1 percent of the time the unconscious is
functioning inappropriately. For winning over panic attacks, the unconscious *needs no fixing* and *needs no supervision* by your conscious
mind. It's perfectly fine. It simply needs to be permitted to do its work
without intrusion. It is the conscious mind's intrusion that is the problem—that little voice that says, "What if these sensations get worse?
Something bad will happen. Watch out!"

THE EMERGENCY RESPONSE

A couple of summers ago, when my wife and I were living in Massa-
chusetts, we drove to the Outer Banks of North Carolina for a week's
vacation at the ocean. Here is the scenario, as we were heading
south.

I am looking forward to being with my brother and his wife during
that week on the beach, so part of my mind is drifting to images of
playful times as I drive down Interstate 95. Another part of me is
aware of how crowded the highway has become now that we are close
to Philadelphia. I move to the outside lane to keep up speed. Driver's-
ed classes teach us to keep a comfortable distance of one car length
for each 10 miles per hour. But today, in this lane, no one thinks of
such things. The task is to keep close to the car ahead of you so that
no one else can squeeze in from the slower lane. You jockey for
position and keep a heavy foot on the gas pedal. I'm cruising at just
under 65 miles an hour, and no one's breaking in.

Suddenly I see a small car, three cars in front of me, sharply
swerve into the right lane and back again. In an instant the second car
ahead of me swerves in a like manner. My immediate thought is,
"We're as good as dead. Here comes the crash." My eyes flash to the
rear mirror and back again. Just like a giant ripple in the stream of
cars, the Chrysler ahead of me also veers out, almost hitting the truck
to its right. And now I'm on top of it: a large eight-foot-long metal

bumper, lying diagonally in front of my car, ready to slam into the left front tire. Before another thought registers in my mind, I veer out and back into my lane, circumventing death.

The thought of our demise seems to slow the pace of all of us in the fast lane. My wife and I simultaneously let out a deep sigh. My heart seems to be pumping out of my chest, my armpits are soaked, and I have a throbbing headache. I place my hand over my heart— partly to verify the pounding, partly to contain it.

Of course I was not having a panic attack. My body and mind had just given a peak performance. Together, they had totally transformed their functions. From the instant that small BMW swerved to the time I passed by that bumper was probably less than eight seconds. In those moments, the pupils of my eyes dilated to improve their vision, absorbed in detail every movement of the cars in front of me, flashed to the rearview mirror to assess the distance and speed of the cars behind; meanwhile peripheral vision registered the vehicles to my right; and all this data was fed instantaneously to my brain. My hearing automatically became acutely sensitive to any relevant sounds. The blood flow to my hands and feet decreased and the excess blood was redirected to my deeper skeletal muscles. Blood also pooled in my torso to provide an abundance of nourishment to any vital organ in need during the emergency. My heart increased its pace to whatever degree was necessary to get blood near my vital organs. My blood pressure thus increased. My breathing accelerated to provide for the increased oxygen needs of my rapidly circulating blood. That newly oxidized blood rushed to the brain, where the increased supply of oxygen stimulated my thought processes and significantly improved my reaction time. The muscles in my arms, hands, legs, and feet tensed in readiness for instructions from the brain, and responded with precision. My liver released increased amounts of glucose (sugar) into the bloodstream to power my muscles and feed my brain and heart.

It is truly phenomenal, this body of ours. Nothing that humankind has ever created can come close to its performance. My conscious thought processes were not responsible for saving my life. Instead, they had one task: to prevent fear from interfering with the task. My life was in the hands of my autonomic nervous system, which signaled the release of adrenalin and coordinated all efforts of the brain and the body with literally split-second timing.

Here are the major changes that take place in the body during such an "Emergency Response":

The blood sugar level increases.
The pupils dilate.
The sweat glands perspire.
The heart rate increases.
The respiration increases.
The muscles tense.
The blood in the hands and feet is reduced.
The blood pools in the head and trunk.

These are normal, healthy, lifesaving changes in the body's physiology, produced by communication from the brain to the autonomic nervous system, the endocrine system, and the motor nerves of the skeletal muscles. When the brain receives word that a crisis is at hand, it flips the "Emergency" switch. All systems react simultaneously and instantly.

TRICKING THE BRAIN

In all likelihood, you have recognized some of these changes as symptoms of panic attacks. Your panic attacks are not identical to the body's natural, healthy Emergency Response. However, since this is a self-help book and not a medical textbook, I will take some liberties with the technical details. View it this way: panic attacks are produced when panic deceives the brain into thinking there is imminent danger. Here you are, standing in the aisle of the grocery store, not bothering a soul. Flip. On goes the Emergency switch. "Red alert! All systems prepare for battle!" shouts the commanding voice of the brain, through the nervous system to the skeletal system, the muscles, the circulatory and respiratory systems, the endocrine system, and most of the organs of the body.

Since this is an unconscious response produced at an illogical time, you are consciously surprised and frightened. The reason you have more symptoms than those I just listed is this: panic now induces anxiety. Anxiety exaggerates the normal, healthy Emergency Response, and anxiety also feeds on itself. Remember that I said that during an Emergency Response the best thing for the conscious mind to do is to prevent fear or doubt from interfering with the task at hand.

Panic, however, instructs you to focus on your body *(wrong!)* and worry about what will happen next *(wrong!)*. Those two instructions are responsible for any extreme symptoms of anxiety that you experience during a panic attack. They can cause these changes:

The heart may seem to skip a beat or beat irregularly.
The stomach may feel as though it is "tied in knots."
The hands, arms, or legs may shake.
You may have difficulty catching your breath.
You may feel pains or tightness in your chest.
The jaw, neck or shoulders may feel tight and stiff.
The mouth may become dry.
You may have difficulty swallowing.
The hands and feet may feel cold, sweaty or numb.
You may develop a headache.

Although several other changes are also possible (I mentioned them in Chapter 1), I list these here because they are all clearly exaggerations of the normal, healthy Emergency Response. For instance, during a crisis the autonomic nervous system produces what is called a "sympathetic stimulation" throughout the body. Along with the other changes I have mentioned, the sphincter muscles of the stomach contract while blood flow to the digestive system is decreased. Anxiety will then increase the secretion of acid into the stomach, thus increasing the chance of heartburn, nausea, and pain in the upper abdomen and chest.

In addition to exaggerating the normal physical changes of the body, focusing your attention on your body, and inviting you to worry about the future, panic produces a fourth problem: it prolongs the symptoms.

After a normal, healthy Emergency Response, the brain signals the end to the sympathetic stimulation of the nervous system. The body begins its swing back to "normal mode." Panic and anxiety, on the other hand, tend to let symptoms linger. The headache throbs for the rest of the day, or the stomach churns through the night, disrupting your needed rest. The body feels depleted, exhausted; the mind seems to hang in a fog.

To summarize:

1. The body and its organs, as with all living organisms, maintain a balance between activity and rest, between expansion and contraction. A shifting from one of these poles to the other creates a healthy, natural rhythm.

2. The body is specially designed to handle extreme activity. It responds to an emergency automatically, through instinct. It is well equipped to perform at an instant's notice.

3. Panic disrupts the natural balance of the body by sending false emergency signals to the brain and by telling you to doubt your body's natural abilities.

To conquer panic attacks as they occur, you must know and believe the following:

1. You can trust your body and your unconscious to perform their essential roles during a crisis.

2. The body also has a response which is exactly opposite to and equally as powerful as the Emergency Response. (This is the Calming Response, which we will discuss in Chapter 10.)

3. When panic flips the Emergency switch on, you can consciously flip it off.

4. And, with practice, you can consciously stop panic even before it takes control.

9

Why the Body Reacts

If the brain is such a brilliant machine with an incredible capacity for intelligence, why doesn't it block out panic signals? How does the brain end up at the mercy of panic? (It is the brain that signals all the physical symptoms of panic, so the brain, as executive, must take responsibility.)

For that answer, we must delve deeper into the workings of the mind and the brain. Most of the time I will use the words "brain" and "mind" synonymously, but occasionally they must be distinguished. For our purposes, I will define the brain as the primary center for regulating and coordinating the body's activities. It also generates thought, memory, reason, emotion, and judgment. Whereas the brain is an actual physical object, the mind is a concept, representing the ability to integrate the functions of the brain: perceiving our surroundings, experiencing our emotions, and processing information intelligently. In a sense, the brain is the workhorse of the mind. This is why I will speak so much about altering your thoughts and beliefs. They are the keys to your brain's activity.

In a nutshell, here is what the brain does:

1. It receives a stimulus,
2. it interprets the meaning of that stimulus,
3. it selects a response, and
4. it enlists the body to cooperate as needed.

For example, if you accidentally touch a hot radiator, (1) that stimulus travels up the nerve endings of the finger through the spinal cord to the brain, (2) the brain interprets the stimulus to mean "I'm touching something hot. This is burning and uncomfortable," (3) the brain selects to remove the finger from the radiator, and (4) it returns a communication through the nerves to the muscles in the arm, hand, and finger. Your hand instantly jerks away.

You might label that behavior as an "instinctual" response, to jerk your hand off a hot object. It is also a learned response. The early experiences of your life, dating back to infancy, have trained your brain to interpret a hot radiator in that manner.

The brain interprets sensations based on two criteria: memory and sensory-based images. Every moment of your life is recorded in your memory with varying degrees of intensity. I have a distinct memory of poking a stick in a small fire when I was four years old. That memory is reinforced through a sensory-based image: the smell of the burning lumber, the sight of those flames, the touch of my hand on that stick. Interestingly, I don't have an image of that stick breaking, causing me to fall into the coals. My next memory is sitting on the counter of my neighbor's kitchen. I can see several adults around me, feel the ointment covering the minor burns on my knees, and recall them offering me a soft drink.

The memory of events like these lives on, reinforced by sensory-based images. The actual event is not the only thing recorded in the memory. In addition, our internal reactions are etched in our unconscious mind. A few minutes before I fell into that fire, my mother had instructed my six-year-old brother and me to "stay away from that fire." So in addition to the immediate pain I experienced from the burns, I suspect that in my memory I also hold the sense of guilt I must have felt for having disobeyed.

WELL-WORN PATHS

Our beliefs and values develop largely out of our life experiences and their ensuing memory. As adults, each of us probably notices that certain of our patterns and habits stem from our childhood experiences. Such things as our religious beliefs, our social skills, our use or abuse of alcohol, our choice of partners, are based in part on our childhood memories and in part on past adult experiences.

This past learning is of tremendous benefit to us today. So many decisions are simple for us because we already have the "circuits" in place. We don't need to put much conscious effort into remembering our phone number or writing a letter or tying a ribbon on a package. But as children, each of these tasks was monumental. Can you remember? As we mastered each skill, we literally created new neurological circuits in our brain, circuits which we have now used for years. They become like well-worn paths. Every time we learn new skills, we create new circuits.

But as I discussed in Chapter 8, with every positive there seems to be a negative. Here is the rub: strong beliefs can *block* the natural protective mechanisms of the brain and mind. Left to its own, the unconscious mind will seek health. But social learning and certain traumatic experiences tend to override the circuits.

After the panic response has become established, the mind stops working creatively in your favor. Instead it seems to be set on "automatic pilot" and stops seeking out solutions. The mind focuses on the problem instead of on its solution. When you walk into a situation which is similar in time or place to one in which you previously had a panic attack, the image of that last time rises up in your mind. This image alone can produce the same muscle tension as in your last panic episode. The mind will then notice that muscle tension and interpret it to mean "trouble." Instead of paying attention to all of its many problem-solving options, the mind focuses on its negative images, its messages to tense, and all of your disturbing body sensations.

A panic attack may completely surprise you—consciously. But unconsciously a step-by-step process has taken place prior to your panic symptoms:

Step 1: When you enter a situation which is associated with panic, the brain registers this stimulus.

Step 2: It interprets the meaning of this stimulus as "harmful" or "dangerous."

Step 3: It then, based on memory of past experiences, doubts your ability to cope effectively.

Step 4: It therefore selects "emergency" as its default response, compounded by "anxiety" (since it doubts that you will cope well.)

Step 5: And the brain enlists the body in the Emergency and Anxiety Responses.

After enough of those experiences, you develop a conditioned response. The brain takes less and less time to evaluate each new situation. Instead, it more and more automatically selects the Emergency and Anxiety Responses. You have created a "well-worn path."

This is why people who have their first panic attack in a car may gradually develop a fear of any form of transportation. The brain stops screening the stimulus. If a person has a panic attack in a restaurant, bank, or other closed space, eventually the mind might say, "All such situations are dangerous."

IMAGES AND INTERPRETATIONS

Since images can produce brain responses equally as well as the actual experiences do, this creates further limitations. If you have experienced panic during public speaking in the past, simply the *image* of seeing yourself giving a talk next week can produce uncomfortable feelings right now. In your fantasy of the future you imagine having a rough time of it. You don't call up a view of yourself standing in front of the group, well organized and prepared, feeling confident, speaking distinctly, being well received by your audience. Instead, you envision yourself in front of the group, then you ask yourself, "What if I begin to panic?" That suggestion triggers an image of you panicking during your speech. And right now, one week before the event, you begin to have those physical sensations that you expect to have during the event. This is how powerful the tools of the mind are.

Here is a key point. Much of your ability to control will be based on this principle: People, places, and events are panic-provoking only *after* we apply meaning to them. A store is just a store, a speech is just a speech, a drive is just a drive, until the brain interprets them as "dangerous" or "threatening." To conquer panic, then, you must intervene at the *point of interpretation*.

TAKING AWAY CHOICE

There are two reasons why the brain selects the Emergency Response at inappropriate times. The first is that it is prevented from gathering relevant information. Many of our observations and beliefs about life were established during our youth, well before our adult intellect was mature. Other beliefs are formed after fearful moments or traumatic events. When these beliefs are fixed in place, they prevent the brain from evaluating new situations with an "open mind," so to speak. Once a belief is established, it closes off the mind from constantly reevaluating the facts associated with the belief. When the beliefs are useful ("Hot objects can burn you"), we benefit. But when a faulty belief is in place ("All forms of transportation are dangerous to me"), our lives become restricted and uncreative.

If you suffer from panic attacks, this means that a faulty belief prevents your brain from receiving a critical message. Remember that with all brain activity, at Step 1 the brain receives a stimulus (e.g., entering a restaurant or thinking of giving a speech) and at Step 2 it interprets the stimulus. It is at Step 2 that the brain is missing a message. The faulty belief "This is an emergency!" prevents an accurate interpretation of the situation: "There is *no physical danger*." (Of course this is not so straightforward for the post-myocardial patient or the patient with chronic obstructive pulmonary disease. He must be able to assess if he requires medical attention and, at the same time, keep himself from becoming panicky.) The brain doesn't bother to look around this new scene, gathering information to make an assessment. Instead, it receives an immediate message which forces the Emergency Response.

The second reason the brain selects the Emergency Response is by default: it doesn't know of another, more appropriate response. From an evolutionary standpoint, the human intellect is a relatively recent development compared to the Emergency Response, which can also be found in all lower animals. Perhaps our intellectual and psychological defenses have not evolved enough to adequately handle certain social threats, so our physical defenses respond first. The fact remains that the Emergency Response produces a handful of significant changes in the body that are strictly designed to help in a physical crisis, yet actually handicap us during a social or intellectual problem. Who needs to be trying to pass a final exam in mathematics while the hands are sweating, the mouth dry, and the muscles tense?

My position, however, is that we have the intellectual and psychological capability to defend against social threat well enough not to need the intrusion of the Emergency Response. This book tells you how to identify these capacities, how to master them, and how to use them against panic. Your first task is to work on changing your interpretation of events. Over a period of time you must slowly reinforce this message: You are *not* confronting a physical emergency. To begin this change you must start to believe it, to remind yourself of it: "This is not an emergency." (Heart or lung disease patients should replace this statement throughout the book with, "I can stay calm and think.'') Sooner or later it will be one of the messages you tell yourself at the moment you sense panic creeping in. Eventually it becomes one of the automatic, unconscious interpretations of the brain.

It is perfectly fine for you to become highly alert and to experience an increase in your heart rate and respiration during a panic-provoking situation. These types of responses are positive and mean that you will have the capacity to think more sharply and clearly. As you face these fearful times and places, clear, sharp thinking will be your ally. Your goal should not be to eliminate all these sensations. A certain amount of anxiety and worry can be beneficial. For instance, in research comparing the test scores of students who enter exams either completely relaxed, somewhat anxious or very anxious, the students who were somewhat anxious performed the best. When we anticipate an event with excitement or anxiety, the adrenal glands secrete hormones that stimulate our creative intelligence, which we will need when facing such events. This same process takes place when you face panic. The goal is to keep your alertness while you change your interpretation. That alertness gives you a conscious choice, so that you don't have to respond with your old and automatic fears.

You will now learn a series of strategies that allow you to remain alert and sharp to all that is taking place around you and within you, while at the same time consciously flipping off that Emergency switch. With practice, you will be able to consciously stop panic before it begins.

10

The Calming Response

For all its apparent complexity, our body operates with great simplicity. In the autonomic nervous system, which controls all involuntary bodily functions, the sympathetic branch produces the Emergency Response. As with most other living organisms, if the nervous system can produce one extreme, it is capable of producing the opposite extreme. This is a basic tenet of physics: every action has an opposite and equal reaction.

And so it is. The sympathetic response (or Emergency Response) is balanced by the parasympathetic response, or what I call the "Calming Response." When a crisis has passed, the brain doesn't just stop sending those emergency communications. An entirely different set of nerves sends *new* signals to all the affected parts of the body. Those signals tell the heart and lungs to slow down and instruct the muscles to stop contracting. The blood pressure decreases, oxygen consumption is reduced, and blood sugar levels return to normal. These restful changes take place not accidentally, not haphazardly, but by instruction.

When I ask my clients what one thing above all they would like changed, their response is: "To feel *calmer* during those panicky times, so that I can *think more clearly*." The fact is, you already have the capacity to turn off the Emergency switch—you just don't know it. You fear you are losing control, but your body has a built-in control which is yours for the asking: you can consciously activate the parasympathetic nervous system response. The central purpose of the parasympathetic or Calming Response is to halt and reverse the Emergency Response. Its circuits cause every internal system to return to its normal state. Thus your parasympathetic system, with controlling fibers in all the essential parts of your body, can cancel out the Emergency Response.

Dr. Herbert Benson was the first to label this calming process the "Relaxation Response," and he continues to pioneer in the medical research into this beneficial phenomenon. I have chosen not to use Dr. Benson's term for one reason: to many panic-prone people, relaxation tends to imply "letting go" or "losing control." Because of this, they resist learning skills that promote relaxation. The word also is associated with meditative practices: not moving, emptying the mind, not thinking. The truth of the matter is that relaxation exercises and meditation do work. They are excellent tools to produce the Calming (or parasympathetic) Response. But these techniques of calming the mind and body must be modified to help you as you begin to face panic.

During the actual moment of panic you need skills which clear your head of extraneous thoughts, which sharpen your mind, and which keep you actively alert. You need the ability to immediately confront panic and regain control of your body on short notice. This chapter, along with Chapters 11 and 12, explains how to elicit the Calming Response through formal exercises. Later chapters will teach you how to apply this skill to the moment of panic.

MEMORIES AND IMAGES

Before you learn the techniques for producing the Calming Response directly, reflect for a moment on times when you have naturally felt at ease, peaceful and calm inside. Perhaps you can remember walking into a church when it was completely empty. A church can be awe-inspiring: huge stained-glass windows, ceilings that seem as though they could touch the sky, a peaceful quietness that invites you to sit and empty your mind. Imagine sitting alone in a church, repeating a simple prayer or letting your mind drift easily. There are no crowds to contend with, just you alone with your peaceful thoughts.

The process of prayer itself invites a calming of the body and mind. In addition to renewing our relationship with God, we quiet ourselves. And as we become calm and quiet we gain perspective on troubled times. Anyone who has successfully turned to prayer during a crisis knows this feeling.

I am not advocating any religious undertaking. But if you are religious, I promise you that by letting yourself *calmly, slowly,* and *meaningfully* pray during a stressful time, you will literally relax the major muscles of the body and significantly reduce any current anxiety.

Other situations can produce this same sensation for you. When I sit by an open fire, watching the flames flickering, skipping from log to log, changing size and shape and color, I become pleasantly mesmerized by those flames. My worries and problems seem to drift away as my attention is consumed by the fire, its crackling sounds, its sweet smell.

Remember, as a child, lying in a field and watching the clouds slowly take shape? First comes a clear impression of Lincoln's face. Three or four minutes later it's a long train, slowly ambling across the sky. Without effort those clouds freely drift into pleasant patterns, allowing your eyes to relax their gaze.

Imagine fishermen sitting on the shore or in a boat, as still as their lines in the water, hour after hour. Their tranquil faces express a relaxed and easy quietness. Think of your own times of stillness and calm in the past. Have they ever come from rocking gently on the porch, back and forth, back and forth . . . no real effort, no pressures, just sitting and drifting? Or perhaps that peacefulness has come when you have risen early in the morning or stayed up alone late at night for some private time.

FOCUSING THE MIND

When we focus on neutral or comforting thoughts and images, clear and measurable physiological changes take place in the body. As an experiment, read again the "Memories and Images" section. This time, read slowly while you let yourself imagine each scene as I describe it. (Try that now.)

If that experience begins to produce the Calming Response within you, here is what may be changing:

Your oxygen consumption is decreasing.
Your breathing is slowing.
Your heart rate is decreasing.
Your blood pressure is lessening.
Your muscle tension is reducing.

There is a growing sense of ease in the body and calmness in the mind.

You can contrast this with how you felt when you were reading earlier chapters when I described anxiety-provoking times. *Our images have tremendous influence over our bodies.*

I am not describing to you some simplistic idea like "Just relax and you'll feel better." I am identifying the opposite and equally powerful capacity of the nervous system—the parasympathetic response, or Calming Response—which is essential to counterbalancing the Emergency Response and all anxiety. And it is a capacity you already use. Any time you feel comfortable and at ease, it is because of this Calming Response. Each time you fall asleep, it is because your Calming Response has quieted down the body and mind enough to allow sleep. What science has gradually discovered in the past twenty years is that we actually can activate this Calming Response through conscious effort. In the field of psychology, this discovery is as important as the achievement of NASA in placing the first humans on the moon. Our mental processes can alter the biochemistry of the body. An entirely new frontier is now open to us.

TAKING CONSCIOUS CONTROL

Typically, the responsibility for tensing and calming the body has been left to the unconscious mind. You probably are not aware of it when the muscles of your body become tense. I am not consciously aware of the number of muscles in my neck, my back, my arms, or my hands which are contracting in order to help me write this sentence on my notepad. My unconscious does that detailed work for me so that I can consciously consider how to express my thoughts to you.

But muscle tension is a major component of anxiety and panic attacks, and if you are not aware of it, it works against your progress. It is during these times of difficulty that we need to become skilled at consciously noticing and changing our muscle tension.

When you become anxious, your muscles automatically tense; that is the rule. The reverse is also true: when the muscles are not tensing, your mind cannot become anxious. In fact, to loosen and relax the muscles is an excellent method of activating the Calming Response. (By the way, muscles don't actually "relax": they are either not contracting or contracting to some degree. When I teach people calming techniques, I speak of "relaxing" the muscles to mean "letting go" of any muscle tension they notice.)

Unfortunately, most people who are afraid of a panic attack will physically tense their muscles and psychologically become anxious as a means of "remaining in control." They consider their tension to be a necessary way to stay on guard. But whenever you are highly tense and anxious, your ability to think logically is greatly diminished. The solution (to brace yourself) contributes to the problem. Reducing your muscle tension automatically reduces anxiety and invites the Calming Response. Your mind gets rid of all those useless negative thoughts so that you can concentrate on the situation at hand. Any of the relaxation techniques and meditations that are being taught these days actually increase your ability to think clearly and therefore increase your self-control.

Much has been written about such relaxation techniques over the past twenty years. The first popular movement began in the mid-1960s, when transcendental meditation (TM) was introduced into the United States. In 1975 Dr. Herbert Benson's bestseller *The Relaxation Response* brought scientific and medical credence to TM and other relaxation/meditation techniques. However, much earlier, in 1938, Dr. Edmund Jacobson created a medically sound method for reducing tension. He described his design to the professional community in his book *Progressive Relaxation*. In 1962 he presented his method in the popular book *You Must Relax*. Dr. Jacobson's "progressive relaxation" technique continues to serve as one of the cornerstones for behavior therapy today. Teaching relaxation or meditative techniques to persons with anxiety disorders and a broad range of physical disorders is now a standard practice within behavioral medicine and psychology.

In the Western world, these practices were "discovered" within the last fifty years and have yet to become part of our culture. However, the true beginnings of the meditations and breathing patterns that elicit the Calming Response date back thousands of years, where they served as the principal techniques of all major Eastern religions to achieve peace, clarity, and oneness with God. In those times, the practice of religious exercises was widespread, since religion served as the psychology, the philosophy, and the science of each culture. Yet the "new" techniques that are slowly receiving scientific validation and credibility in the 1980s in the Western world are the centuries-old methods from India, Tibet, China, and Japan, found in Buddhism and Zen Buddhism, Hinduism, yoga, pranayama, Taoism, and T'ai Chi Ch'uan. The skills presented in the several chapters to follow are based on the scientific complexity of Western medicine, research, and psychology. At the same time, they represent the simplicity so often found in Eastern philosophy.

In the next chapter you will learn of the pervasive physiological effects of one of our body's simplest functions: breathing. Breathing is so instinctual that we have long taken it for granted. To control panic, however, breathing is our most powerful somatic tool. Without its help, we can fall prey to over twenty-five symptoms; with its help, we can calm the body and clear the mind. Our breathing patterns are always involved in panic; they are either part of the solution or part of the problem.

11

The Breath of Life

Breathing is an essential function of the body. With each inhalation, oxygen is delivered to the bronchial tubes of your lungs. Passing through the millions of tiny air sacs, the oxygen moves into your arteries, where it is captured by your blood cells. As blood circulates out of the lung area, it is bright red because of its high oxygen content. This oxygen-rich blood is pumped through the heart to all parts of the body. Every cell throughout the body then exchanges its waste products for oxygen. (The blood returning to the heart is duller in color because of its diminished oxygen content.) The heart pumps the waste-filled blood back to the lungs. As you inhale more fresh air, a form of combustion takes place, in which the blood cells absorb oxygen and release carbon dioxide. And the cycle begins again.

If your lungs do not take in enough air, your blood will not be oxygenated or properly cleaned. Your complexion will be pale, since blood vessels with low oxygen content are a dark blue. (If you look at your hands now, you can probably see some blue blood vessels. This is the normal color of your veins, which are returning blood to the lungs for a fresh supply of oxygen.) In addition, your digestion is impaired, and your organs and tissues are not fully nourished. A lack of oxygen in the blood can contribute to anxiety, depression, and fatigue.

The respiratory system regulates breathing in order to maintain a balance of oxygen and carbon dioxide within the bloodstream. In normal circumstances, your rate of breathing is determined by the amount of carbon dioxide that must be expelled from your bloodstream and the amount of oxygen needed to satisfy the demands of your immediate activity.

Panic and breathing patterns are intimately related. The less you understand about the process of respiration, the greater the power of panic. This is so because changes in breathing alone can produce over two dozen sensations within the body. If you are unaware of your ongoing breathing patterns and if you don't realize that the mechanics of respiration alone can be solely responsible for those uncomfortable feelings, then you will become frightened.

If your fear includes being uncertain whether your heart or lungs are functioning properly, your alarm will take on panic proportions. People who have heart or lung damage, such as from a myocardial infarction or a chronic obstructive pulmonary disease (see Chapter 6), may experience this kind of panic when they begin to have trouble breathing or think that they are having another heart attack. Other panic-prone people, who notice symptoms and interpret them as "I can't breathe" or "I'm having a heart attack, I'm going to die," will immediately feel the effects of panic. These thoughts automatically and instantly switch on the body's Emergency Response.

The most important task during those moments is to stay rational. Panic can cause you to become so emotionally tangled up in your fearful expectations that you fail to take supportive action. Your mind becomes cloudy, your symptoms escalate, and your thoughts run in seven different directions. At the same time the symptoms in your body continue to grow in strength, often for two reasons. First, you continue to frighten yourself by your thoughts. And second, you ignore the changes in your breathing and instead focus on your symptoms. Mastering your thoughts is a target of later chapters. In this chapter you will learn just how extensively you can control your symptoms by the way you breathe.

I want to give you some details about the mechanics of respiration. At first glance, this information may seem too technical to be useful. Nothing could be further from the truth. Actually, the contribution that respiratory patterns play in the cause and cure of panic has been virtually ignored by sufferers and health professionals alike. My professional experience has taught me to use the respiration process as a central focus of treatment. Once a client of mine can control his breathing patterns in a variety of situations, I believe he is 50 percent along on the road to success. For some people, identifying and mas-

tering breathing patterns will completely end their symptoms and resolve their problem.

SIGNALS OF CHANGE

When it comes to taking a breath, our lungs don't have much say in
the process. As a basic life-sustaining force in all mammals, breathing
has evolved as a relatively simple function controlled neurologically
by what is called the "respiratory center" in our hindbrain, located
just above the spinal cord. When a signal arrives from the brain stem,
the muscles around the lungs contract, which increases the space
within the chest. This diminishes the pressure within the lungs relative
to that outside the body. The lungs now are "forced" to inhale in
order to equalize their internal pressure with that of the environment.
A second signal is then sent to instruct those muscles to stop contracting. As the muscles relax, pressure increases in the lungs and air is
forced out. This basic mechanical process is the typical method of
breathing. Only in special situations does our breathing fall under the
control of our more evolved, or higher, brain centers.

The brain, of course, makes all its executive decisions based on
the information it is currently gathering. What information does it pay
attention to as it selects a breathing pattern for any given moment?
You might expect that it simply attends to how much oxygen we need.
In reality, adjustment of respiration is based more on the amount of
carbon dioxide in the body than it is on the amount of oxygen. This is
in part because carbon dioxide plays such an important role in maintaining a proper acid-base balance (or pH balance) in the body and in
producing energy (metabolism).

To understand the relationship between breathing and panic, we
need to look closely at all the factors that relate to increased respiration. The brain will signal the respiratory system to increase its rate
and depth of inhalation based on specific chemical and neurological
signals, including those that indicate an excessive amount of carbon
dioxide in the blood, not enough oxygen in the blood, reflexes from
our joints and muscles as they begin to move, an increase in body
heat caused by metabolism and emotional arousal. As the breathing
rate increases, the excess carbon dioxide is deposited in the lungs and
exhaled, more oxygen is passed into the bloodstream from the air sacs
in the lungs to assist in metabolism, and body heat is lowered by

increased evaporation of water through the lungs. When the brain and the chemical receptors in the arteries find that "things are back in balance," the brain signals a return to a normal breathing pattern.

This balancing process becomes a little more complex when we introduce the other influences on breathing patterns. The first is the body's autonomic nervous system. You have already read about this in the previous chapters on the Emergency Response and the Calming Response. An increased breathing rate is one of the many automatic and instant responses of the body's alarm system. It can take place independently or as a component of the mass action of the Emergency Response.

The second influence on breathing patterns is conscious thought or emotion. If you stand at the edge of a pool and contemplate swimming a lap, your breathing will automatically increase in anticipation of the activity. If you think about arguing with your boss at work while you are standing in the kitchen, washing the dishes, you will also increase your rate of breathing, and usually without any conscious awareness. Any of the "active" emotions—anger, fear, joy, or excitement—require energy from the body and therefore stimulate increased breathing. Conversely, when you feel sad or depressed, breathing slows, less oxygen is needed, and less carbon dioxide must be expelled.

The third influence is the tension of stress. Studies consistently show that during episodes of stress, people breathe more rapidly and, therefore, levels of carbon dioxide in the blood drop significantly.

TWO TYPES OF BREATHING

Studies have revealed another important phenomenon which plays a significant role in mastering panic. It seems that not only do people under stress begin to increase their respiration rate, but they shift from breathing into the lower parts of their lungs to breathing into the upper portions of the lungs. Figure 4 illustrates these two kinds of breathing: upper chest (thoracic) and diaphragmatic. In upper chest breathing the chest lifts upward and outward. The breathing is shallow and rapid. In diaphragmatic breathing, each inhalation is deeper and slower. Below the lungs is a sheetlike muscle, called the diaphragm, which separates the chest from the abdomen. When you fill your lower lungs with air, the lungs push down on the diaphragm and cause

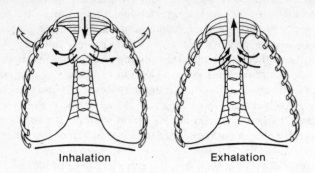

Inhalation   Exhalation

Figure 4. Two kinds of breathing: upper chest (thoracic) breathing (above)
and lower chest (diaphragmatic) breathing (below).

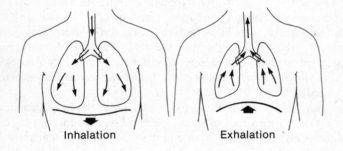

Inhalation   Exhalation

your abdominal region to protrude. (This makes it appear as though
your stomach is expanding and contracting with each diaphragmatic
breath.)

As research continues, we are learning more and more about the
importance of these two breathing patterns. One study of 160 men and
women found that those whose typical breathing pattern was slow
and deep were more confident, emotionally stable, and physically and
intellectually active. Those whose habitual breathing pattern was
rapid and shallow were more passive, dependent, fearful, and shy.

This rapid upper chest breathing style is a normal, brief response
to any threatening or anxiety-provoking situation. However, it now
appears that this is a rather stable ongoing feature of people who are

chronically anxious or phobic. In studies where chronically anxious subjects were specifically asked to begin breathing in their upper chest, these people reported increased psychological and physical symptoms.

On the other hand, slow deep breathers have a slower resting heart rate and a less "trigger-happy" Emergency Response. The habit of slow, easy, diaphragmatic breathing invites the Calming Response, promotes good health, and provides long-term protection for the heart.

These studies tell us that both short-term and long-term breathing patterns are directly related to psychological strength and the subjective experience of anxiety. By changing your habitual breathing pattern you can increase your defenses against panic. By changing your breathing pattern during an anxious episode you can reverse your body's panic-provoking symptoms.

THE HYPERVENTILATION SYNDROME

Although changing your long-term breathing patterns will be beneficial to you, your most important ally will be your breathing during the moment of panic. As mentioned earlier, a change in your breathing should directly correspond to your activity level. For instance, if I am out running for exercise, it won't be long before I am breathing rapidly from my upper chest. My body is now demanding increased oxygen, and metabolism is producing larger amounts of carbon dioxide, which must be exhaled. I can keep that breathing pattern up for as long as I'm running.

What would happen if I stopped running but forced myself to continue breathing at that accelerated rate? I would continue to exhale large quantities of carbon dioxide (CO_2), but my body would no longer be depositing that amount of carbon dioxide into my bloodstream. Immediately my blood CO_2 level drops. When that takes place, CO_2 begins to leave my nerve cells, raising the pH level in the cells and making them more excitable. Because of this I may begin to feel nervous and jittery. Changes in the pH level remove calcium salts in my blood, which increases the excitability of my peripheral nerve endings, causing tingling around my mouth and fingers and toes. At the same time, this diminished level of CO_2 will suppress my Calming Response: my pupils dilate, my hands and feet begin to feel cold, my heart continues to race, lights seem brighter, sounds louder. Simultaneously, the blood vessels in my brain constrict. This lowers the amount and the rate of oxygen transferring into those tissues. And this action will produce most of my uncomfortable symptoms: dizziness, faintness, distortions in vision, difficulty concentrating, and a sense of separateness from my body (depersonalization).

Most of these symptoms will develop in under a minute of this form of breathing, called hyperventilation. And all these changes are reversed by slowing the rate of breathing. Although uncomfortable, none of these short-term changes in the body's chemistry will cause lasting harm.

Most people who hyperventilate never realize they are doing so. They don't report that they are having a problem with their breathing. Instead, they complain of various specific or vague symptoms throughout their body. Specialist after specialist will search for thyroid, cardiac, gastrointestinal, respiratory, or central nervous system problems. Misdiagnosis, which is common, can lead to operations on the spine, the abdomen, or other organs. Just as likely, though, the patient will be labeled by the physician as anxious or neurotic and referred to a mental health professional who also fails to identify hyperventilation as the culprit. It is true that many people who are prone to hyperventilate are also anxious. But I would be anxious too, if I continued to spontaneously experience such dramatic and undiagnosed symptoms!

**PHYSICAL AND PSYCHOLOGICAL COMPLAINTS
CAUSED BY HYPERVENTILATION
Cardiovascular**

uncomfortable awareness of
    the heart (palpitations)
racing heart (tachycardia)
heartburn

Neurological

dizziness and lightheadedness
poor concentration
blurred vision

numbness or tingling of the
    mouth, hands and feet

Respiratory

shortness of breath
"asthma"
chest pain
choking sensation

Gastrointestinal

lump in the throat
difficulty swallowing
stomach pain
"swallowing air"
nausea

General

tension, anxiety
fatigue, weakness
poor sleep, nightmares
sweating

Musculoskeletal

muscle pains
shaking
muscle spasms

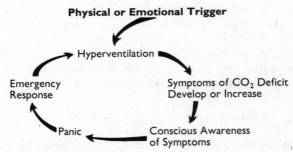

Figure 5. Hyperventilation in the cycle of panic.

Figure 5 shows how hyperventilation can be part of the vicious circle of panic. The process is as follows: (1) Any kind of emotional or physical disturbance can stimulate (2) hyperventilation, without the person being consciously aware of the change. (3) The symptoms of hyperventilation develop rapidly. (4) As soon as the person notices enough uncomfortable symptoms (5) he becomes panicky ("I can't breathe!" or "I'm going to faint!"). Before these thoughts are even completely registered in the mind, (6) the body has reacted to this interpretation with its Emergency Response (to face whatever is threatening the body). This further supports rapid upper chest breathing and the cycle is re-created, with an increase in the number and intensity of symptoms.

Only minor degrees of hyperventilation are necessary to initiate its effects of increased heart rate, constriction of blood vessels, and a shifting of the blood acid-base balance toward alkalosis (a high pH level in the blood, causing lightheadedness). If you want to see how quickly these changes occur, try this: breathe in and out as rapidly as you can for no more than fifteen seconds. Then sit back and notice the sensations in your body.

People who tend to hyperventilate appear to develop a general sensitivity to breathing patterns. The amount of carbon dioxide in their lungs at any time can change considerably relative to people who don't tend to overbreathe. Carbon dioxide levels drop markedly with any deep sigh, and recovery to normal levels takes longer. This instability, combined with the habit of upper chest breathing, makes them even more susceptible to panic.

Once the problem is identified, recovery and control can be just as dramatic. In one study, more than 1000 patients diagnosed as hyperventilators were taught breathing and relaxation skills. On the average, all their symptoms were gone within one to six months. Seventy-five percent were completely free of symptoms at a twelve-month follow-up, and 20 percent experienced only occasional mild symptoms which were no longer troublesome.

THE FOUNDATION SKILLS

There are two important things you need to learn about your breathing in order to conquer panic. First, you should learn how to breathe from your diaphragm and make that breathing pattern a part of your daily life. Old habits die hard, so you will have to work at this one. But by shifting to this slow, diaphragmatic breathing you will, over time, bring your blood carbon dioxide levels back to a more stable position, less sensitive to brief respiratory changes.

Second, you will need to become skilled at shifting to this kind of breathing whenever you begin to feel panicky. During panic, one goal is to turn off the Emergency Response and encourage your body's Calming Response. Proper breathing will promote this shift.

All methods of eliciting the Calming Response will require one or both of two types of breathing: what I call "natural" and "deep" breathing. This simple exercise will teach you both of these breathing techniques:

1. Lie down on a rug or on your bed, with your legs relaxed and straight and your hands by your side.
2. Let yourself breathe normal, easy breaths. Notice what part of

your upper body rises and falls with each breath. Rest a hand on that spot. If that place is your chest, you are not taking full advantage of your lungs. If your stomach region (abdomen) is moving instead, you are doing fine.

3. If your hand is on your chest, place your other hand on your stomach region. Practice breathing into that area, without producing a rise in the chest. If you need help in accomplishing this, consciously protrude your stomach region each time you inhale.

By breathing into your lower lungs, you are using your respiratory system to its full potential. This is what I mean when I use the term *natural breathing:* gentle, slow, easy breathing into your lower lungs and not your upper chest. It is the method you should use throughout your normal daily activities.

4. *Deep breathing* is an extension of this normal process. With one hand on your chest and one on your abdomen, take a slow, deep breath, first filling your lower lungs, then your upper lungs. When you exhale, let your upper lungs go first (causing your upper hand to drop), then your lower lungs (causing your lower hand to drop). This deep breathing is used at the start of the Deep Muscle Relaxation exercise in Chapter 12 and also in exercises in Chapters 14 and 15.

5. Practice the natural slow breathing and the deep slow breathing several times, until you become familiar with each process. Remind yourself to practice the natural breathing technique often throughout each day. No matter how awkward it feels now, with practice it will eventually come naturally and automatically.

These are very important techniques. Just like the relaxation exercise, they are foundation skills which will later assist you in managing your symptoms. Soon you can incorporate them into relaxation exercises. But don't "overload your circuits" by trying to remember too many things at once. For a while, simply practice natural breathing several times during each day.

NATURAL BREATHING

   Give this exercise its proper attention.
1. Gently and slowly inhale a normal amount of air through your nose, filling only your lower lungs.
2. Exhale easily.

3. Continue this slow, gentle breathing with a relaxed attitude, concentrating on filling only the lower lungs.

One reminder: if you take too many deep breaths in a row instead of these slow, gentle breaths, you will produce a sense of lightheadedness—the same feeling people get when they hyperventilate. It means only one thing: you have just reduced the body's level of carbon dioxide. This is not harmful in the short run, only uncomfortable if you are not expecting it or don't know why it is occurring. All you have to do is return to natural breathing and that symptom will disappear.

You may have heard someone suggest breathing into a paper bag when you hyperventilate. That is logical: when you breathe in the bag, you use up all the oxygen in that small area. Less oxygen goes into your bloodstream, more carbon dioxide is added, and your symptoms disappear. Breathing in the natural manner described in this exercise will accomplish the same goal. In fact, some persons who have suffered from hyperventilation-type panics have completely cured themselves by learning one skill: natural breathing.

If clinical studies are accurate, your body's physical improvement will begin long before you consciously recognize any change. Therefore, you will probably need to have faith that a change in breathing habits will help you. Your breathing pattern is the foundation upon which everything else in this book is built. Unless it is in place, other attempts to control your symptoms will not get the physiological support they require.

If you have never had the opportunity to learn a formal method of producing the Calming Response, now is an excellent time to begin. In Chapter 12 you will find a full description of two techniques. The first is called Cue-Controlled Deep Muscle Relaxation, which combines progressive relaxation and imagery training with verbal and physical cues, such as a special word and your breathing pattern. After several weeks of practice, the brain creates learning pathways based on the exercise. Then, during a tense time, the experienced person can more rapidly develop the Calming Response by repeating those cues. In Chapters 14 and 15 you will learn how to use the cues from this exercise during the moment of panic. In addition, the Deep Muscle Relaxation (DMR) will provide you with a valuable tool: the ability to tell when your major muscle groups are becoming tense. Such awareness can serve as an early warning sign so that you are not surprised by increased levels of anxiety.

The second exercise presented in Chapter 12 is a meditative technique. It involves sitting comfortably and quietly while focusing on a single word or phrase and maintaining a passive attitude. A great number of scientific studies substantiate the ability of this kind of meditation to reduce the symptoms of anxiety and to promote health. This exercise can be learned more rapidly than the DMR, but it does not directly teach awareness of muscle tension.

If you have never learned a formal relaxation exercise, take the time to read through Chapter 12 and choose one of the two methods. Begin as soon as you are ready, since the techniques I will present in later chapters presume a basic understanding of and proficiency in these methods. If you have learned formal relaxation or meditation in the past, yet still have problems succeeding at some of the new techniques in this book, you may choose to practice the Deep Muscle Relaxation or meditation again. Many of my clients who have successfully controlled panic attacks make formal relaxation or meditation time a continuing part of their daily activities. They consider it "preventative medicine," just like getting regular exercise or eating a proper diet.

12

Releasing Tensions

When a person thinks about a situation related to his anxiety, mental images activate the muscles into particular patterns of tension, as though bracing for a blow to the body. Dr. Edmund Jacobson was the first to propose that physical relaxation and anxiety are mutually exclusive. In other words, if one learns how to recognize which muscle groups are tense and can physically let go of that tension, then he will diminish emotional anxiety at that moment. The first exercise in this chapter gives you an opportunity to learn how you personally experience tension. Called Cue-Controlled Deep Muscle Relaxation, it is based on well-researched and time-tested methods for training your mind to notice the subtle cues of muscle tension—and to release that tension.

Some people find that a passive technique to quiet the mind and relax the body is more suited to their personal style. You may prefer to practice a meditation exercise, presented at the end of this chapter, instead of the Deep Muscle Relaxation. Both of these methods are useful in learning the general skills of clearing the mind and calming the body.

CUE-CONTROLLED DEEP MUSCLE RELAXATION

This exercise, which takes approximately twenty minutes, trains your body's large muscles to respond to the cues you give. Your task is to consciously notice what muscle tension feels like in specific areas of your body and to consciously release that tension. Learning this particular technique is not essential to conquering panic. It is, however, one of the best ways to learn about your tension and how to alter it. If you have learned a different technique which produces these results or if you have already mastered this skill, feel free to move on to the next sections of the book.

On page 162 you will find a full transcript of Cue-Controlled Deep Muscle Relaxation. When I teach a client this method, I give him or her a prerecorded audio-cassette tape with these instructions. For your convenience, this prerecorded tape may be purchased by writing: Reid Wilson, Ph.D., P.O. Box 269, Chapel Hill, NC 27514. Or if you own a tape player, or can borrow or buy one, then ask a friend with a soothing voice to read these instructions onto a blank tape for your use. If this is not possible, you may simply read each step of the instructions to yourself silently and pause to follow that instruction or record the tape with your own voice. I suggest that my clients practice the exercise once a day, every day, for five weeks.

Why so often for so long? Because this is a straightforward, mechanical exercise which physically trains the muscles to release their tension. At certain intervals during the exercise, you are asked to repeat a cue word, such as "loosen" or "relax." It seems to take about five weeks of practice before the physical loosening of the muscles becomes associated with that cue word. (You will be creating new "circuits" between your brain and your muscles, as I described in Chapter 10.) Once that learning has taken place, the muscles will be prepared to release their tensions rapidly when that cue word is spoken (along with several other "cues" which I will mention later).

There are three stages to this twenty-minute exercise:

Stage 1: Tense and then relax each muscle group. You will be instructed to tense a particular muscle group for a few seconds, then release the muscles and allow them to loosen. (ten minutes)

Stage 2: Allow all the muscle groups to loosen and relax. (five minutes)

Stage 3: Support and reinforce that muscle relaxation through imagery. (five minutes)

How to Follow This Guide

Each day find a comfortable and quiet place to practice. Take the phone off the hook or arrange for someone else to take calls. This is a special time, just for you.

Begin by sitting comfortably in a chair; take off your shoes and loosen any tight clothing. Close your eyes and take three deep breaths, exhaling slowly. On each exhale, say the word "relax" silently. Or, you may select a word which produces more comfort for you, such as "loosen," "quiet," "peace," or "calm."

First, you will tense and relax each muscle group once (Stage 1). During each relaxation phase, you will repeat the word "relax" (or your selected word) with every exhale.

Next you will follow in your mind a visual image of the sun warming and loosening all the muscles of your body (Stage 2). You needn't feel frustrated if you don't actually "see" the sun in your mind's eye, or "feel" the sensations of loosening or warming. It is essential, however, that you maintain your attention on each muscle group as it is mentioned and imagine the possibility of warmth and loosening of the muscles. You may be surprised at your growing ability over time if you don't try too hard. Just open your mind to the possibility of change.

During the last few minutes of the exercise you will be asked to "go to your safe place" in your mind's eye (Stage 3). Take a moment now to picture a scene which symbolizes comfort, relaxation, safety, warmth, and the absence of outside pressures. You might imagine yourself in some location where you were relaxed in the past: a vacation spot, fishing, sitting on a mountaintop, floating on a raft, soaking peacefully in the bath, or lying on a chaise lounge in the back yard. Or you could choose to create an image of your ideal vacation dream (like your own private South Seas island) or fantasy (such as floating on a cloud).

Regardless of the image you choose, spend a few minutes developing all your senses within that scene. Look around you in your mind's eye to see the colors and patterns of the scene. Hear any sounds appropriate to the environment: perhaps birds singing, wind blowing, ocean waves crashing on the shore. You may even develop an aroma, such as honeysuckle or flowers, perhaps the salt air or the fresh odor after a rain shower. Enjoy all your senses in an easy, effortless manner. This is the kind of image you can use for your "safe place."

At the end of the exercise, open your eyes, stretch your body, and slowly rise from the chair.

Several guidelines will help you as you begin:

1. The more you practice a skill, the greater your ability. So, be dedicated to this project and practice, practice, practice.

2. During the ten seconds of tensing, tense only the muscle groups described. Let the rest of your body be relaxed and loose.

3. Always continue breathing while you are tensing a muscle group. Never hold your breath while tensing.

4. During each fifteen-second relaxation phase, focus on your breathing and mentally say your cue word—"relax" or "loosen"— with each exhalation.

5. Don't evaluate or judge how well or how poorly you do during each practice. This is not a test. Simply practicing each day, no matter what you experience, will ensure progress. You are creating new, unconscious circuits in your brain. How you feel consciously is not a measure of your progress.

6. Some days you will find it quite hard to concentrate. Your mind will tend to wander to a variety of thoughts: "I've got to get back to my housecleaning." "What should I make for supper?" "This isn't working. I'm still tense." "I've got to remember to pay those bills." These kinds of distracting thoughts are normal; everyone experiences them. It does not mean that the process is failing.

As soon as you notice that you have drifted off course, let go of those distracting thoughts and return to your task. Do not feel angry or disappointed with yourself. Do not let that be a reason to quit the exercise. Your body and mind are still benefiting, still learning about control, still creating those new circuits. Stay with it.

7. You may do the exercise any time during the day or evening. It is best to avoid starting immediately after a meal, since your body is busy with digestion then and you are less alert mentally.

8. Do not expect immediate and magical relief from the practice. This process is used solely to train your muscle groups to respond to a cue.

Some people *will* notice changes from the practice. You may find that you are more alert and rested, have an improved appetite and sleep better, are in a more positive mood and feel less overall tension. If any of these take place, consider them "icing on the cake." Your primary task is to practice once a day for five weeks.

The following are questions and comments by several of my clients who were practicing the cue-controlled relaxation exercise. You may find that they speak for some of your concerns.

SUSAN: Can you practice this at bedtime?

DR. W.: There are two concerns related to practicing the exercise just before bedtime. One is that you may fall asleep right in the middle of the exercise. Second, you may feel quite rested after the exercise and therefore no longer feel inclined to fall asleep. Experiment with the best times of day for you, when you can have privacy and can remain attentive to the suggestions.

JUDITH: I tried listening to the tape in the afternoon. And just as I was getting to that point where I was starting to unwind, I jolted myself. Now is that being afraid to relax? In other words, it was taking control of me and I didn't like it. I jolted right out of it, and I shut it off.

DR. W.: The jolting of an arm or leg is a physiological response that can occur when shifting from one level of consciousness to another. People probably have experienced it if they have ever nodded off in a meeting, or when they start to drop off to sleep at night. I just finished working with a man who would have jerks while in deep sleep at night and would wake up frightened by them. He thought they meant something was wrong with him, but they mean nothing of importance. They are a natural physiological response. Think of it as your muscles discharging stored-up tensions as they continue to loosen.

HELEN: I'm having difficulty finding a "safe place." My mind keeps changing images. I imagine being in my house, but I just associate bad memories with that image. I've spent so long in that house being sick that it's not a comfortable place. Then my mind shifts to a couple of other scenes.

DR. W.: Try creating an image of yourself somewhere with supportive people present—enjoying yourself. And any time you need to be there—any time you're feeling uncomfortable or unsafe—mentally drop yourself back into that pleasant scene with supportive friends. You can simply create a fantasy scene and imagine supportive people there. In that scene see yourself with a gentle smile on your face. If you are imagining yourself in some other pleasant scene and you get a twinge of anxiety, switch the image to this new, safe place.

HELEN: Another thing I can't do is close my eyes. I have to stare at something, like the floor.

DR. W.: It doesn't matter whether your eyes are open or closed. Simply develop the scene until it is pleasant enough for you to have a light smile on your face or some other symbol of safety and comfort. If you want to stay in that scene, stay in it. If your mind floats back to another simple, pleasant scene, fine. Any time you need to be back in that safe place, just be there. The great thing about our visualizations is that we can change them in any way we want. If there's something wrong with the scene that doesn't make you feel safe enough, create something comforting for yourself. Buy a new house in your mind! Just build whatever you need, because your unconscious mind can take care of you. Your unconscious mind is what runs you when your conscious mind is busy worrying. You really need to know this: your unconscious mind runs your entire body automatically. It's ironic that some people think that to quiet the conscious mind is to "lose control." Because when your conscious mind quiets and drifts, your unconscious mind takes care of you. And the unconscious is much more skilled than the conscious mind. What do you think runs the show when you're asleep?

SUSAN: You're saying something really important here. As you're talking, a light goes off in my head. I'm sitting here smiling inside, because you're telling us we can bring in thoughts and images that will take care of us. I've been feeling like I must always be realistic, and maybe I need to stop trying so hard.

DR. W.: Fantasies move your body into a particular state of being. If you have a fantasy of an anxiety-provoking scene, your body reacts negatively to it, physically. Here you have an opportunity to create a setting for your body to act normally. No one here is forcing their breath to inhale or exhale. You are doing it unconsciously. You can hold your breath for only so long, just as you can hold your bladder for only so long. Eventually your natural bodily response will take control.

When you refuse to let your conscious mind quiet down, you're fighting that natural unconscious process. In fact, our bodies are most efficient when the conscious mind rests in this manner. When the Calming Response is activated, the activity of all the major systems of the body slow down. Why? Because they are now running at peak efficiency. It is like coasting down a hill on a bicycle: very little energy is expended to achieve the same results. So all systems of the body are getting a rest. Doesn't your mind deserve to stop working so hard? . . . your lungs, your heart, your stomach?

DONNA: I want to listen to the relaxation tape; it's a reward to me. I like the feeling I have on that tape. But I have to get everything done that's supposed to be done or I can't reward myself with playing the tape. Or if I'm having a really tense day, then I know I need the tape and I'll go to it. And that's why I'm on this every-other-day schedule for listening to it. Because I only reach my goals about every other day. I'm having a problem justifying taking the twenty minutes, I guess. I would like help in changing that.

DR. W.: So the tape is beneficial to you, but you won't give yourself permission to enjoy it on a daily basis. You seem to take your responsibilities seriously. Therefore, you need to reevaluate just what those responsibilities are. Consider for a moment how panic has limited your activities and your ability to keep up your other responsibilities. If you don't heal yourself, you can't live life to your potential.

It's your obligation to heal yourself. Your priorities may be wrong if you feel that you have to earn the right to heal yourself. You should ask yourself, "What am I doing for myself today?" Every day you should ask yourself, "How am I taking care of myself?"

ELIZABETH: I'm not feeling the nice warm feeling when I'm in that safe place; I'm only picturing it. And it makes me mad that I don't feel it. I can see the picture fine, but I'm not getting the feeling.

DR. W.: When you are sitting comfortably listening to the tape, and you are seeing the picture but not feeling the feeling . . . what do you do at that moment?

ELIZABETH: I try to shift scenes, I think. I try to find the feeling.

DR. W.: What are you thinking at that moment? Are you thinking, "Gee, this is irritating"?

ELIZABETH: Yeah, that's right. And getting angry about it.

Dr. W.: At that point you should say, "Oh, that's interesting, now I'm angry at myself." Then let that thought go and return to following the tape. It doesn't matter what your sensations are; that is not important. What is important is that you maintain a passive and alert attention. When you are angry at yourself for not achieving your goal, that is attachment to the process. As soon as you say, "Where is that feeling of warmth? Why can't I notice it!" that is an active, critical attention. Whenever you have a critical thought, simply notice it, let it go, and return your attention to the tape. There is no struggle or effort needed.

ELIZABETH: So you're saying, "Just accept it for what it is—it will work"?

Dr. W.: Exactly. Your job is only to stay singleminded, attending to each moment without struggling, doubting, or worrying. As soon as you start commenting on the process, you should let go of those thoughts. Your mind will wander, you can't help that. It's going to say, "I haven't got time for this, I have too many other things to do," or "I better stop this," or "Why aren't I getting this? Where is it? Come on!" As soon as you are consciously aware of those comments, just say to yourself, "Oops, I'm struggling again," and bring your mind easily back to the tape.

JACK: If the purpose of the exercise is to relax our muscles, why do we need to tense them?

Dr. W.: With chronic tension, we tense certain muscles (like our shoulders or neck) without knowing it. But if you consciously choose to tense a muscle, there is a paradoxical response: as you tense the muscle and let go of it, it relaxes to the degree of tension it held. The tighter you squeeze the muscle, the more it will unwind when you relax it. It is just like that principle in physics: for every action there is an equal and opposite reaction. Think of a rubber band. The more you stretch it, the quicker it "relaxes" when you let go. That is why in this technique you begin by tensing your muscle groups on purpose. If you pay close enough attention during the relaxation phase, you will actually feel some of them loosen.

JACK: I still don't understand why it's called "cue-controlled."

Dr. W.: Through constant repetition or practice, the brain can be taught to respond to a particular cue. That's how children learn to speak or read. They receive constant repetition of certain words and sounds. Eventually it becomes automatic, meaning that the brain has been fully trained and new circuits are in place. By repeating this exercise thirty-five times over five weeks, you are training the brain to develop new circuits for the Calming Response. At the same time, you are repeating a word ("relax" or "loosen") many times during each practice, you are breathing in a special easy manner, and you may even be noticing new and pleasant feelings in your body. Those three changes will later serve as "cues" to trigger muscle relaxation when you need it.

CUE-CONTROLLED DEEP MUSCLE RELAXATION

Stage 1: Muscle Tensing and Relaxing

Find a comfortable chair and sit down. Loosen any tight clothing, take your shoes off, and begin to relax. [Pause.]

Take three deep breaths, and on each exhalation repeat the word "relax"* silently to yourself. [Pause.]

Take a mental check throughout your body, noticing any areas of tension. [Pause.] Use your natural diaphragmatic breathing throughout the rest of this session. Allow your breathing to relax those tense areas.

During the relaxation phase for each muscle group, repeat the word "relax" to yourself silently with each exhalation.

Now turn your attention to your *hands*. Squeeze them tightly, tightly. [Pause 10 seconds.] And let them go, dropping them to your lap. Just relax. On each exhalation now, repeat the word "relax." [Pause 15 seconds.]

Turn your attention to your *arms*. Squeeze your arms tightly together. Hold them tightly, as hard as you can, tightly, while you're breathing. [Pause 10 seconds.] And let go. Drop your arms to your lap. And relax. [Pause 15 seconds.]

Bring your attention to your *shoulders*. Lift your shoulders up to your ears, tightly, hard as you can, and press, while you're breathing. [Pause 10 seconds.] And let go. Now with each exhalation, repeat under your breath the word "relax," letting go more and more. [Pause 15 seconds.]

Bring your attention to your *forehead*. Gently raise your eyebrows, and hold

* Substitute the word "loosen"—or another comforting word—for "relax" throughout the tape if that word offers more pleasant associations.

them there while you're breathing. Hold it. [Pause 10 seconds.] And let go. Relax. [Pause 15 seconds.]

Now bring your attention to your *eyes* and your *nose*. Squeeze your eyes and nose tightly while you're breathing. Tightly. Hold it, hold it. [Pause 10 seconds.] And let go. Letting that tension melt away. Relax. [Pause 15 seconds.]

And bring your attention to your *tongue*. Press your tongue to the roof of your mouth, firmly, tightly. Hold it, hold it. [Pause 10 seconds.] And let go, relaxing your tongue. Repeating the word "relax" to yourself on each exhalation. [Pause 15 seconds.]

Now press your *lips* together. Press them firmly, tightly, while you breathe through your nose. Tightly. Hold it, tightly. [Pause 10 seconds.] And let go. Let go of your mouth and your jaw. Now feeling relaxed and calm. [Pause 15 seconds.]

Turn your attention again to your *mouth* and open your mouth wide, very wide. Breathe. Wide, hold it, hold it. [Pause 10 seconds.] And let go. And just relax, throwing away the tension. [Pause 15 seconds.]

Now lean forward in your chair. Bend your arms, bring them up to shoulder height and attempt to touch your elbows to your back, flexing the muscles in your *back* and your *chest*. Hold that position. Press, while you're breathing. Press, while you hold it. [Pause 10 seconds.] And let go. Sit back in your chair again. Just relax, letting go of those muscles more and more. [Pause 15 seconds.]

Turn your attention to your *stomach*. Now extend your stomach and tighten those muscles firmly. Tightly. Hold it, tightly, hold it. [Pause 10 seconds.] And let go. Relax. [Pause 15 seconds.]

Turn your attention to your *buttocks*. And tighten your buttock muscles by squeezing them together. Hold it, squeeze, hold it, tightly. [Pause 10 seconds.] And let go. And relax. [Pause 15 seconds.]

Now bring your attention to your *thighs*. Slightly lift the left leg and squeeze all the leg muscles in the left leg now. Squeeze them and hold it tightly, while you're breathing. Tightly. [Pause 10 seconds.] And let go. Drop that leg. Let go of all those muscles. And just relax. [Pause 15 seconds.]

Now slightly lift the right leg and squeeze all the leg muscles tightly, firmly, squeeze tightly. [Pause 10 seconds.] And let go. Drop that leg. Completely relax the muscles in the right leg. With each exhalation, repeating the word "relax." [Pause 15 seconds.]

Turn your attention to your *calves*. Keeping your heels on the floor, point your toes up toward your face and lift the balls of your feet off the ground. Tense those calf muscles. You'll feel it in the front of your legs as well. Hold it, hold it. [Pause 10 seconds.] And let go. Drop your feet and relax those calf and lower leg muscles. That's it. [Pause 15 seconds.]

Bring your attention to your *feet*. Curl your toes, turning them down as if you're pressing them into the sand. Hold those muscles tightly. Hold them, toes curled, hold them, while you're breathing. [Pause 10 seconds.] And let go. [Pause 15 seconds.]

Stage 2: Complete Muscle Relaxation

Now relax all the muscle groups in the body. Just let them all go, with your breathing, relaxing any tense areas. [Pause 15 seconds.]

Imagine the sun shining down, warming the back of your head, producing a soothing, warm, relaxed feeling in the back of your head. [Pause 5 seconds.] Let that feeling flow through your face, and down into your neck, that warm comfortable relaxed feeling [5 seconds]. From your neck into your shoulders, into your shoulder blades, soothing, relaxing, loosening those muscles over your shoulders [5 seconds], to your arms [5 seconds]. Your upper arms relaxing, loosening those muscles over your elbows to your lower arms, relaxing, soothing the lower arms [5 seconds]. Loosening the muscles over your wrists to your hands, relaxing those hands [5 seconds]. Letting the tension flow out of the fingertips [5 seconds], as that warm, soothing, relaxing sun continues down the back, the chest, relaxing every muscle that comes in contact with that soothing, warm feeling [5 seconds]. Down to the stomach [5 seconds], the lower back [5 seconds], the intestines, warming, soothing, relaxing [5 seconds].

And the more you notice these sensations, the greater will be your relaxation [5 seconds]. Down to your pelvic region, warm, soothing, and relaxed feeling. Loosening muscles [5 seconds]. In your thighs [5 seconds], upper legs [5 seconds], warm, loosening, comforting feeling across your knees [5 seconds], down into your lower legs [5 seconds], your calves [5 seconds], your shins [5 seconds], throwing away the tension, feeling comfortable and relaxed.

That soothing, warm comforting feeling over your ankles [5 seconds] into your feet [5 seconds]. Relaxing the muscles in your feet. Allowing those tensions to pour out of your toes [5 seconds]. And feeling relaxed and calm [5 seconds].

Your whole body now, comfortable, relaxed, loose. Everyone knows the sensation of comfort that comes from feeling warm and safe [5 seconds].

Stage 3: The Safe Place

Now I want you to go to that safe place. Visualize yourself now in that safe place. Again producing the sensations of comfort, relaxation, and safety that come from that place for you. [Pause 5 seconds.] And you know the feeling. And you know the experience of feeling safe and relaxed, in a place and time without pressure, without responsibilities. Where time seems to stand still or go unnoticed, even if only for a while [5 seconds].

Continue to bathe in this comfort [5 seconds]. Perhaps there are certain sounds in that place which offer added comfort. Sounds which add to your experience of safety and comfort. [Pause 15 seconds.] There may even be a pleasant aroma or fragrance [5 seconds].

Possibly you have chosen this particular area because of its special atmosphere, the view you can see from that special spot. And you can enjoy that view now. [Pause 15 seconds.] Continue to drift and float in that image until you hear my voice again.

[Pause for 3 minutes of silence.]

You can continue to feel your mind enjoying this experience. You can memorize these feelings [5 seconds]. And you can bring these feelings with you to a future time and place, where they will be most useful to your well-being, to your best interest. [Pause 15 seconds.] You can absorb these feelings like a sponge. [Pause 15 seconds.]

Begin to slowly close this imagery, as you count to yourself from one to five. You can begin to reorient yourself to the room, allowing slight movements of your fingers and your toes now, of your feet, of your hands and arms, and begin to reorient your entire body.

Now, you're ready to open your eyes and enjoy the rest of your day and evening, feeling refreshed and alert.

MEDITATION

You may, after considering both methods, prefer meditation to Cue-Controlled Deep Muscle Relaxation as a way to release tensions.

Meditation is a family of mental exercises that generally involve sitting quietly and comfortably while focusing on some simple internal or external stimulus, such as a word, one's breathing pattern, or a visual object. In Deep Muscle Relaxation, the individual engages in a number of mental and physical activities. In meditation, the person is physically still and has a much narrower focus of attention.

There are a number of potential benefits to learning meditation, and I will explain them later in this chapter. These benefits fall within two general categories: First, meditation helps you to gain control of your physical tension by eliciting the Calming Response. Studies show that during meditation, as well as during Deep Muscle Relaxation, the heart rate and respiration rate slow down and blood pressure diminishes. Over time, meditators report feeling less daily anxiety and they tend to recover more quickly after highly anxious times. Thus within this category, meditation and Deep Muscle Relaxation provide similar gains.

The second category of benefits offers the greatest distinct contribution to those who experience panic. Learning the skills of meditation can dramatically increase your ability to control your fearful thinking by teaching you new ways to respond to your automatic thoughts, emotions, and images. The typical panic-prone person dwells on his worries, pays close attention to fearful thoughts, and responds emotionally to his negative images. Instead of being in control of these experiences, he is controlled by them.

To learn to meditate is to learn how to step away from these experiences, to become a detached, quiet observer of your thoughts, emotions, and images, as though you were watching them from the outside. Anyone who has experienced panic knows that the negative thinking during panic is so powerful that you can't simply say to yourself, "These thoughts are ridiculous. I am not about to die." That only invites a mental argument that increases panic: "Yes, I am! My heart's racing a mile a minute. People die under this kind of stress."

Any type of self-change strategy requires as a first step the skill of self-observation. In order to reduce your anxiety reaction and halt your negative thinking, you must be capable of stepping back from them far enough to put them in perspective. Chapters 13, 14, and 15 will teach you how to gain that perspective and use it to control panic. This chapter gives you the foundation skills needed to implement those techniques.

There are two types of meditation that you may choose from. Since they each accomplish similar goals, you can practice either or both of them. The first is "concentration" meditation.

The four essential features of this meditation are: (1) a quiet place, (2) a comfortable position, (3) an object to dwell on, and (4) a passive attitude.

Just as with the Deep Muscle Relaxation technique, you should use a quiet place in your home or elsewhere to practice. Then, assume a comfortable body posture and begin to invite a passive attitude within your mind (meaning that you don't need to worry about or become critical of distracting thoughts—you just note them, let them go, and return to the object you are dwelling on). The difference is that during meditation you select one object to focus on continually during the twenty minutes. You may choose a word (such as "calm," "love," "peace"), a religious phrase ("Let go and let God"), a short sound (such as "ahh" or "omm"), a feeling or a thought. You gently repeat that word or phrase silently at an easy pace. (For instance, if it is a one-syllable sound, you might say it once on the inhale and once on the exhale.) Or you may use your breathing pattern as the focus of your attention.

Both in meditation and in relaxation you are attempting to quiet your mind and to pay attention to only one thing at a time. An especially important skill to develop is that passive attitude. There should be no effort involved in the meditation. You pay attention to instructions, but you don't struggle to achieve any goal. You don't have to work to create any images; you don't have to put any effort into feeling any sensations in your body. All you have to do is remain aware, be in a comfortable position, dwell on the phrase, and easily let go of any distracting thoughts until those twenty minutes are over. That is the passive attitude.

The second meditative technique is an "awareness" meditation. In concentration meditation, you dwell on one object; all other awarenesses are considered distraction. In awareness meditation, each new event that arises (including thoughts, fantasies, and emotions), becomes the meditative object. Nothing is distraction.

The process is as follows. Find a quiet place to sit comfortably for twenty minutes. Begin by focusing on your natural breathing pattern. Mentally follow each gentle inhalation and exhalation, without judgment and without comment. (Those who become anxious when attending to their breath may focus on a single word or sound instead.) After a few minutes, allow your attention to shift easily among any perceptions that rise up. As each new thought or sensation registers in your mind, observe it in a detached manner. As you observe it, give that perception a name.

For instance, in the first few minutes of meditation you are focusing your awareness on each breath. As you loosen your attention you soon notice the tension you are holding in your forehead muscles. Without effort or struggle, subvocalize a name for the experience—perhaps "tension" or "forehead tension"—and continue observing. Sooner or later, your perception will shift. As your detached observing mind follows your awareness, you take notice of a mental image of a man's face with the corners of his mouth turned downward. Do not become involved with the image; don't analyze its meaning or wonder why it appeared. Simply notice it and name it—"frown" or "sad face"—while you maintain your uncritical perspective. When you do become lost in your thoughts, involved in emotions or focused on a decision, return your full concentration to your breathing pattern until you regain your detached observer. Everyone gets caught up in their experiences from time to time during meditation. Don't be self-critical if you continually drift off and don't fight to expel those perceptions. In concentration meditation you merely relax, let go, and focus back on your meditative word. In awareness meditation you relax, let go, and follow the flow of your perceptions from a distance. *What* you observe is not important. *How* you observe is the key: without evaluation and without involved comments.

WHAT YOU CAN LEARN FROM MEDITATION

You needn't become a skilled meditator in order to gain benefits from meditative practice. In fact, highly anxious people will find that the Deep Muscle Relaxation exercise is easier to follow, and they may wish to choose that technique as a long-term method to relax their muscles and quiet their mind. It is the process of *practicing* meditation that provides the valuable understanding that can be directly applied to controlling panic, even if you only practice the technique for several weeks.

Consider that during panic we become consumed by our momentary experience. We notice the unpleasant sensations in our body and become frightened by our interpretation of their meaning ("I'm going to faint," or "I won't be able to breathe"). We notice our surroundings and become frightened by how we interpret what we see ("There's no support here for me. This is a dangerous place right now"). We reinforce these sensations and thoughts by conjuring up terrifying images of ourselves not surviving the experience. Most of our thoughts, emotions, and images are out of proportion to reality. To gain control of these moments we must become skilled at disengaging from our personal distortions. We will not develop this skill by waiting until our next panic to practice. By then it's too late, because panic has control. The best time to learn a basic skill is during nonanxious periods. Then, we introduce that new skill gradually over time into the problem situation.

Here are the valuable learnings you can glean from meditative practice:

1. Meditation is a form of relaxation training. You learn to sit in a comfortable position and breathe in a calm, effortless way.

2. You learn to quiet your mind, to slow down the racing thoughts, and to tune in to more subtle internal cues. You acquire the ability to self-observe.

3. You practice the skill of focusing your attention on one thing at a time and doing so in a relaxed, deliberate fashion. By reducing the numbers of thoughts and images that enter your mind during a brief period, you are able to think with greater clarity and simplicity about whatever task you wish to accomplish.

4. You master the ability to notice when your mind wanders from a task, to direct your mind back to the task, and to hold it there, at least for brief periods. At first there may be a longer time span between when your mind wanders and when you realize it. With continued practice, you learn to catch yourself closer and closer to the moment in which you lose track of your task.

5. Through meditation you desensitize yourself to whatever is on your mind. You are able to notice your personal fears, concerns, or worries and at the same time step back and become detached from them. In this manner you can learn about your problems instead of being consumed by them.

6. If you regularly practice meditation and are able to feel more relaxed during that time, you gain the experience of mastery: your voluntary actions produce pleasurable changes in your body and mind.

7. As you acquire the knowledge of how you feel when you are calm, then you can use that feeling as a reference point during your day. For instance, if you feel calm after meditation in the morning, you will have a greater chance of noticing the subtle cues of tension later in the day. In other words, meditation (as well as Deep Muscle Relaxation) helps you become more alert to what circumstances are stressful in your life. You then have time to intervene in those circumstances before your tension builds to uncomfortable proportions.

8. In the upcoming chapters you will learn the importance of noticing your thought process leading up to and during panic. You must develop the sensitivity to notice those thoughts, to then let those thoughts go, and finally to turn your attention to some specific supportive tasks. That is no simple feat! By practicing meditation you

practice those three steps without simultaneously struggling with the frightening experience of panic.

9. Some people attempt to overcome the anxious thoughts leading up to panic by replacing them with positive thoughts. For instance, if they are thinking, "I'm about to lose control and go crazy," they will begin to simultaneously tell themselves, "No, I won't. I've never gone crazy before. I'll calm down soon." Sometimes this is quite a successful strategy. At other times, though, it can backfire by producing an internal quarrel. In arguments, of course, we tend to "dig in" in order to defend our position, and that's what can happen here: the fearful thoughts only get stronger. A central strategy you will learn in the coming chapters is first to stop completely those fearful comments by shifting your attention to some neutral task. Then, after disrupting your fearful thoughts for a few seconds or a few minutes, you will be better able to introduce positive, supportive suggestions without risking the internal battle. The two meditative techniques in this chapter teach you this basic skill. In Chapter 14 you will learn two of these disruptive processes—the Calming Counts and the Calming Breath— which are actually brief forms of meditation.

WHICH METHOD IS BEST FOR YOU?

One essential purpose of practicing the Deep Muscle Relaxation or meditation is to give your mind and body the peaceful rest that comes whenever you elicit the Calming Response. By practicing one of these methods daily for a number of weeks, you learn how you feel when you calm down. You discover that you don't lose control as you let go of your tensions; you actually gain control. Choose whichever method interests you, then give yourself time to catch on to the technique.

I have outlined a number of benefits that can come from meditation. If you are a person who is plagued with many anxious thoughts, you will probably have an easier time with concentration meditation rather than awareness meditation, since it provides you with a specific mental focus. Research suggests that people who experience predominantly physical symptoms of anxiety can diminish these tensions best through regular practice of active techniques such as Deep Muscle Relaxation. Engaging in some form of regular physical exercise—such as walking, dancing, or active sports—can also help control anxiety that is expressed physically. Even if you prefer the Deep Muscle Relaxation, I suggest that you spend some time with meditative practice. Use meditation to teach yourself how to disrupt your intrusive thoughts while you use Relaxation to gain a sense of calmness.

Whichever approach you choose, your initial concentration will take great effort. Take your time, and don't be self-critical if you notice few immediate positive results. Use the time as practice, not as a test. If nothing more, the simple task of sitting quietly for twenty minutes each day can bring rewards.

13

The Independent Observer

In the first nine chapters you learned about the complexity of panic. Now we will begin to apply that information to a specific task: controlling an actual panic episode. To do so, we must first make the complex simple. When you face panic you will want to rid yourself of unnecessary worries or questions and replace them with a few simple thoughts. In order to think clearly during panic, you must understand how panic attacks take place.

You are already familiar with your physical symptoms, and I have discussed them in Chapters 1, 8, and 11. But panic is not those symptoms alone. If it were only the physical discomforts, panic could disappear from your life as rapidly as it enters. In Chapter 7 I identified the manner in which panic becomes more than just the physical. It invades your mental processes as well. In fact, a panic episode often *begins* in reaction to your thoughts ("I wonder how I'll feel today? I wonder if I'll feel nervous again?").

For a panic attack to grow in intensity, two phenomena must take place:

1. You must closely observe your current experience.
2. You must comment on those observations.

To reduce panic you can change either one of these two steps. Let's look at each of them more closely.

Imagine that you are interested in buying a house. To begin your search you are spending a Saturday with a realtor, viewing four different houses within your size, location, and price range. At each site you will probably spend thirty to forty-five minutes walking through the rooms and around the yard. What are you doing during that time? What is your mental process?

The first thing you do is *observe*. Your eyes are scanning each room slowly: you are noticing the layout of the kitchen, the size of the bedrooms, the number of baths, and so forth. You look for moisture in the basement, insulation in the attic, and check the condition of the exterior.

Let's call this part of us—which objectively gathers information— our "Observer." When you take a first look through a house, it is best to simply "flip on" the Observer within you. In that way you can gather much more information about each potential home. You may even take a notebook to record the facts you need to make an intelligent decision.

That's Step One. Step Two is to begin to *comment* about the data you have collected, to consider your personal preferences as to size, design, location. You analyze each house according to your needs and desires. Here is what might go on in your mind as you view a house for the first time. Notice how the thoughts come in two stages:

[As you drive up the driveway] OBSERVER: "The drive is concrete; there's a two-car open garage. The house is Colonial style, and the yard is manicured." COMMENT: "Looks good. We could use a carport. Maybe we could even enclose it one day. The outside looks well cared for. Colonials aren't my favorite, though."

[As you enter the kitchen] OBSERVER: "This is bigger than mine, with an island in the middle. Open entry into a breakfast nook. No windows in the kitchen. Also opens into the living room/dining room combo. Walk-in pantry. And lots of cabinet space." COMMENT: "Wow! This is what I'm looking for! Plenty of space to spread out, plus we can eat most meals without lugging things into the dining room. And lots of storage would be a treat. Major drawback is the lack of natural light. It's so nice to be able to look outside from the kitchen. But I think I can live with it. Let's see if the rest of the house is as nice."

There is a clear and distinct difference between the Observer statements and the Comments. The Observer simply notices and reports objectively any data it receives. It is like the attitude of the judge in a courtroom: "Just the facts please, ma'am." The Observer applies no biases, preferences, personal desires, or judgments to the facts.

In Step Two we comment on our observations. Now we *are* influenced by our desires, beliefs, values, hopes, fears, and judgments. ("I love it/hate it/am afraid of it/don't care for it/want it/want to change it/doubt I can have it/wish it never happened/hope it works," and so forth.)

It is when we comment on our observations prematurely that our problems begin. Imagine that as you drove up to that house you said, "It's a Colonial. Colonials aren't my favorite. That's a strike against this house already; the inside probably won't do, either. Why don't we go on to the next one." Your quick judgment would prevent you from continuing to gather information. In this case, you would have missed the opportunity of seeing your ideal kitchen. And the quality of that kitchen might have offset the exterior design. When we are quick to judge, we lose valuable information.

Prejudice is the judging of people, situations, or experiences prior to objectively observing them. One of the greatest tragedies of racism, sexism, and ageism is that so many talented people are arbitrarily dismissed without regard to their unique qualities and talents. The same process occurs during panic. Our beliefs or fears are so predominant that we never objectively observe the situation. With only a minimal amount of data, we quickly interpret the situation as an emergency and, therefore, begin our panic routine. We blend a two-step process into one step. We no longer take time to take advantage of our detached, objective, data-gathering Observer. We instantly analyze and interpret each new piece of information as though we are certain of its meaning.

The interpretation of events is the mental process that produces the panic response. As I discussed in Chapter 9, during a panic-provoking time the brain lacks relevant information about exactly what is going on, and it doesn't know a more appropriate way to respond. Therefore, it selects the same old response it used in the past to handle a similar situation. The brain pushes the panic button because we withhold new information from it. We do not slow down enough to collect current information; we fall back to our preconceived notion that we are "out of control." By using the skills of your Observer at the moment of panic, however, you will gather current, relevant information about your body and your surroundings. This vital data will guide you toward gaining control of your anxiety attack.

You already have an excellent capacity to observe. In fact, panic happens only to those who are capable of paying close attention to small details. It is important to renew your acquaintance with this skill, so that you may begin to use it during panic-provoking times.

Instead of taking the time to observe the threatening situation, the panic-prone person will quickly observe and interpret the situation in one swift moment. In my work with clients over the years, I have found three primary ways in which they "contaminate" the responsibilities of the Observer by adding negative comments during this important first step. I call them the "Worried Observer," the "Critical Observer," and the "Hopeless Observer." Here are some examples of these Negative Observers.

The Worried Observer. "My heart rate has increased. . . . Oh no, what does that mean? Am I starting to have a heart attack? I must be."

"My speech is scheduled for next week. . . . I know I'm going to start stammering. Then everyone will watch me shake in my boots. I'll be so embarrassed."

"There are a lot of people shopping here today. . . . That means that the checkout lines are going to be endlessly long. I'll have to stand there forever. I'll probably start to get dizzy again. I might even faint on the spot."

THE WORRIED OBSERVER

- Anticipates the worst
- Fears the future
- Creates grandiose images of potential problems
- Expects and braces for catastrophe
- Watches, with uneasy apprehension, for any small signs of trouble

Over time, the Worried Observer creates anxiety.

The Critical Observer. "Last week when I drove to the store I had no symptoms. This morning I became anxious and never made it to the store. . . . I'm doing terribly! I'm so angry I failed! I'm such a weak person."

"Tonight is the Webers' party, and I'm afraid about going. . . .

Well, that's typical. Every little thing bothers me! I feel like a two-year-old. When am I going to grow up and face the world!''

"They're thinking of having the family reunion in Florida. . . . Oh, great. Guess who's going to spoil everything again. I'm too afraid to fly, I won't shop by myself, I don't like highways. What am I doing to this family!''

THE CRITICAL OBSERVER

- Makes certain you understand how helpless and hopeless you are
- Doesn't hesitate to remind you of the mistakes you have made and that you are lucky to have anything or anyone in your life
- Points out each of your flaws regularly, in case you might have forgotten them
- Uses any mistake to remind you of what a failure you are

Over time the Critical Observer produces low self-esteem and low motivation.

The Hopeless Observer. "Susan wants me to go out to lunch with her. . . . There's no way I can survive a restaurant. I just can't handle it. What's the point. I'll never be in control.''

"I used to be so outgoing. Now I hardly leave the house unless I'm taking the kids somewhere. . . . I've dug myself into a hole, and I'll be here for years.''

"I feel physically drained today, and I wanted to get some work done around here. . . . Why bother.''

THE HOPELESS OBSERVER

- Suffers over your present experience
- Believes there is something inherently wrong with you
- Believes that you are deprived, defective, or unworthy, that you are missing what it takes to succeed
- Expects that you will fail in the future just as you have failed in the past

- Expects that you will continue to be deprived and frustrated
- Believes that there are insurmountable obstacles between you and your goals

Over time the Hopeless Observer creates depression.

All three of these ways of commenting contaminate your natural ability to observe. They distort information about your life in a hurtful way. They don't encourage your progress, your independence, or your self-esteem. Instead, they invite you to surrender your efforts and give in to failure.

If we study the experiences of people who have significantly restricted their lives out of fear of panic, we can see more clearly the destructive patterns of these Negative Observer comments. Listen to the statements of each of these clients during one of our first sessions. Imagine how these thinking patterns literally halt their progress.

ANN C.: I watch myself. I'm always trying to keep this grip on myself. I'm monitoring every little thing that I do, and in the final analysis I decide that I'm not in control.

Ann tells us that she has the skill to observe herself. But she takes that ability and moves it to a Worried Observer extreme. She becomes the Detective, watching her every move to discover clues that will prove she is out of control. Since she is completely focused on herself, since she notices every small change, and since she *expects* the worst, sure enough, she always concludes, "I'm not in control."

DONNA B.: I judge my level of success in recovery by how well I get through a bad feeling. If I stay out of bad feelings and keep going, then I feel like I'm almost healed. But if I lie down or quit, then I'm very negative about myself. I only support myself when I've been successful.

Notice that Donna, too, has that Observer skill. But she makes extreme interpretations of the facts. When she has a great day, she is certain her problems are over forever. Her standards are so high, however, that if she has any kind of setback she labels herself a "failure." She views her actions through Critical Observer eyes, and she can never be good enough. The Critical Observer allows no room for mistakes.

KAREN L.: I started to feel physically sick today, like an allergic reaction. Then I said to myself, "How much is physical and how much is psychological?" I started arguing in my mind, "Should I drive myself to therapy or not? I don't think I can." Finally I gave in to myself and asked my husband to drive me. I just didn't think I could handle it, and I didn't want to struggle anymore. Now that I'm here, a part of me doesn't really care, but another part of me feels disgusted with myself for not fighting.

Karen's statements reflect all three of the Negative Observer contaminants. Her Worried Observer questions, "How much is physical and how much is psychological?" Her Hopeless Observer surrenders, "I can't handle it. I don't want to struggle anymore." Then her Critical Observer delivers the final blow, "I'm disgusted with myself for not fighting." Can you imagine what it is like to treat yourself this way on a daily basis? This is how anxiety, low self-esteem, low motivation, and depression can become central parts of a panic-prone person's life.

SHERYLL W.: In my own case I'm too keen an observer, in a negative way. I'm observing myself constantly, but it's always with fear. Like Claire Weekes says, "Headphones on your feelings."*

Sheryll's Worried Observer amplifies any minor change in her feelings: "Oh, no, what was that?" "Is it still there?" "Is it getting worse?" "Will I be ready to handle it?" Why is she fearful? Not because she is having uncomfortable physical symptoms, and not because she is paying attention to her body. It is because her Worried Observer is saying to her, "Any moment now you might be overwhelmed with a severe anxiety attack. Stay on guard!" To the Worried Observer, your current experience is irrelevant. Instead, it remembers how bad the past has been and imagines how frightening

---

* Dr. Claire Weekes is a pioneer in the study of anxiety and panic. She has written three books on these topics.

the future will soon be. Your Worried Observer can actually supersede any rational thoughts. If the Worried Observer is thinking of past trauma and imagining future danger, your brain has no choice but to interpret these fantasies instead of interpreting your current reality. The brain then responds to the presumed danger by automatically shifting into Emergency gear. *To stop the physical symptoms of panic you must stop the Worried Observer.*

DONNA: I know I get angry with myself whenever I get tense for no reason.

There is usually some reason why we get tense or anxious during a time when there is no actual threat. Either the events of the past are remaining with us, or we are anticipating events of the future. Using the Observer, we can objectively review those events and our reactions to them. Based on that information, we can choose the most supportive action to take. Donna's Critical Observer, however, prevents her from thinking in a caring manner about her needs. Instead it says, "There's no reason to be tense! What the hell is wrong with you!" Because her Critical Observer is so strongly embedded within her belief system, it prevents any current facts from entering into the picture.

Each of these contaminated Observers operates on a pre-existing negative belief system. Each one of them, therefore, keeps the mind closed and prevents intelligent decision-making.

ANN: When I begin to notice symptoms I become paralyzed and I start listening in on my body. And my immediate reaction is to run away from it. I have tried to sit, or to "handle" it, but physically it depletes me so much that I have to run. I'm feeling symptoms now, and my immediate reaction is to get out of here. I don't feel I have the energy, the physical or the emotional energy, to see it through, because I've been like this for twelve years. I feel like I'm going to drop dead next week because of the effects, because of the toll this has taken on my health.

Ann's comments reflect the stance of the Hopeless Observer. She becomes "paralyzed" and completely absorbed by the symptoms she notices. She feels so "depleted" of energy that she can't imagine surviving her symptoms. Since she has been this way for twelve years, she has decided that nothing will ever change this pattern. Every anxious episode seems to pile on top of the last one, and her burden gets heavier and heavier. Eventually, she imagines, she will collapse from the toll. This is the type of contamination that leads to depression.

Since our actions are based on our interpretation of the facts and not the facts themselves, all of these Worried, Critical, or Hopeless Observer comments prevent us from taking positive action. Turn back to the three Worried Observer examples on page 175. Read each one, then imagine what kind of action these interpretations might produce. Do the same for the Critical and Hopeless Observer statements. See if you notice any pattern among the nine examples. (Try it now.)

Most likely you saw that these kinds of conclusions were drawn:

I'd better go lie down.
I think I'd better cancel.
I ought to leave while I can.
I'm not going to keep trying.
I might as well not be around people anyway.
I'll tell them to go without me.
I quit.

In other words, these contaminated Observers lead to passivity and inaction. They invite you to surrender to helplessness, to stop trying, to wave the white flag.

The Worried Observer, which is usually present just before or during physical symptoms, goes one step further. It provides a distorted interpretation of events for the brain. Take the first example: "My heart has increased its rate. Oh, no, what does that mean? Am I starting to have a heart attack? I must be." The brain makes this interpretation: "I'm losing control." The brain then responds appropriately to an inappropriate interpretation: "All systems to Emergency Response!"

That is why sometimes immediately after you question whether symptoms are developing, those symptoms become stronger, almost magically. After such an experience you tell yourself, "Good job. I was paying close attention and caught myself before the panic snuck up on me. I'd better stay on guard more often."

But there is nothing magical about it. Do you see the vicious circle? Your solution creates your problem:

1. You pay close attention to your physical sensations.
2. You become suspicious of a minor sensation.
3. You interpret that sensation to mean the beginning of an anxiety attack or other serious disturbance.
4. Your brain turns on the Emergency Reponse to "save" you.
5. You vow to be even more sensitive next time.
6. Back to Step A.

What is the alternative to this passive, fearful, guarded cycle? How does one get out of these old, repetitive patterns? Three general tasks are required at panic-prone moments:

Step 1: Think with your Observer.
Step 2: Calmly interpret the facts.
Step 3: Choose an appropriate action.

By eliminating the Worried, Critical, and Hopeless comments, your Observer instantly becomes one of your strongest resources.

THE OBSERVER

- Takes times to collect all the relevant information
- Is detached from strong emotions
- May feel concern, yet thinks calmly
- Is devoid of prejudices
- Gains a perspective on the situation
- Sees problems in a different light
- Is objective

Who can possibly face a challenging situation with confidence while mentally reciting a litany of fears, criticisms, or doubts? The Observer dismisses such comments and focuses on the important information at the moment: "What is taking place in my body right now? What is special about my current situation? (Have I been afraid here before? Is it reminding me of a past or future fear?) What sense can I make of my current reaction?" These types of questions can be asked and answered based on a momentary reflection, as though you are stepping back from the scene for a short time. ("Hmmm . . . I'm starting to get tense again. How come? Nothing special is bothering me; I'm just sitting here watching TV [pause for reflection]. Oh, yeah, that character on the show was just fighting with her husband. I think that's when I started getting tense.")

The ability to slowly and objectively size up a situation is a crucial first step, because this information determines what action you will take next. If, in the above example, you quickly think, "Oh, my gosh, I'm starting to have an anxiety attack. How bad will this one be?," you become a powerless victim of panic by not pausing for even a moment before surrendering to the symptoms. But if, instead, you stop to think, "I'm reacting to the fighting on TV," now you have something you can grasp, something which seems plausible.

Gathering the facts and interpreting the facts are two different steps which should be treated as such during panic-prone times. In Step One ("Think with your Observer"), your Observer is concentrating on your present experience. It doesn't get emotional or excited. It is unattached to the facts that it gathers. Even looking around for a cause of the current tension can be done in a detached manner. Not a frantic rush of thought, such as, "Oh, I feel a little jumpy right now. I've just woken up. Why do I feel so jumpy? Oh, no, I probably didn't sleep well, or I had bad dreams. Oh, damn, here it comes, the start of another terrible day." You must remember that you have time to think methodically, "This is not an emergency." In fact, the more time you give yourself to think, the greater chance you have of using your Observer's skills.

In this example, if you are thinking more slowly, your Observer might say, "Hmmm . . . I'm feeling a little jumpy right now. I've just woken up. [Pause for reflection.] There is probably some logical reason why I'm feeling this way, even though I'm not certain what it is." This example raises an important point. Notice that the Observer didn't come up with the exact cause of the tension. Sometimes the cause isn't obvious or immediately known. At those times the Observer makes a new factual statement: "There is some logical cause for my sensations, even though I can't put my finger on it immediately." It does not say (as the Worried Observer might), "I've *got* to know what's causing this, *now!*" Instead, it carries out its responsibility, which is to calmly collect and report information.

Your body may be shaking, your legs may be weak, your breathing may be fast. But your Observer can separate itself from those symptoms. It can report, in a detached manner, the facts that it gathers. It notices them but does not get preoccupied with them. *To become preoccupied with the symptoms is to encourage the symptoms.*

The Observer does not try to fix the problem. Instead, it observes the action without disturbing it. All of us who have had to react to a sudden physical emergency in the home or on the highway have first-hand experience with the skills of the Observer. After the crisis has passed, most people will be able to report in great detail everything that they saw or thought. It is as though time slowed down and every second during the crisis lasted a minute. This detailed memory is produced by our Observer. Like a film camera, it records, in an objective manner, every single piece of relevant information. During the moment of panic, your first task will be to watch and listen through that same Observer's camera.

Step Two is to calmly interpret the facts that your Observer has reported. Now you are determining the relationships among the facts you have gathered. In response to the observation about the TV show ("Oh, yeah, that character was just fighting with her husband. I think that's when I started getting tense"): "Since I have trouble facing conflicts in my own life, I bet that's why I'm overreacting to this scene. I don't need to become so involved in these feelings right now."

In the second example ("Hmmm . . . I'm feeling a little jumpy right now. I've just woken up"): "It won't be helpful to focus on these symptoms right now."

In other words, Step Two ("Calmly interpret the facts") answers this question: Based on what I now know from observing, what do I seem to need? Again, you take a calm moment to explore that thought.

In the early stages of this learning skill, I recommend that you slow down your thinking during Step One and Step Two. I suggest that you take at least ten times (!) longer than you do now, simply to gather your information. That sounds like forever, but "slow down" is a relative term in this situation. The panic-prone person probably takes less than two seconds before concluding that she is losing control. *No* objective thinking takes place. In most panic-provoking moments all you need is less than twenty seconds of observing in order to realistically assess the situation. Then another ten seconds will often be enough time for you to interpret the information. At that point you are ready for Step Three: "Choose an appropriate action."

(The following chapters are dedicated to this task.) This suggestion of thirty seconds is only to give you a general sense of the time needed. Of course, each situation and each person will require varying degrees of time. Some of my clients can accomplish these steps in less than five seconds:

OBSERVER: "I'm tense."
INTERPRETATION: "I don't need to be."
ACTION: Take a deep breath, sigh out loud on the exhale, let go of tense muscles.

In an example requiring a little more time, our thoughts might run like this:

OBSERVER: "I'm feeling anxious right now. How come? Hmmm . . . maybe it's because Jim's going on a business trip for three days. I've been nervous during those times in the past."
INTERPRETATION: "I need to find a way to reassure myself these next few days."
ACTION: "Why don't I talk about my concerns to Jim before he leaves. Who knows, maybe it'll help. Plus, I'll talk with Judith. Her husband travels a lot, and she'll probably have some advice. I want to have some ideas before Jim leaves on Wednesday."

To further illustrate these first two steps, let's review the nine hypothetical examples used earlier in the chapter. This time I will remove the Negative Observer comments, leaving simple Observer statements (Step One), followed by possible interpretations (Step Two). Remember that Step Two answers the question, "Based on what I now know, what do I seem to need?" What specific action to take in each scenario is not presented yet; that will be Step Three.

OBSERVER: My heart rate has increased. I'm starting to worry what that means. INTERPRETATION: "This is *not* an emergency. I can calm my worries and calm my body."
OBSERVER: "My speech is scheduled for next week. Right now I'm afraid I might perform poorly." INTERPRETATION: "It's OK to be concerned about my talk. I also probably need to gain some confidence in my ability before then."

OBSERVER: "There are a lot of people shopping here today. That means the lines will probably be long. I've been uncomfortable in lines before." INTERPRETATION: "This is *not* an emergency. I need to pace myself while I'm here. I want to leave here later with at least a few groceries, and I don't need to rush myself. I'll do the best I can."

OBSERVER: "Last week when I drove to the store I had no symptoms. This morning I became anxious and never made it to the store." INTERPRETATION: "When I don't meet my goals, I tend to become harsh on myself. That's not helpful. I need to support myself and set a new goal."

OBSERVER: "Tonight's the Webers' party, and I'm afraid about going." INTERPRETATION: "It's OK to be afraid about the party. Social events are usually tough for me, so this is normal. But it would be best if I stayed calm and busy until it is time to get ready."

OBSERVER: "They're thinking of having the family reunion in Florida. I've been so afraid of flying that I haven't been on a plane in six years." INTERPRETATION: "Nothing is going to be decided immediately. I have time to think about my options."

OBSERVER: "Susan wants me to go out to lunch with her. I often feel trapped in a restaurant." INTERPRETATION: "I need to believe that Susan will be supportive of me if we go. And I need some control over the logistics of lunch."

OBSERVER: "I used to be so outgoing. Now I hardly leave the house unless I'm taking the kids somewhere." INTERPRETATION: "This pattern is hurtful to me. I need to find some activities that will help me feel better about myself."

OBSERVER: "I feel physically drained today, and I wanted to get some work done around here." INTERPRETATION: "If I do nothing all day I'll end up angry with myself. I need to start by accomplishing some very small, brief tasks. I need to take one step at a time."

14

Finding Your Observer

In Chapter 10 I described the Calming Response, which can counterbalance the symptoms of panic. In Chapter 13 I introduced the concept of the Observer, which can give you needed perspective during anxious times. This chapter will detail for you specific methods for producing the Calming Response and eliciting your Observer at the same time. During a panic-provoking moment, that is exactly what you want to do. By calming the body and clearing the mind of negative comments, you will become mentally sharp and alert, ready to take care of yourself within seconds.

THE FIRST IMPORTANT STEPS

The best way to master a new skill is to break it down into learnable "chunks." For instance, when you learn to type, you begin by repeatedly typing a few letters, in order to master the proper finger movements. Again and again you repeat those patterns until your confidence builds. You then practice typing more letters in a row, then more complex sets of letters. You are always instructed to type slowly at first so that you may concentrate better; speed will come later. The process then continues in gradual stages: two-letter words, three-letter words, five-letter words, phrases, and finally full, punctuated sentences.

The same diligence and patience are needed here. If you have never mastered a formal relaxation or meditation technique, daily practice will build your skill and confidence. Slowly you will be better able to recognize when your mind and body are tense and when they are comfortable. Mastering any of the techniques in this chapter requires time. Remember when you first learned to ride a bike or rollerskate? During your early attempts you probably said, "I'll never catch on. I'm so clumsy." But you persisted, and you learned.

Some people may feel these methods won't be powerful enough to affect their panic attacks, which are overwhelming. I say to these of you what I have said to my clients over the years: if you are committed to controlling anxiety attacks, you can do it. If you want to learn these new behaviors in order to conquer your anxiety attacks, then practice, practice, and practice some more. No one needs to be continually devastated by this problem.

In the Deep Muscle Relaxation technique, by allowing your muscles to rehearse again and again those contractions and relaxations you are giving them a chance to create new pathways in the brain. Soon those pathways will be strong enough to operate without practice. By repeating the structured experiences in this chapter again and again, you will create new pathways for these needed skills as well. Anyone who plays a musical instrument knows how much time and effort is required to first learn those hand movements. After persistent practice, those same movements come reflexively, without conscious thought.

Remember that your primary goal is to find a long-lasting method for regaining control over panic. This is a one-step-at-a-time process. The learning of a new skill should be undertaken during low-anxiety times, when you are not feeling under stress. Once you have mastered the skill, then begin to apply it to the panic-provoking times. No one learns to type after they have been hired as a typist. And no one should expect these methods to work as effectively at first as they will after practice.

Let me begin with a few brief experiences. For the first one I would like you to follow these guidelines:

Calming Counts (Practice Version)

1. Sit comfortably.
2. Take a nice, long, deep breath and exhale it slowly while saying the word "relax" under your breath.

3. Then simply close your eyes.
4. With your eyes closed, let yourself take ten natural, easy breaths.
5. Purposely count each exhale, starting with "ten," until you reach "one."

Practice this experience now, and as you begin to read the words again, let yourself read them slowly, as though you have shifted into a more gentle, quiet state. Let your natural breathing remain calm, gently inhaling into your abdomen as described in Chapter 11.

I would now like you to try this same process a second time, with jone additional step:

CALMING COUNTS

1. Sit comfortably.
2. Take a long, deep breath and exhale it slowly while saying the word "relax" silently.
3. Close your eyes.
4. Let yourself take ten natural, easy breaths. Count down with each exhale, starting with "ten."
5. This time, while you are breathing comfortably, notice any tensions, perhaps in your jaw or forehead or stomach. Imagine those tensions loosening.
6. When you reach "one," open your eyes again.

Practice this now, starting with a deep breath. Now please try the experience a third time, this time taking twenty breaths and counting each exhalation, from "twenty" to "one." Practice this now.

As you open your eyes and before you become active again, take a moment to mentally scan your body. What do you notice? What has changed? How do you feel in general right now? If your body is feeling a pleasant kind of heaviness, lightness, or tingling, if you felt some of your muscles unwind, if your breathing seems calmer, then you are learning firsthand about the Calming Response.

Did you have trouble keeping track of the numbers? Did you become distracted by other thoughts? Did you make any "Worried,"

"Critical," or "Hopeless" comments during the three exercises? Usually, the better able you are to passively concentrate on the counting, the calmer your body and mind become. The more you "work" at trying to concentrate, the harder this task becomes. Your job is *not* to focus intently on how your breathing is changing; it is *not* to evaluate how the exercise is progressing while in the middle of the experience. It is simply to let each exhale be a "marker" for the next number in your mind—inhale . . . exhale . . . "twenty" . . . inhale . . . exhale . . . "nineteen" . . . and so forth. When some other thought comes into your mind, gently dismiss it and return to the counting.

YOUR OBSERVER AND THE CALMING RESPONSE

Whenever your breathing settles down and your mind focuses on a few simple thoughts, you are inviting the Calming Response. During the Calming Counts, when you notice your breathing just enough to count each exhalation, and notice and gently let go of any unnecessary comments, you are using your Observer. This exercise is an excellent way to teach yourself about your Observer and the Calming Response.

The Calming Counts can be applied specifically toward controlling panic attacks. One way is to incorporate them within relaxation or meditative techniques to help you concentrate more completely. We know from experience that if, on a daily basis, you structure a period of private time to quiet your mind and relax your body, panic will find less and less opportunity to intrude into your life. The more rested you are physically and psychologically, the better protected you become. If you are having difficulty concentrating during these structured quiet times, the Calming Counts can be helpful.

The Cue-Controlled Deep Muscle Relaxation, described in Chapter 12, is one method of developing the Calming Response by using your Observer. At the same time it prevents the tensions of the day from piling up. If you practice this method, you will notice Worried, Critical, or Hopeless Observer comments rising up from time to time during the twenty mintues (which you should acknowledge and gently dismiss). The final portion, in which you are instructed to "go to your safe place" in your mind, requires the greatest skill of passive concentration. If you find that you have difficulty maintaining an easy, quiet concentration during that time, use the following counting exercise in place of your visual image: Instead of "going to your safe place," begin counting silently with each exhalation, from "one hundred" to "one." Follow the Calming Count instructions.

ONE HUNDRED COUNTS

1. Sit comfortably.
2. Take a deep breath, exhale slowly, and silently say "relax."
3. Breathing in a relaxed, natural manner, count silently from "one hundred" to "one," using each exhale as one count.
4. If you happen to notice any tension in your face, jaw, stomach, or other areas, easily suggest in your mind that they relax.
5. As you notice any irrelevant thoughts, easily let them go and return to your counting.
6. If you lose track of your counting, simply return to some number close to where you were.
7. When you reach "one," gradually open your eyes as you think about feeling refreshed and alert.

If you enjoy private time to unwind from the tensions of each day, I suggest that you also experiment with meditation, which is the sister to relaxation exercises. As I described in Chapter 12, the four essential features of meditation are a quiet place, a comfortable position, an object to dwell on and a passive attitude.

Here is a modification of that meditative process which uses the Calming Counts. I have designed it especially for my panic-prone clients, because it offers two distinct advantages over traditional meditation. First, it gives you a stronger sense of being in control, since you must consciously keep track of the descending numbers. Second, it reduces the number of irrelevant thoughts that drift into your mind. This is most helpful during the times when you become flooded with Negative Observer comments. The Calming Counts give you a specific and neutral task: to count with each exhale until you reach "one." This task will be in direct competition with your Negative Observer comments, therefore your mind will become less involved with such self-destructive thoughts.

MEDITATION OF ONE HUNDRED COUNTS

1. Sit in a comfortable quiet place.
2. Take a deep breath, exhale slowly, and say "relax" silently.
3. Begin counting at "one hundred" while breathing naturally. Use each exhalation to mark the next number, until you reach "one."
4. When extraneous thoughts enter your mind, simply note them and let them go. Return to your focused counting.
5. When you reach "one," begin counting again at "one hundred."
6. When you reach "one" the second time, count forward with each breath, from "one" to "ten." During this final ten-count sequence, suggest to yourself that you will open your eyes at "ten," feeling alert and refreshed.

When you finish this or any other exercise in this book, do not immediately begin to evaluate how well or how poorly you performed. There are many variables that determine our responses to any particular exercise. For instance, on certain days when you are more anxious, your concentration may not be strong. Nonetheless, practicing the structured experience that day, difficult as it is, may give you greater benefits than if you had a "good" practice during a less pressured day. Any time that you consciously choose to quiet your mind and relax your body, you are promoting your health.

As you become more skilled in producing the Calming Response through daily formal practice of relaxation or meditation, you may begin to use a briefer technique, which I call the Calming Breath.

THE CALMING BREATH

1. Take a deep breath, filling first your lower lungs, then your upper lungs.
2. *Slowly* exhale, saying "relax" (or a similar word) under your breath.
3. Let your muscles go limp and warm; loosen your face and jaw muscles.
4. Remain in this "resting" position physically and mentally for a few seconds, or for a couple of natural breaths.

If you need or want to have your eyes open because of your circumstances (you are driving a car or are with a group of people), feel free to do so. During your early weeks of learning, however, find opportunities to practice this exercise with your eyes closed. This will improve your body's chances of responding to your suggestions.

During the Calming Breath you will be taking advantage of the "cues" you have developed in practicing the formal relaxation or meditative techniques: you are repeating a special word, breathing in a special manner, and giving the body a chance to develop the same pleasant sensations it has during the Calming Response.

This is another skill, like the Calming Counts, that you should practice throughout your day, whether or not you are feeling tense. Even if you have never practiced any lengthy relaxation exercises, you can immediately begin using the Calming Counts and the Calming Breath. Such techniques, used several times each day, have been found to reduce the buildup of normal everyday tensions. If you begin to use it regularly during non-crisis times, you will create new pathways in the brain which promote mental calmness and muscle relaxation. Then, when you need this skill during a panic-provoking moment, it will come almost as "second nature."

In addition to releasing tensions, all of the structured experiences in this chapter will teach you how to rid yourself of unhelpful thoughts by first noticing them and then dropping them. Almost every time you practice one of these techniques, you will experience random thoughts floating up in your mind. The more you practice letting go of them, the greater skill you will develop, so that during actual problem times you will apply this new skill easily. Then, instead of noticing a stray thought during a Calming Counts practice, you will be disarming negative thoughts which are producing tension within you. That is why you should never become discouraged about your progress in these techniques. The more difficulty you face while learning these skills, the better prepared you will be for the problem times. I cannot stress enough that repetitive practice will reward you tenfold over time. These methods need to become as automatic as your panic response is, because in the moment of panic you want to focus on only a few simple thoughts. The more these skills become second nature to you, the better they will serve you during troubled times.

15

Taking a New Stance:
The Supportive Observer

For most of us, the world is full of decisions to be made, options to select, choices to consider. Every day we must discriminate dozens of times among an array of alternatives, from selecting the right combination of clothes in the morning, to choosing what to eat at each meal, to deciding which projects to tackle for the day. How do we make these decisions?

Within each of these arenas we develop, over time and through trial and error, our individual tastes. If I were to ask you to describe your favorite foods, the music you enjoy most, or your ideal vacation spot, you would probably describe the qualities you look for in making your choice. For instance, "I like a vacation spot with lots of sun but that's not too hot. Somewhere that isn't too crowded. And it would have to have water: either a pool, a lake, or the ocean." We discriminate among actual vacation spots based on the characteristics we value.

By becoming aware of our general tastes and preferences, we make each specific decision easier. I don't stand in the kitchen every morning, stupefied over whether I should have cereal, eggs, pancakes, French toast, oatmeal, granola, or just a glass of juice for breakfast. Since I am by now quite familiar with my likes and dislikes, I can choose within a few moments' time (usually cereal and coffee).

FILTERING THE FACTS

It is the same with any of our decisions. The more we develop our sense of taste, our preferences, our values, our leanings, the less time we need to spend picking from an array of choices. Imagine how annoying it would be to have to spend a half-hour reviewing each selection on a restaurant menu before picking out an entree. At some point we must trust our judgment. We must take a stand.

To make a decision we move through three stages. First, we observe and register the information available to us ("This menu has steak, pasta, and fish"). Second, we interpret that information, based on our own knowledge, experience, and preferences ("I had steak last night, and I'm not in the mood for pasta; I think I would like the stuffed flounder."). Finally, we take action based on our interpretation (we order the flounder.) In other words, during the interpretation phase, we screen the information through our personal inclinations before we choose an action.

This discriminating process doesn't always work in our favor. When the panic-prone person screens all collected information through one of the Negative Observers, he reduces his options in a self-defeating manner. Each of the Negative Observers has its own special attitude about the world.

For instance, here is a typical stance of the Worried Observer: "In all likelihood, things are going to turn out badly. I should be extremely careful before taking any action. What choice will keep me from experiencing any discomfort whatsoever? I must avoid problems. I need to feel completely comfortable. I'm willing to give up a lot if it will ensure that I'll feel safe. If I make the wrong choice, it could prove catastrophic."

The Hopeless Observer might filter all choices through this attitude: "I've always been uncomfortable in these situations, and I probably always will. Nothing's going to help. The same problems I have had in the past will continue tomorrow, next week, and next year. I'll never feel better. Things are just too difficult."

The Critical Observer may screen choices in this manner: "You'd better not make another mistake. The chances are that if you try anything new or bold, you'll screw it up and embarrass yourself again. You don't have what it takes to change. You are only good at failing."

Our minds are always interpreting and commenting on our experience of the world. Part of what you need to acquire in order to control panic is the ability to recognize your Negative Observer comments and disrupt them. If you don't disrupt these negative attitudes about yourself and the world, you will continue to feel controlled by panic, since these attitudes will prevent you from taking successful action.

Let me give you a model with which to consider this idea, illustrated by Figures 6 and 7. During every moment of the waking day our minds are observing the environment through our senses. Everything that we see, hear, touch, smell, and taste is a stimulus which is recorded by what I call our Observer. But if our minds allowed this vast array of sensations to register fully in the brain, we could not make sense of the world. It would just be one confusing, overwhelming mess. Therefore, all stimuli which are recorded by the Observer go through a filtering process so that we can choose an appropriate response. That filter reduces the stimuli to a few simple ones, which we then interpret. Based on our interpretation of this filtered-down, simplified version of what we have observed, we decide how to respond. (See Figure 6.)

For instance (see Figure 7), you have decided to go out to lunch today. You drive into the parking lot of a restaurant. At that moment all of your sensations are recorded by your Observer, including sight: the color, size, shape of the building, the number and kind of cars in

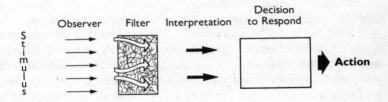

Figure 6. Simple decision-making process.

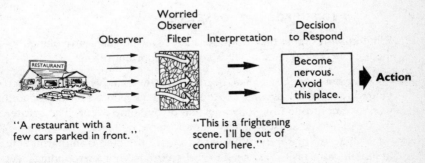

Figure 7. Decision-making with Worried Observer filter.

the lot, and so forth. In the next instance you filter all that data down to a few concepts and interpret them: "This is the restaurant that I wanted. It doesn't seem too crowded, either." Based not on all the various stimuli but on your filtered interpretation of them, you choose a response: "I'll eat here."

Now suppose, instead, that sometime in the recent past you had a panic attack in a restaurant. Today you decide to go out to lunch with a friend. You drive up to the restaurant and observe the same stimuli as in the above example: the size, shape, and color of the building, the number of cars in the lot. Perhaps you even see people eating in booths by the window. Only this time you filter all that identical data through your Worried Observer. Now your interpretation is completely changed: "This is a frightening scene! I'll be out of control here! It's not safe!" Now your decision changes, because our decisions are always based on our interpretation of the facts, not the facts themselves. This time you decide, "I'm going to become a nervous wreck if I stay here. I'd better avoid this place. How do I get out of here?"

This is why I say that in order to control panic you will have to learn to disrupt your Negative Observer comments. But, as they say in physics, nature abhors a vacuum. Your mind must always comment on your observations. If you disrupt worried comments during a panic-provoking moment but neglect to replace them with new and different comments, then those same negative thoughts will float back into your awareness. In other words, your mind will always use some filtering system; if you remove your Negative Observer filter you must replace it with a more beneficial one.

THE SUPPORTIVE OBSERVER

What qualities must this new filter have? During panic-provoking moments, the typical person needs several important resources:

1. A sense of choice: You need to feel free to move, free to change your direction. You want to know that you won't be trapped and won't be controlled by someone else or by some event. The greater the freedom you sense, the more comfortable you feel.

2. A sense of safety: You need to feel protected from harm, safe to pursue your task. You need to feel secure in your surroundings. As you feel increasingly safe, you feel more at ease.

3. A sense of support: You need to feel stable and secure. You need to feel respected, nurtured, and cared for. You need to feel good about the choice you make. The more supported you feel, the easier it is to try new activities.

4. A sense of confidence: You need to believe in yourself, have faith that you will make it. You need to hope for and expect the best. You need to trust in your own abilities, to believe that you will succeed. The more confident you feel, the more power you have over your actions.

In essence, you need to develop within you a new Observer—a supportive, confident part of you which offers you a number of safe choices. I call this part the Supportive Observer.

I am not suggesting that you can completely erase all the worried comments you make when facing panic. For many people, those comments come like clockwork, automatically, whenever they consider facing a panic-provoking situation. Instead, I am suggesting that you add another perspective which will support your healthy, positive intentions, a perspective which can come into play as a new filter during panicky times.

THE SUPPORTIVE OBSERVER

- Reminds you of your freedoms and choices
- Gives you permission to feel safe
- Supports all your efforts
- Invites you to feel confident
- Trusts you and lets you trust yourself
- Expects a positive future
- Points out your successes
- Looks around you for support
- Believes that you can change
- Knows that there is always more than one option in decisions
- Focuses more on solutions than on problems

To do so will take a little time and a lot of practice. One of the best ways to start is to regard the Supportive Observer as a new attitude that you can instill within yourself. That attitude has a particular manner of thinking about things. And it has a distinct voice.

"I CAN . . . IT'S OK . . ."

With the Negative Observer, the voice within you is usually harsh, dramatic, and extreme: "I *can't* let myself feel this way." "This is going to be *terrible*." "I'll be the *laughingstock* of the company." "I'm being *ridiculous*." "*Nothing* will work."

The Supportive Observer, on the other hand, is permissive, accepting, and flexible. It gives you more freedom and more options. It is constantly working to keep you from feeling trapped while at the same time helping you move forward toward your goals. That is the gift of the Supportive Observer: it helps you feel safe while it helps you take action.

The Worried Observer mislabels your emotions. When you begin to feel symptoms of anxiety, your Worried Observer filter says, "I'm terrified!" By this knee-jerk reaction it prevents you from noticing any gradual improvement in your ability to cope. The Supportive Observer gives you time to notice your emotions. It helps you label feelings more realistically. When you notice some anxiety, it keeps those sensations in check: "I'm beginning to feel a little afraid right now." It can notice the subtle changes in your tension level, when it increases and when it decreases.

The Hopeless Observer underestimates your capacity to cope: "I can't. It's impossible." The Supportive Observer says, "I'm not ready, yet. Let me back up a step and try a safer task." It reminds you that you can be in control and that you can master your problems.

Two introductory phrases most aptly express this attitude: "I can . . ." and "It's OK. . . ." Listen to how the Supportive Observer within you might think as you drive into that restaurant parking lot.

> Well, here we are in the parking lot of the restaurant. I'm starting to feel nervous. Last time I ate out I had that panic attack.
>
> I don't have to do this if I don't want to. It's OK to tell Susan that I'm just not feeling up to it. She really will understand. I don't have to keep this a secret from her.
>
> I can also go inside and see how I do. I don't have to have the same reaction I had last time. I can feel safe in there. If I need to, I can get up and leave. Or I can tell Susan that I'm nervous and get her support. There's no reason I have to stay through the

whole meal if I don't want to. The worst that could happen is that I won't finish what's on my plate. I can handle that. So can Susan. I don't have to take care of her. In fact, she'll probably support me.

But I'm starting to breathe fast. . . . This is *not* an emergency. It's OK to think about what I need right now. . . . Let me just take a few Calming Breaths. I can let my muscles loosen a little. I can take time to calm down.

I think I'd like to go in, just to practice my skills of managing this scene.

Notice how permissive that voice is. It knows that the more freedom you feel, the better you will feel. It is not demanding that you perform. You can stop whenever you want. It also reminds you that you can seek the support of others: you don't have to go through all this alone. In fact, you will find that when you give yourself permission to tell others, you will feel a great relief. The more you force yourself to contain all your thoughts and feelings, the more trapped you feel and the stronger your symptoms become.

Until you establish a sense of free choice within you, your primary need will be to escape. But once you establish that sense of freedom, you can consider moving closer to your goal. And with every step forward you again offer support and choice.

You also offer permission to reduce your symptoms. "This is not an emergency. It's OK to calm down a bit." It is also OK if you remain somewhat nervous. There is no reason for you to have to feel perfectly calm while you are trying a new behavior. If you panicked in a restaurant recently, it is normal to feel a little uncomfortable. You can expect that and accept it, because eventually you won't be frightened. Eventually you will have managed this same situation enough times to trust that you won't fall apart, go crazy, or humiliate yourself.

Figure 8 illustrates how the Supportive Observer is used to replace the usual Negative Observer filter. Through a permissive, supportive attitude about your actions, the general interpretation of the scene changes from "This is a frightening scene—I'll be out of control here" to "It's OK to take a chance here—this is a place to practice my skills." Instead of deciding to become nervous and run away, you can then decide to move ahead, one step at a time, just for practice.

STOPPING THE NEGATIVE OBSERVER

We always have a particular filter in place through the day because in order to make sense of our world we must analyze the facts through our beliefs and past experiences. Not only does the filter screen all our experiences, it seems to direct the focus of our internal attention. Some days we seem to be stuck with a Negative Observer filter in place. No matter what we do or where we go, we become obsessively preoccupied with our worries and problems. We begin repetitious, unproductive, negative thinking about some concern in our lives. We spin our mental wheels and get nowhere. If the pattern persists, it only complicates our problems, because it increases our anxiety. If I begin to think, "I'll never finish this book. I'll never get to the end. I'll never pull it all together," by using my Hopeless Observer I have begun a meditation of a particular sort, a *negative* meditation. I am focusing on one simple idea over and over. But instead of producing the Calming Response, I am encouraging my own anxiety and tension. The more anxious and tense I become, the more susceptible I am to panic.

To break such a pattern, first you must begin to notice the moments when you are focusing on Negative Observer comments. Often we are not aware that our minds are rushing through negative thoughts. As you begin to pay attention to such thoughts you will start to notice these moments more frequently. When you become aware

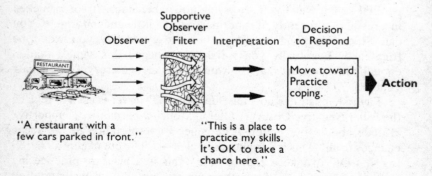

Figure 8. Decision-making with Supportive Observer.

of a repetitive, unproductive, negative thought pattern, first decide whether you want to stop it. Ask yourself, "Are these thoughts helpful to me right now?" Simply by asking the question you have momentarily disrupted the negative thinking. If you decide to stop the negative pattern, then let your Supportive Observer reinforce your decision. "I'm in control of my thoughts. I don't need to be run by these ideas. It's OK to stop focusing on this."

Then begin the Calming Counts. If you want to briefly clear your mind, start at "ten"; take a deep breath, exhale slowly while repeating the word "relax," then gently count your natural breaths from "ten" to "one." This takes less than one minute. If you think you may need to take longer, start at a higher number.

STOPPING THE NEGATIVE OBSERVER

1. Stop and listen for your worried, self-critical, or hopeless thoughts.
2. When you become aware of a negative thought pattern, decide that you want to stop it.
3. Reinforce your decision through supportive comments ("I can let go of these thoughts").
4. Begin the Calming Counts.

Even if your negative thoughts return a minute later, you have briefly disrupted them. This is a method of bringing your Observer to the foreground during a time of trouble. Several minutes later you may want to disrupt those negative thoughts again with a second set of Calming Counts. Slowly, you will begin to "step back" and see your worries from a new perspective. You will become less preoccupied, and your tension level will have a chance to decrease.

This structured experience is adaptable to many public situations. For instance, you can begin the Calming Counts while waiting to give a speech. Instead of dwelling on negative thoughts such as "Everyone will notice that my hands are shaking" or "I know I'm going to make a fool of myself," you can preoccupy your mind by keeping track of your counts.

This same negative thinking process takes place when we anticipate facing our fears. For example, imagine you are scheduled to attend your neighbor's party tonight. You usually avoid such parties because you become nervous in groups. But this week you decided you will fight your fears by attending this gathering of friends. It is now 11:30 A.M. You notice that you have spent the last thirty minutes repeating useless Worried Observer comments silently in your mind: "I can't do this. I'll never last. What if I get trapped there? I don't want to get trapped. I can't go. I just can't handle it. I'll never last." At this moment your Observer breaks in.

OBSERVER: "I keep repeating the same thoughts in my head about tonight. I'm scared. I've decided to go, but I keep thinking about how to avoid it."

SUPPORTIVE OBSERVER: "These thoughts are only making me more scared. They aren't helpful. I need to stop them."

ACTION: Sits down for a minute and does ten Calming Counts.

OBSERVER: "Now that I am quieter, I notice how tense my stomach is. I'm still scared."

SUPPORTIVE OBSERVER: "Probably I'll be a little anxious all day. It's OK to be somewhat tense since I'm taking on a challenge tonight. I need to pace my day and keep myself fairly busy until it's time to get ready. That's a good way to take care of myself. I also want some support tonight so I don't feel like I'm going through this alone."

ACTION: Makes a list of a few worthwhile projects for the day which require some concentration. Shares concerns with a supportive person who will be attending the party. Monitors stomach tensions periodically through the day, using the Calming Breath to relax the stomach muscles when needed.

Notice what happened at the beginning of this example. I described the Observer as "breaking in" during your negative, obsessive thinking. This is probably something which already takes place within you now. You will become entangled in some negative thinking, then all of a sudden, some part of your mind will "step back" and comment on what you are doing. This is the moment you want to seize; this moment is the opportunity for change.

Begin to listen to your Observer rising up. When you notice it, *keep it!* Let yourself gather the facts of the moment objectively, then shift to some suggestion or plan which will take care of you and at the same time support your positive goals. If you begin criticizing yourself or making comments of hopelessness, simply notice them and then let them go ("Thinking that thought isn't helpful to me right now").

DISRUPTING THE PATTERN

Let's think about the moment of panic and apply this concept of filters. In a simple decision-making process, we move through three stages: (1) we observe relevant information, (2) we interpret that information, and (3) we choose an appropriate action (Figure 9). A panic

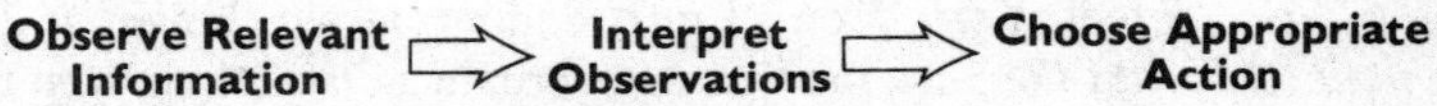

Observe Relevant $\Longrightarrow$ **Interpret** $\Longrightarrow$ **Choose Appropriate**
Information   **Observations**   **Action**

Figure 9. Simple decision-making process.

attack occurs when that process becomes bogged down in the first two stages. First, we observe either our bodily sensations or our surroundings. Second, using our Worried Observer filter, we interpret our sensations as "panic" or our surroundings as "dangerous." Then we turn back and observe our bodily sensations again. We notice they are becoming increasingly uncomfortable. Next, we interpret those increased sensations as "panic," and so forth, in a continuing, escalating mental and physical crisis (Figure 10).

This is how we create panic. We become stuck at the point of focusing on and reinforcing the idea that a problem exists. Our mind gives 100 percent of its attention to the problem and its potential repercussions instead of giving equal time to solutions. It fails to switch to Step 3—choosing an appropriate action—until it has enlarged the problem to monumental proportions. By the time it shifts

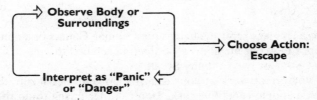

Figure 10. Decision-making during panic.

to the take-action stage, the only solution to this self-imposed over-whelming crisis is to escape.

The essential first step in a panic-provoking moment is to disrupt that pattern. If you do not consciously disrupt the pattern, it will follow its normal course automatically, which typically concludes with your "running away" from some situation in order to avoid what you interpret to be your "loss of control."

At some point during that process, you must stop long enough to notice what you are thinking. If you pay close attention, you will actually hear an Observer statement rise up spontaneously, reporting something about your current experience: "My heart's beating faster," or "I feel dizzy," or "I'm becoming afraid." *That is the moment to disrupt the pattern*. You must create a distraction from the negative thought pattern which typically follows immediately after such an Observer statement ("Oh, no, what terrible thing is about to happen to me?"). Your job is to drive a wedge between your symptoms and your negative, self-defeating thoughts.

Disrupt the pattern at the moment your Observer makes a comment, then seize that moment and instantly turn all responsibilities over to your Observer. Give your Observer some simple task to perform, one that requires no interpretations, no filters; by doing so you will also be inviting the Calming Response to compete with the rising Emergency Response.

There are a multitude of ways to momentarily disengage from the negative pattern and engage your Observer. Here is how: find something neutral or pleasant to do. I have listed a few examples below, some of which will sound silly, I'm sure. They all begin the same way.

OBSERVER: "I'm starting to panic."
SUPPORTIVE OBSERVER: "This is *not* an emergency. I can care for myself by disrupting the pattern."
POSSIBLE ACTIONS:

- Do a formal exercise, such as ten Calming Counts or a minute of repeating your meditative word with each breath.
- Take one or two Calming Breaths.
- If you are at work at your desk, begin gently concentrating on some simple repetitive task. Don't bother trying to do the task well. Instead, concentrate on doing it slowly. For instance, open

your file drawer and begin slowly counting the file folders. Or take out a piece of paper and write a few simple lists of any kind, slowly and methodically. If you are operating machinery, find some basic rhythm in your work and apply your breathing and counting to that rhythm.

- If you are walking down the street, begin slowly looking around while you continue to walk or as you stop and lean against a wall. Give yourself a minute or two of easy Observing, such as deciding what color is predominant in the clothing of the people on that street, or any other simple task. Or pace your walking with your breathing: two steps while inhaling, three steps while exhaling, or any other easy rhythm.

- If you are in a restaurant, or are a passenger in a vehicle, take out your wallet or purse and reorganize your pictures and cards. Or pull out all your dollar bills and order them by serial numbers.

- If you are at home, peel an apple or orange slowly and with concentration. Watch the light mist spray out each time you pull off a wedge of orange. Count each piece as it breaks off. Or reorganize the books on one shelf. Or make up a bed "army style," with attention to detail.

- If you are at a sporting event or a concert, begin studying the program in detail.

As I said, some of these suggestions do sound a little silly. But the point is that to do something which requires simple concentration, which has relatively little importance, and which can be done slowly and methodically, you will need to pay enough attention to distract you from flipping on that Emergency switch. You are essentially calling "time out" on your negative thoughts. You are taking a chunk of time to do nothing but concentrate on your Observer task. No checking back to monitor your physical symptoms, no evaluations of how poorly the interruption is working. Remember, this is Step 1, pure Observing. Any interpretations ("This won't work") which float up during this time—thirty seconds to two minutes—should be gently dismissed.

Gaining control of these initial few moments will be a turning point. Once you have disrupted the pattern, even briefly, your mind makes room for positive, supportive thoughts about the problem. When you gain the edge of time, you gain perspective. You can then, when you are ready, return your Observer to your physical sensations, your negative thoughts, or your environment.

For example, you are driving down the freeway when you begin to feel anxious.

SUPPORTIVE OBSERVER: "I'm starting to get some panicky feelings. But I don't need to get all worked up. This is *not* an emergency. I need to disrupt the pattern."

ACTION: Starts to notice the license plate and color of each car that passes in the outside lane.

OBSERVER: "OK, here I am still driving the car. I've been paying attention to the license plates and car colors as a way of gaining perspective. I don't seem to be getting worse. I'm not losing control. What can I observe about my body? My heart isn't racing like it was. But I am squeezing the steering wheel really tightly with both hands, and my knuckles are white. I feel the knots in my shoulders. It feels like I'm lifting my shoulders up to my ears."

SUPPORTIVE OBSERVER: "I'm in full control of my driving even though I am nervous. I can loosen my grip and still have control of the wheel. I can loosen my shoulders. I'm OK."

ACTION: Takes a deep breath, lets out a sigh, loosens hands on wheel, relaxes shoulders. Concentrates on breathing calmly.

SUPPORTIVE OBSERVER: "My driving skills are good right now. I think I began to panic when I read that sign saying, 'Next exit 9 miles.' I need to reassure myself."

ACTION: Continues Supportive Observer comments. "I'm doing fine. I really caught myself early this time. I deserve a pat on the back. I can be nervous and still drive competently. I'll get where I'm going and back again."

TAKING CONTROL OF THE MOMENT OF PANIC

1. Listen for your worried, self-critical, or hopeless thoughts about your body and your circumstances.
2. Disrupt this negative pattern.
   - Use the Calming Breath or Calming Counts.
   - Find some neutral or pleasant task to occupy your conscious thoughts.

3. As you gain control of your thoughts and your breathing, observe your physical sensations, your negative comments, and your surroundings.
4. Answer the question, "How can I support myself right now?"
5. Take supportive action based on your answer.

In a panic-prone situation, you will not remain in your Observer or Supportive Observer role the entire time. Just as it does during your practice experiences, your mind will float away into Worried, Critical, and Hopeless Observer comments. That is to be expected. As soon as you realize you are thinking negatively, disrupt that pattern. Return again to Observing, commenting with your Supportive Observer, and choosing an action. Whenever you feel in trouble, your first question should be, "How can I support myself right now?" As long as you can find your Supportive Observer, you will never be consumed by panic.

16

Paradox in Action

How does one fight anxiety attacks?

I am sitting in Linda M.'s living room, listening to the story of her five-year battle with panic. The curtains are drawn, as if to keep out the fear. For six long years she has remained behind the doors of her home, too afraid to step outside.

> As soon as I consider taking a walk alone, my heart begins to pound and I get a tingling feeling from my upper body right down to my knees and toes. It feels as if my throat will close. I can't swallow. I try to fight all these symptoms at once, but that seems to bring on the panic. The more I fight it, the worse I become. I ask myself the same questions: "What's making me this way? Why does it continue? Why does it get worse?"

You met Donna B. in Chapter 4. She is an agoraphobic who has suffered from anxiety attacks for over twenty-one years. During her worst months only her bedroom was a safe haven from the symptoms.

> When that panicky feeling starts, I want to fight it. But instead I almost always run from it. And it seems the faster I run, the faster it catches up to me. I've used the expression "quicksand": the more I struggle, the deeper I sink into it. After a while I almost feel the surrender: "OK, fear, you've got me."

Linda and Donna fight the most devastating form of panic, the extreme case in which the individual becomes trapped inside her own home. Yet they illustrate the two primary ways each of us tends to battle our enemies. If we must face them, we gather our resources to fight them head-to-head. Or if we feel inadequately prepared to fight and win, we choose to steer clear of them, to avoid any kind of confrontation.

But with panic these two strategies seem to fail. As Linda describes, the more you fight the symptoms directly, the stronger they seem to grow. The more you avoid panic-provoking situations, the more panic controls your life. Like Donna, the more you run from panic, the faster it seems to chase you.

Our instinctual defenses fail to overcome panic. In fact, they actually support the recurrence of anxiety attacks. We encourage and strengthen the power of panic by treating it as our "enemy," to be avoided or to be battled. If we place ourselves on guard, waiting and watching for the next signs of trouble, we are inviting panic to return sooner. How? By establishing a special "relationship" with panic, a relationship of opposites. To take control of panic you need to understand this special relationship and then learn how to alter it.

THE BALANCE OF POWER

First, let's look at this relationship of opposites. All the activities of our world are built around a dynamic tension between opposing forces. In Chapter 8 I described the balance between rest and activity and between expansion and contraction, using the examples of the ocean tides, a pendulum, summer and winter, day and night, our patterns of work and rest, and the movements of our heart and lungs. I presented them as essential life-sustaining rhythms. The Emergency Response and the Calming Response also form a relationship between two equally powerful and opposing systems within the body which help to maintain our balance of health.

Polarity creates and maintains all types of activity. Every book, play, short story, movie, or TV show involves at least one basic polarity: antagonist "versus" protagonist, a detective "missing" the answers, a man "wanting" a woman, a teenager "struggling between" right and wrong, a poor family "seeking" food or shelter. Without this basic push-and-pull found in conflict, desire, struggle, decisions, or other differences, these "dramas" would not succeed. It is the tension of such unresolved problems that maintains our interest and involvement. In world politics, major activity is found only where a polarity exists, as with the ideological differences between the United States and the Soviet Union, or one country's need to import what it is missing and another's need to export what the other needs.

On a more personal level, all parents have experienced this same dynamic when you take a toy away from a child. Instantly the struggle begins, because now the child *wants* the toy. If you surrender and give the toy back, the child is soon bored with it and moves to some other activity.

Scientifically, opposites attract. Place the north end of a bar magnet next to another magnet. It will repel the other north end and attach itself to the south end. To make sure we continue to populate the earth, Mother Nature creates men and women as attractive opposites, producing desire.

In each of these examples there exists a complementary relationship between two opposites. Think of your own life and the lives of others around you. Whenever we set our minds to a goal, whether it is to graduate from school, achieve recognition, cook a meal, or take a vacation, we create this dynamic tension by choosing something we don't already have. Our positive, goal-oriented drive is produced by the distinction between what we have now and what we want. We are "missing" that degree, that recognition, that supper, or that vacation. And we "seek out" what we are missing. Once we reach that goal, we stop working and come to rest. (Of course, moments later we have some new goal, large or small, because this process takes place constantly.) These polarities, and the ensuing tensions they create, are not bad or wrong; in fact, they are the driving force of all action. If activity is taking place within a given field, you will find a basic tension between two opposites.

Now let's reverse the tables. How do you write a screenplay which will fail at the box office? Here is one way: make all your characters happy and content. Don't let any character worry, or set a tough goal for himself, or realize that he needs something more in his life. Let no one struggle to fulfill a dream. How will your audience react? Zzzzz.

How could we reduce the hostile tensions between the Soviet Union and the United States? One way would be to devote a greater amount of media and government attention to our similarities instead of our differences, thus reducing the degree of polarization. Or we could discover a foe which is more powerful than either country alone (a worldwide disaster, another Hitler, or aliens from outer space). This would shift the dynamic tension toward a new polarity, a new "them versus us."

How could you make yourself depressed? By never setting any goals for yourself, by never striving toward the future. By not believing that things change or that you can change. By expecting that tomorrow will turn out just as badly as yesterday did. How could you deepen your depression? By creating a polarity in your mind between "everybody else" (who can change) and you (who can never be different).

HOW TO INVITE PANIC

Based on this principle of tension between opposites, how might panic attacks continue in someone's life? *Whenever you resist something, that something will persist,* because you have created a polarity. By resisting a panic attack, you support it, and the stronger your resistance, the greater your support. Here are several ways to prolong the existence of panic in your life:

- Fear panic.
- Actively fight against a panic attack.
- Avoid any panic-provoking situation.
- Set a goal of "never ever" having another anxiety attack.
- Worry about the next time you might feel the symptoms of panic.
- Try not to notice tensions.
- Expect to master panic before you face it again.
- Run away from panic symptoms.

Each of these actions invites anxiety attacks by creating a dynamic tension between you and panic. This tension takes on a life of its own and becomes the driving force behind an ongoing process. It provides the energy that sustains the process. This is the pattern that must be disrupted if you are going to take control. And here, too, is the paradox: to win against panic you must stop fighting it or running away from it.

Imagine that you are walking alone on an isolated dirt road in a foreign country. You are enjoying this beautiful peaceful day when in the distance you see a cloud of dust rising. You watch it curiously for quite some time. Soon you begin to make out the forms. Finally you see what faces you. Marching directly toward you are two hundred native warriors, each with battle attire and each carrying a long, sharp spear. They continue to advance, closer and closer. Now they are upon you. What do you do? Do you shove at them? Do you tell them to get out of your way? Do you begin to run away? Attacking and retreating both seem to be poor choices. Either one would provoke an aggressive response.

Take that same road and those same two hundred warriors. This time imagine that as you spot them approaching, you slowly move off the road, sit down, cross your legs, and simply observe them as they pass. What will they do?

Most likely the worst they will do is to jeer at you as they pass. What powerful warrior needs to prove himself by attacking someone who is sitting, passive and defenseless, off to the side? If you run or fight, you are producing just the polarity for which these warriors are prepared. If you do nothing but *passively observe,* you do not attract their attention.

GIVING UP THE STRUGGLE

It is the same way with panic. Your most effective defense against anxiety attacks will involve the use of paradox. Dr. Claire Weekes, in her book *Simple, Effective Treatment of Agoraphobia,* recommends four methods of managing symptoms of anxiety: *face* the symptoms —do not run away; *accept* what is taking place—do not fight; *float* with your feelings—do not tense; *let time pass*—do not be impatient.

Each of these is actually a paradoxical response, one which seems contrary to logic. Logic tells us that in a threatening situation we should flip on our Emergency Response, tense the body, and immediately begin fighting. Or if we imagine we will lose, run like the devil before we get hurt.

Instead, what I am suggesting is that you flip on your Calming Response, relax the muscles of the body, don't fight your physical sensations, and don't run away. It's much like those Chinese finger cuffs we played with as kids. Do you remember them? They were made from a cylinder of thin woven bamboo, just large enough to fit the first finger of each hand into each end. You would give the finger cuffs to an unsuspecting friend and instruct him to place his fingers inside. That was the easy part. When he attempted to remove his fingers, the cuffs tightened. The more he tugged, the tighter the cuffs were. Those darn cuffs defy all logic because they are created paradoxically. To remove your fingers you need to *push* the bamboo together again with your free fingers, not pull them apart. It is the same with quicksand: if you struggle, you sink. If you remain very still (going against all your instincts), you have your best chance of remaining on the surface.

In Chapter 7 you read about Michelle R., who became so fearful of panic that she stopped driving and avoided taking walks, staying home alone, or shopping alone. After a few sessions she realized that she was contributing to her panic symptoms by her Worried Observer thoughts. One morning, just prior to a business meeting, she caught herself thinking questions such as, "What happens if you feel overwhelmed? Or if you get that panicky feeling?" While asking herself these questions she began to develop symptoms, and moments later she produced an anxiety attack. At that moment she recognized that her fearful thoughts of panic can lead directly to her actual panic symptoms.

From this awareness, Michelle made rapid progress. Several weeks later she began to practice driving alone and to take a few short walks. But her Worried Observer comments continued to hinder her.

> We agreed last week that I would return home from the session by driving on the freeway, and I did. Right before I got on the road I started to feel anxious. I thought, "What if I get a panic attack and I can't get off the highway?" I remained tense most of the drive, and my hands were perspiring. But I started thinking that I had an option to continue or to stop, and I really wanted to continue. I felt good that I made the progress. The worst part was anticipating the drive, not the drive itself.

Notice how Michelle succeeded in switching from her Worried Observer comments to a Supportive Observer stance. She said the worst part was prior to starting the drive, because that is when her Worried Observer typically runs through a series of negative fantasies about the future. She began by worrying about some catastrophic event which might take place if she kept driving. Once she began the drive she shifted into a permissive attitude, giving herself choice. "It's OK to stop driving if I need to. Or I can choose to keep going if I want." By always giving herself supportive options, she gained the confidence to continue. And she was able to follow through on her desire, which was to complete her task.

To fight panic paradoxically is to go against our basic instincts. I knew that Michelle needed to experience some success in managing her anxiety before she would be ready for my next instructions. Now that she was able to persist through mild symptoms and continued Worried Observer comments, I presented the idea of paradox: if you stop fighting panic, it will disappear. For the coming week I gave her the following instruction: "The next time you have fearful thoughts about panic, I want you to try, at that very moment, to have a full-blown panic attack. Tell yourself to increase your heart rate, to become dizzy. Try to produce all your symptoms."

As you can imagine, Michelle nervously laughed at my suggestion and questioned my seriousness. I explained the rationale behind this seemingly illogical advice. When we become afraid of symptoms we are supporting those same symptoms by establishing an oppositional relationship. The more fearful we become, the stronger they grow. By removing our fear we destroy this complementary relationship. All the strength is drained out of panic, because it requires our resistance in order to live.

In this same way, if you attempt to stop the symptoms or try to fight them, you are simply supporting and prolonging them. If you practice some kind of relaxation technique and then anxiously wait for it to reduce your symptoms, you will be disappointed. Techniques will not conquer panic; attitude will.

INVITING THE SYMPTOMS

In a paradoxical strategy your attitude must be this: "I want to bring these symptoms under voluntary control. I would like to increase all my symptoms right now." Then consider each symptom which typically bothers you. "I would like to start perspiring more. Let me see if I can become dizzy or make my legs shaky, right now." Through this attitude you accept your symptoms, and you permit them to exist. If you practice any relaxation techniques at that moment, you do so as a way to end your Emergency Response and reduce your Negative

Observer comments so that you can continue to accept and encourage symptoms.

Listen to Michelle's description of her experience the following week.

MICHELLE: I took a long walk on Saturday. First I walked to a shopping mall and bought a few things. That only took about half an hour, so I decided to walk down some residential streets. I felt a little panicky because there were no stores, no telephone booths to turn to for help—unfamiliar territory. I took a few Calming Breaths and reassured myself. Again, I found that my anticipation of trouble caused me more problems than any actual symptoms.

DR. W.: What kind of thoughts did you have?

MICHELLE: I would think, "Here I am . . . People don't know me . . . What if I faint? . . . No one would help me . . . I could start feeling dizzy?" Then I would remember to do my breathing exercise and to say some positive things to support myself.

Remember the exercise you told me about last week, "Try to bring on the symptoms yourself?" I was surprised that the thought came to mind, but at one point I said, "Why don't you go ahead, feel like you're going to faint and see what happens?" And I sort of brought things back into perspective.

DR. W.: How do you mean "brought things back into perspective?"

MICHELLE: Well, for a few moments *nothing* happened. Then I said to myself, "No, you know you're not going to faint. You know this happens to you all the time. You can walk through this neighborhood, and you are going to feel good about that when you are done." It was easy after that.

Something else seemed to change after Saturday. I've noticed an overall difference in my attitude . . . about myself. I seem to be staying away from criticizing myself. I'm not as down on myself. It's as though I started accepting my symptoms and accepting myself. Then Tuesday I spent the night alone for the first time in ages. That went well, no problems.

Michelle's experience with paradoxical intention is typical. When you completely and honestly request that your symptoms increase, they will usually diminish instead. It is important, however, that you don't make a pseudo-request, such as, "I'm beginning to become anxious. Now, I'd like this anxiety to increase . . . but I hope it doesn't, because then I'll never be able to handle it. So this trick better work soon!" By fearing an increase in symptoms and hoping that they diminish quickly based on this "trick," you fall back into the trap of opposing panic, and thereby encouraging and supporting those symptoms.

Here is how we might analyze Michelle's activity that Saturday through the experience of her Observer.

[While walking through the shopping mall] OBSERVER: "I'm enjoying myself here today. I'm surprised and I'm pleased. I've been here a half-hour. I want to walk around for at least another hour to build my confidence. I could walk down some residential streets, but I might start getting nervous." SUPPORTIVE OBSERVER: "It's time for me to take a little bigger risk. I need the practice."

[While walking through the neighborhood] WORRIED OBSERVER: "Here I am in a strange place. People don't know me. What if I faint? No one would help me. I could start feeling faint." OBSERVER: "I'm starting to get worried and panicky. I can feel my heart beating." SUPPORTIVE OBSERVER: "I need to calm myself and feel reassured."

ACTION: Takes several slow, easy Calming Breaths. Tells herself: "This is not an emergency. It's OK to be somewhat anxious right now since I'm trying something new. I can be a little afraid and still take this walk. I am in control."

WORRIED OBSERVER: "There aren't any stores around to turn to for help. There is no phone to use in case I have a panic attack. Oh no, I'll never make it." OBSERVER: "I'm starting to get upset again." SUPPORTIVE OBSERVER: "I need to take care of myself right now. I'll try what Dr. Wilson suggested last week."

ACTION: Tells herself: "Why don't I go ahead, feel like I'm going to faint and see what happens. I'll increase my symptoms right now. I'll try to get dizzy and pass out on the sidewalk." She stops walking and tries to "will" herself into fainting.

[After a couple of minutes] OBSERVER: "No, I can tell that I'm not going to faint. My symptoms aren't increasing even though I'm trying." SUPPORTIVE OBSERVER: "I can walk through this neighborhood, and I'm going to feel good when I'm done." [Her symptoms decrease, and she completes her walk.]

Fighting paradoxically is not only the instruction to increase your symptoms; it is an attitude and perspective to use whenever you face a panic-provoking situation. And it is a basic principle behind most of the practical skills in this book. For instance, in the Deep Muscle Relaxation exercise, you tense a muscle group to make it relax. In a panic-provoking situation, you calm your mind and relax your body. By calming yourself, you become more alert and better prepared to take control of panic than if you were to tense up for the fight.

USING PARADOX DURING PANIC

1. Take a Calming Breath, then begin natural breathing.
2. Don't fight your physical symptoms and don't run away.
3. Decide if you want to use paradox.
4. Observe your predominant physical symptom at this moment.
5. Say to yourself, "I would like to take voluntary control of these symptoms. I would like to increase my [name the predominant symptom].
6. Consciously attempt to increase that symptom.
7. Now attempt to increase all the other symptoms you notice: "I would like to perspire more than this. Let me see if I can become very dizzy and make my legs into jelly, right now."
8. Continue natural breathing, while you consciously and fully attempt to increase all your symptoms of panic.
9. Do not get trapped in worried, critical, or hopeless comments ("This better start working soon! I certainly must be doing this wrong. It'll never work.").

When you are controlled by panic you are run by your Negative Observer voice: "I can't. . . ." ("I can't feel this way." "I can't get anxious, because someone will notice." "I can't handle this experience.") As you begin to gain control over panic, you will notice that your voice shifts to that of the Supportive Observer: "It's OK. . . . I can. . . ." ("It's OK to feel this way." "I can be anxious and still perform my job." "I can manage these symptoms.") Using paradox, you progress to the opposite end of the continuum. You take full responsibility for your symptoms by inviting them: "I want to. . . ." ("I want to make my heart beat faster." "I'd like to see just how much I can perspire right now." "I want to increase all of these

Negative Observer	$\longrightarrow$	Supportive Observer	$\longrightarrow$	Paradox
"I can't..."	$\longrightarrow$	"I can... It's OK..."	$\longrightarrow$	"I want to..."

Figure 11. The shift in attitude toward panic symptoms.

symptoms immediately.") Keep in mind that this shift represents more than just a difference in semantics—it reflects a new attitude.

Start by practicing the use of paradox when you are feeling just a few minor symptoms. If you have trouble mastering the approach, look first at your attitude. Once your attitude is set—your complete willingness to embrace the symptoms in order to diminish their power —your skill will improve dramatically.

Experiment with using humor, because humor can put some distance between you and the symptoms. Try to prove to the world that you are a champion fainter. See if you can tie your stomach in knots so tightly that even the butterflies want out of there.

Don't be disappointed by early setbacks, because once this special attitude is in place, your entire perspective will have shifted. The goal of accepting and increasing anxiety is the object, rather than being free of anxiety. Panic comes when we try to control our anxiety and we fail. Since you are no longer trying to control your symptoms, it is much harder to experience a sense of failure. And when you don't think "I am failing right now," panic usually won't set in.

To win over panic, you stop fighting it. To rid yourself of panic, you let it exist. To conquer panic, you stop resisting. And that is the paradox.

17

Choosing Solutions: A Matter of Time

If I wanted to order a birthday gift for my brother out of a catalogue, I would start by flipping through the pages, browsing through the photographs. Coming across a picture of a denim shirt, I might visualize my brother working in his yard on a Saturday. I momentarily imagine him wearing this shirt while working. Is it his style? My mind's eye briefly runs through images of him in other kinds of work clothes. Would he like it? I picture him opening a gift package and smiling. Now I see him holding up that new denim shirt and nodding his head in approval. I think he would like it, so I place the order.

When the mind takes on the task of predicting the future, it does so by comparing each possible option with known information. The mind will judge the likelihood of something happening by how easily it can recall other examples of the same thing. If I had difficulty imagining my brother working in the yard, or if I had no memory of him appreciating clothes as gifts, I would dismiss the work shirt idea and continue browsing.

Our mental images are not necessarily "pictures" we see in our mind. They can be any internal, sensory-based experience of the past or future, including sounds, touch, taste, smell, or bodily sensations. In choosing that work shirt, for instance, I might get a "sense" of what denim feels like against the skin, and I might compare it with the feeling I would have wearing a lighter-weight shirt.

We use mental images all day long. Whenever we are not 100 percent attentive to what we are doing in a specific moment, we mentally drift into the past or the future. We review past experiences as though we are watching old film clips. We project ourselves into the future, imagining how a situation will turn out. If we are considering a new behavior, we often rehearse it mentally, seeing if it will work for us. When we awake in the morning we consider our upcoming activities, not merely by stating what they are but by seeing them unfold in our mind's eye. We adjust our attitude based on our visualized expectations of the day.

CHANGING THE PROPHECY

Our mind contains a record of every moment of our past, registered, in part, through mental imagery. It is this imagery which programs our current state of mind. Each day, the thoughts and emotions we focus upon create further mental images. The longer we hold a mental image and the stronger the sensory experience within that image, the more influence it has on our activities. As we approach an event, the mental images most likely to arise are those which we have held long enough and intensely enough to be projected into the front of the mind.

For instance, in theatrics there is a system of acting called the Method: the actor recalls emotions and reactions from his own past experiences and utilizes them to develop the role he will play. During the weeks of rehearsal he retrieves again and again those memories in an effort to develop the special traits of his character. By opening night of the play, the Method actor is capable of becoming one with his role—his movements, voice tone and inflection, gestures, and facial expressions are a natural blend of his own experiences and those of his character. He now plays the part instinctually.

Consider another example. In prepared childbirth classes, the instructor explains to the woman and her partner each of the stages of labor and delivery. Within each stage she teaches a special breathing pattern that supports the changes of that stage and describes what physical and emotional changes take place. Then, week after week, the instructor reinforces these stages and their associated techniques. The participants are encouraged to practice the breathing patterns every day. During classes the instructor leads the partners through guided visualizations of the birthing process, identifying within each stage the cues for special breathing, for relaxing, and finally for the "pushing" of delivery. Such detailed, repetitive practice prepares the couple through mental imagery and greatly increases their chances of remaining in control of this dramatic and sometimes surprising event.

Actors preparing for their roles and future parents preparing for the birth of their child are two examples of the positive use of mental imagery. There are also times when our memories can work against us. If you have had a number of panic attacks in the past, and if you are facing an event similar to those past times, you are likely to pull up into the front of your mind the images of those past panics. Our nervous system cannot tell the difference between an actual experience and one which is vividly imagined. So, while you are merely contemplating the idea of some future activity, those images produce actual physiological changes.

It is much like a self-fulfilling prophecy. You predict an outcome based on a mental image of past experiences. As you predict that outcome, your mind then produces an image of that invented future. Your nervous system responds to the prediction as though it is reality, causing you to experience the new event in advance in the same way you did the past events. For instance, a woman who fears driving alone entertains the idea of taking a drive by herself. This idea stimulates images of past anxious moments while driving. She imagines how those past events might recur during her next drive. She feels herself become physically tense in reaction to those ideas, then tells herself, "I'm too anxious to drive."

Because of its dramatic, immediate, and powerful physical and psychological intensity, a panic attack becomes a vivid image which is chiseled into your mind, programming it for the future. Any reasonably similar situation seems to call up that strong image, and your psycho-physiological response follows immediately. But if the mind can be programmed by visual imagery, we can reprogram it by controlling the mental images we contemplate. We can even "install" new and equally powerful images to support our goals.

A PROBLEM-SOLVING MODEL

In the previous chapters I have outlined the steps to conquering panic. The final step is to give your mind and body sensory experiences powerful enough to compete with the sensations of panic.

Whenever we have a problem to solve, we call up past memories or future images at the same time that we are focusing on the present situation. Even during the simple process of balancing a checkbook, our mind simultaneously experiences the current problem (''$423.00 balance minus $12.00 check equals what?'') and recalls the knowledge of arithmetic from our memory.

In the process of selecting a new car, we observe a certain car at the dealership while simultaneoulsy comparing it to the image of our last car. While still in the dealer's lot we get in the driver's seat, experiencing its comfort, viewing the layout of the dashboard. Simultaneously we imagine how we would feel driving down the highway in this particular car.

Anytime we solve a problem we do so by pulling up the needed resources within us and applying them to that problem. Sometimes that resource is the memory of a skill which can solve the problem, like recalling how to subtract. Sometimes that resource is the ability to imagine how well our proposed solution would work in the future, like picturing the trunk of that new car holding all our luggage for a vacation.

We take our memories and our images of the future and apply them to our present situation in order to make sense of it. We hold the present up to the light of our perspective. We step back just long enough to understand the present based on any other relevant information we can retrieve from within us. This is the only way we can make a rational decision (see Figure 12).

During panic this built-in, normal problem-solving skill falls apart. The mind instantly shifts away from the present and into a negative image of the past, or it immediately pictures some catastrophic future event, or both. The body automatically responds to the mind's im-

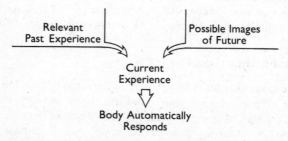

Figure 12. Making sense of our current experience.

ages, not to reality. Since the mind is focusing on an anxiety-provoking image of the past or future, the body automatically provides the Emergency Response (see Figure 13). The mind reinforces that Emergency Response by continuing to focus only on the problem and not on the alternatives to the problem.

As you begin to learn how to control panic, you should assume that this instant-response pattern will continue for some time. Don't expect to rid yourself overnight of something which you now experience involuntarily. Assume that the process illustrated in Figure 13 will probably take place as you face any uncomfortable situation. Now, what do you do next?

DOUSING THE FLAMES

This is the moment when you have a conscious choice to make. You cannot consciously control the mental pattern which instantly produces your Emergency Response. But you can control what you do as soon as you notice that you are spinning your mental wheels. Now is the moment when you make the choice to use your Supportive Observer. From your past, you pull up a memory of any of your Calming Response skills. You might recall that voice inside you which can say, "This is not an emergency. It's OK to think slowly about what I need." Or perhaps you remember the way you take a Calming Breath, how your body responds to a nice, long exhalation. Or you recall the instruction, "Think of some task to preoccupy your thoughts." Having some past memory of your coping skills might stimulate an image of yourself surviving this problem, feeling com-

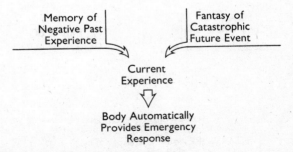

Figure 13. Faulty mental processing during panic.

fortably in control once again. It is these problem-solving resources which you add to your current experience to give you a problem-solving perspective.

And perspective is exactly what you want during the moment of panic. Mentally, you step back just long enough to retrieve some supportive thoughts or images. Then you add them to your current experience (see Figure 14). You don't add fuel to the fire by flashing onto an image of the last time you panicked or by beginning to study every single physical sensation in your body. Instead, you begin dousing the fire by looking outside your body, by considering any one of your many options.

In fact, you invite alternatives: "I could keep thinking about how tense and nervous I feel right now, or I could just let myself take a few slow Calming Breaths the way I've practiced in the past." Now, given that choice, which would *you* pick? "I could run away from these feelings right now, or I could imagine staying here and slowly feeling in control of the situation. Or I could imagine staying here 'til I feel a little calmer, then I could leave. Whichever I choose is OK."

An old slogan from activist days of the 1960s says, "You are either part of the solution or part of the problem." In politics, it means that if you are doing nothing to change a bad situation then you are directly contributing to the problem. This is exactly the way you should view your role during a panic-provoking moment: if you are not actively thinking about ways to support yourself, then you are probably experiencing negative thoughts and/or images which are feeding the flames. The next few times you begin to get minor anxiety symptoms, experiment with consciously changing your thoughts to ones which

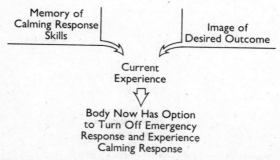

Figure 14. Supportive mental processing to end panic.

are positive and supportive. Find out: by shifting your focus, do you deny your panic its fuel?

ADDING A COMPETITIVE EDGE

The next chapter, called "The Guide," is designed to help you experience some of the thoughts and images that can serve as your resources during a panic-provoking time. Since the mind has powerful recall of an experience as dramatic as panic, you need to entertain positive images and memories of equal power. Fortunately, high drama is not the only way to memorize an experience for later recall. The other way is through repetition. For this reason I have designed Chapter 18 to be used as a script for an audio recording or to be read aloud by a friend, in a slow soothing voice. (Or you may purchase a prerecorded tape of The Guide by writing: Reid Wilson, Ph.D., P.O. Box 269, Chapel Hill, NC 27514.)

The Guide permits you to focus your attention on a specific goal or task. Each time you listen to The Guide, you should first decide on a positive goal for your future. You may change the goal each time you follow The Guide, or you can reinforce a specific goal again and again. Here are some examples of specific positive goals.

"I will feel safe in restaurants and comfortably enjoy my meals with friends."

"I will be able to regularly fly in a plane across country."

"I will feel in control at parties and not need to drink alcohol to relax."

"I will look forward to the adventures of my life without fearing panic."

"I will remain calm and keep within my normal breathing pattern as I climb the steps to my apartment." (This is for post–myocardial infarction patients or those with a chronic obstructive pulmonary disease.)

"I will notice some of the signals of tension during the days before my menstruation and will take steps to increase my comfort." (For premenstrual syndrome.)

"I will become aware of my breathing whenever I begin to hyperventilate. I will bring my breathing under control." (For hyperventilation syndrome.)

To see how you might respond to The Guide, think for a few moments about a personal goal you would like to explore. Then read Chapter 18 to yourself silently, pausing to consider each idea. The script will guide you through several processes.

First, you will spend some time simply becoming comfortable while you learn how to respond to the ideas within The Guide. You will be instructed that you need not work or struggle to see any images in your mind's eye or to feel any particular sensations. Just let yourself consider these ideas gently, taking whatever comes.

Second, you will be given an opportunity to practice developing your Observer, that part within you which provides a calm perspective on your problems. This is the same part of you which will "step back" during a panicky moment long enough for you to begin thinking in a helpful way.

Third, you will be introduced to the voice of a Supportive Observer. Let yourself experience each statement as an indication of the supportive attitude you can develop within yourself. Once you have created that attitude internally, you will begin to hear the voice of your own personal Supportive Observer during hard times. Until then, consider this voice a friend. Feel free to absorb the ideas offered, and notice how your body responds.

Fourth, you will be asked to begin focusing on your specific goal for this Guide. During this portion you will be invited to mentally drift into the future as far as needed to imagine a time when this specific problem has long been solved. There is no need to wait until you have accomplished a particular goal in order to feel the good feelings that success brings. By imagining that you have resolved any problems standing between you and your goal, you get to experience just how nice it is to end the struggle. At the same time, you have the chance to develop a picture of success that can compete with that old Hopeless Observer image of failure. And, as you might guess, holding on to a positive image of your future will provide a distinctly different feeling in your body than holding on to the expectation of failure.

Before you turn to Chapter 18, I want to stress again the importance of The Guide. It is a tool not to be used just once but to be repeated again and again. Its power is in that repetition; its messages, over time, become your own messages. You may find, as others have, that each time you experience The Guide you hear different messages or you pay attention to different suggestions.

It takes approximately twenty-five minutes to read The Guide slowly. Treat it as you would a peaceful, meditative time: find a quiet place and a comfortable seat, choose a positive goal, let yourself listen easily to The Guide, and keep an open, passive attitude about any of your experiences. There is no need to consciously work at having any image. Simply invite the image to come, letting your unconscious produce any of your desired responses. If a negative image floats up, say to yourself, "I don't choose to focus on that," and let it go. This is designed as a positive experience with safe, comfortable ideas and images. There is no reason for you to spend any time with negative thoughts or images. If you do, assume they come from one of your Negative Observers, who should be dismissed.

Even though you should not force yourself to have any particular experience while listening to The Guide, you will need to concentrate your attention. The conscious mind is easily distracted. You must constantly return your attention to the task at hand. The more you totally involve yourself in the statements and questions within The Guide, the greater your gains will be. With involvement, patience, and persistence your learning will continue.

18

Seeing Results: The Guide

[Author's note: This special chapter, to be read slowly and reflectively, is designed to reinforce many of the learnings within this book. For instructions on its use, please review Chapter 17.]

You might want to begin by sitting comfortably, adjusting your body in the chair so that each part is fully supported. Your hands can rest comfortably in your lap as both feet rest on the floor. Feel the support of the chair on your back, allowing those muscles to loosen and relax. Your head can rest easily, supported by your neck.

As you become more comfortable you can sink more deeply into the chair, letting your muscles loosen, relax. You needn't be distracted by sounds around you. In fact, the less attention you pay to your surroundings the more you will be able to turn your attention inward to your own thoughts, ideas, feelings. If you like, you may let your eyes close.

Take a moment to notice how you can relax in that chair. Adjust your body in any ways that increase your comfort. Each of us has our own way of finding a private time; this is a time just for you. No worries, no troubles. No one to bother you. It is like putting all your problems outside the door. This is your special time, which you deserve. Just for you.

I don't know when you last let yourself have a special time, a chance for the body to unwind from the tensions of the world, the everyday tensions that creep in unnoticed.

As you take a mental scan through your body, you might notice areas that feel some tension. Simply become aware of each area. Pause alongside that area of tension, simply observing it. Perhaps you can picture it symbolically, like a knot tied tightly. You can imagine that each breath you take brings relaxation to those muscles, loosening those knots and warming them. Gently. And with each exhalation you can let that area be soothed in comfort.

It is unnecessary for you to become completely relaxed. It's OK to notice certain areas of tension and leave them undisturbed. In fact, the more you notice your tensions the easier it will be to become aware of those areas of your body which are at ease.

A part of you may wonder whether you are even able to feel fully comfortable right now. But at the same time, another part of you may feel free to entertain ideas, images, memories—wondering how much you can really benefit from this experience. And during this time, you can make any adjustments in your body that would increase your comfort.

During this quiet time I want to remind you that you need not work at this experience. Simply open your mind up to entertain a new perspective. To slow down. To soothe the self. And this can be done without effort, without any expectations. Just listening easily, without effort. You needn't even raise your expectations to any particular level in your mind. Nothing need disturb you. Just let your muscles relax more and more as your mind remains in control, letting go more and more tension as you listen to my voice, letting go of any thoughts which rise up to bother you. Like dropping a pebble into the water, you can let those negative thoughts fade away as a sense of calmness, peacefulness, ripples through the body.

There is nothing you have to do, no work. Just enjoy this quiet time, a time to let go of pressures and worries. Perhaps with every breath becoming more and more comfortable, more and more safe. Slowing down, soothing the self. The closer you come to feeling at ease now, relaxing comfortably in your own unique state of mind, the greater the opportunity for you to feel an inner peace tomorrow and the next day and next year. And with that peace comes clarity—an ability to see beyond the pressures of daily living, toward a positive future where you are in control of your life, making choices for yourself. So the closer you come to just enjoying your experience now, the more you will notice these feelings in the future. Like having "a piece of the Rock." Feeling stable, grounded, strong. All these things come in time.

Every time you hear a word like "strong" or "stable," you can have your own sense of what that word means to you. Your own special understanding of "strong," or "safe," or "wrapped in a sense of protection."

Each of us has our own way to feel safe, a sense of being well protected. You can learn over time how you best feel safe and protected. A small sense of safety can seem to grow more and more. Safe, warm, pleasant. And over time, as that sense of protection grows, new opportunities will open to you, as you feel safer and safer. In the same way that you have felt safer sometime in the past than perhaps you do now, you can look foward to a greater sense of safety in the future. And the greater safety you feel inside yourself, the more you will be able to fulfill your life's goals.

THE OBSERVER

All through the day you are observing your surroundings. When you arise in the morning you look outside to the sky, noticing the blue or gray or white above. You step outside and experience the temperature on your body. You take time to gather the information you need before choosing the clothes that will best protect you today. This same observer notices the colors, the design, the feel of the clothes you wear, helping you choose the best match, the most comfortable fit. You look in the mirror to gain perspective, to see if all is satisfactory. A light smile may come over your face as you support your choice. And you are always free to make another choice that supports you in a different way.

It is so nice to step away from our problems, to let them go enough to gain some distance. Just as a vacation gets us away from the pressures of home. Walking along the beach during the quiet of the early morning can bring a peace and serenity to the soul. During this private time, the problems back home can feel so far away if you let them. There is a time and place for everything and sometimes it's time to say, "Time out . . . I deserve this quiet time, just for me." And then your Observer can see problems from a safe distance.

If you would like to get to know your Observer better, you can take the time now. If you are able to visualize, just allow your mind's eye to entertain the image of some safe, comfortable place. It doesn't really matter where you are or who you are with. Perhaps you have been there before or have always wanted to go there. It can be a real place or an imaginary one.

Take time to simply look around you. There is no need to comment about what you see, you may just purely observe: the colors around you, the objects you see, the shapes and patterns. Whether you are alone or have someone with you. There may be some special sounds that you can hear, perhaps birds flying by or the wind against the trees. You may even smell aromas: the salt air, honeysuckle blooms, or perfume, whatever is in your scene.

Now let yourself experience some object up close: look at its colors and patterns, feel its texture. Notice how much more there is to study. Taking time to pay attention to your surroundings.

The more time you have to observe your surroundings, the safer you can feel.

THE SUPPORTIVE OBSERVER

So you can slow down, taking time to think about how to feel support. Just as that chair supports your back so that you can comfortably entertain new ideas, you can find support within to use as you comfortably face your future.

Over time you will develop your own unique voice which supports your hopes, your dreams, and your plans for a safe, secure, and comfortable future. You will create your own voice to satisfy your personal needs—all in good time. As you are learning to listen for your own inner voice, you might be guided by these thoughts which I am about to share. You can absorb these thoughts and turn them into your own voice. You may change them in any way you wish. But for now, you might just listen to these words as if they were coming from within you. Allow your Observer to note how you might feel if you actually believe these words, and how you might see your future if you believe these words, how your daily life might change if you believe these words. If anything you hear does not suit you, you may simply dismiss it or ignore it, and have your own thoughts instead.

Here is the attitude of your Supportive Observer: "Every human deserves to feel free. I am an important person. I deserve to feel free. I don't have to be controlled by my surroundings. I deserve to feel safe and protected wherever I am. Safe and protected."

Just let these words sink in. No need to doubt them or doubt yourself. Simply entertain the idea. Without effort. "No matter what I am doing or where I am going, I can have freedom of choice. I always have options, no matter what. I have the right to choose how

I feel at any moment. I can decide what I want to do at any moment. I am free to come and go according to my comfort. No other person in this world is allowed to control me. No place or event is allowed to control me. *I* get to choose how comfortable I feel at every moment. The more freedom I feel, the more comfortable I will be in the days and weeks to come.''

Continue to permit yourself to take in these words. They are merely ideas that will continue to sink in if invited—like opening the door for a friend. ''It's OK to think about what I need. The more I know about my needs, the safer I will feel. I can slow down and think for myself. I have time to think before I act and when I slow down I can support myself. I deserve to feel support.

''I can trust my body, just as my body trusts this chair and then lets its muscles loosen their grip. As I learn to trust my body I will feel even greater support. As I learn to trust my body I will have more and more control of my body. I can take all the time I need to learn to trust my body.

''I deserve to be respected, nurtured, and cared for. I can respect myself no matter what I choose to do. I don't have to prove anything. I don't have to change. I am already a worthy human being.

''My first job is to take care of myself. The more I respond to my need for rest and love and care, the more I will be capable of giving to others. Right now is a time to feel that rest, love, care.''

Just as a funnel can direct and concentrate water flowing into it, you can allow these ideas to flow inside you. They can be like seeds planted in fertile ground, nourished by the soil and water, warmed by the sun. And each day these feelings can grow a little stronger. Possibly imperceptible at first, with little noticeable change after a week. But once they sprout to the surface of your mind, you will know that these roots have formed, grounding you in your own support.

''There is nothing wrong with feeling confident about the future. The more support I feel, the easier it will be to try new experiences. I can take all the time I need to feel safe and comfortable. 'A journey of a thousand miles starts under one's feet.'

''All of life is made up of activity and rest. I can take as small a step forward as I choose. I can rest when I want; I don't need to constantly push. I simply keep one eye on my goal, chipping away a little bit each day. Everything in this universe is constantly changing. I am always changing. No one can stop that. But one thing never has to change. I can always support myself. No matter where I am or what I am doing, I can always think of supporting myself. Perhaps I'll say something special, like 'I deserve to feel comfortable now,' or 'I am lovable and capable.' "

Just hearing these words can create a calmness within you. You may find in the days and weeks ahead that some of these words surface in your mind. And as they do, you can have a growing confidence in your ability to care for yourself in any situation.

Listening to your Supportive Observer is like hearing the voice of a friend. Take a moment now to speak silently from the stance of your Supportive Observer. Offer yourself any message you wish. And as you do, let yourself absorb that message, believe it, if only for a moment. Say anything supportive that you wish, silently to yourself, now.

After you have heard that message and taken it in, see if you can picture the face of someone sharing that message with you. Perhaps it is your own supportive face, or the face of someone close to you or someone strong and confident who wishes to share that strength and confidence.

Imagine that you are being given that same never-ending fountain of strength and confidence, flowing inside you now. Filling your body with a sense of comfort, safety, protection. Imagine, if you like, how your face changes when you are feeling strong and confident. How you stand and how you hold your head. Imagine, if you like, standing in front of a full-length mirror, seeing yourself strong and confident. Or simply entertain the idea. Absorb yourself in the possibility.

SEEING RESULTS

You are listening to these words for a reason. You have your own special needs and desires to be fulfilled. While you continue to allow yourself to feel a sense of strength and confidence from that never-ending source within you, reflect for a moment on your goal. A specific goal; a positive goal. As soon as you have brought that specific, positive goal to mind, I would like you to do something very special. Every day we permit our mind to imagine the future. We imagine how our day will turn out, we imagine what a project will look like when it is finished. We imagine how we will feel if we succeed at a task.

Imagination is nothing more than entertaining an idea. We can change our image as easily as we change our mind. Your images are simply a way to see things exactly as you'd like them. No troubles, no problems, no pressures. Just things the way you'd like them. Feeling the way you want to feel. Experiencing the things and people you desire.

So I would like you to do something very special with your imagination. Simply let your mind drift forward in time, just as we do when we are daydreaming or when we dream during sleep. Drift forward in time, as far forward in time as you would like or as you need. Settle down at some time in the future, long after you have accomplished this goal of yours.

Simply entertain the possibility of change. No need to struggle with any images, just easily allow whatever rises up in your mind's eye.

See yourself having already accomplished your goal. It is unimportant how small or large a problem it had been. You now have the ability you've always wanted, the ability you knew was inside you. All those problems between you and your goal have faded into the background. All your doubts or fears have dropped away. Because now you have already reached your goal for some time. And you can now enjoy all the changes that come with attaining that goal.

Let yourself fully experience how you feel now that you have made it. And look around; how does your world appear to you now?

Step in front of that mirror. How does your face express your success, your pride, your sense of accomplishment?

Look around you again. Who is near you to support and enjoy these changes? Someone you know, or someone new?

Now that you have made it, take a little time to enjoy these changes. Perhaps you would like to experience some of the new doors which you can now open, as you continue to feel strong and confident. That same strength and confidence is reinforced by having successfully reached your goal. Follow your interests now as you imagine opening a door or two with comfort and ease, stepping through to new, pleasant, and enjoyable experiences.

Perhaps one of these will be an old door which you had thought you could never open. But now, having reached your goal some time ago, that door opens effortlessly, to your surprise and pleasure. Step back and watch yourself moving smoothly through an event which in the past might have proved uncomfortable. Watch the smile slowly come across your face after you glide through that scene with comfort. There is no need to pay attention to your body. It knows exactly how to respond to your cues. Instead, you can look around you, possibly noticing any other smiling faces. Remembering your right to feel secure and safe wherever you are. While your body simply reflects your trust in it. Allowing it to do its job as your mind looks forward to a positive future. Always keeping one eye on your goal. Your positive goal.

You can feel very proud, having accomplished those things you set out to accomplish, consistent with your values. And memorize that success. It's yours; you're entitled to it. It can fill every cell, every molecule of your body.

And while you are feeling that success, you might as well take a moment to just look back and review all those steps you took to find yourself so comfortably here. From the comfort of hindsight, you can look back and be pleased with the ways you managed to deal with those obstacles you encountered, those conflicts which seemed so insolvable at the time but are now in the distant past. And appreciate the opportunity that you had to learn what you now know and wouldn't trade for anything. You can have these insights and take them with you into your future. Each time that you listen to these words, what you learn can become more and more an integral part of your personality.

Sometime in the future you may find yourself using these skills, these understandings, spontaneously, at the exact time that you need them. And feeling so pleased that you are automatically supporting yourself in that situation, without effort or work.

Receive all experiences as practice. And since it is only practice, you can continue to permit each experience to bring a new understanding, a new strength. While you keep an eye on each new positive goal you set.

Everything is practice; there are no tests.

When that moment in the future comes, you might find yourself taking a nice long, slow deep breath, releasing all those tensions collected over the years. A sense of relief. "I can trust my body. I can look outside of myself now. Out toward that positive future that I deserve. Out toward the safety and comfort I deserve no matter where I am."

While you are looking forward, in one way or another you can put aside past experiences that are no longer useful to you. There may even be a few things that you would like to discard altogether. Anything which is not beneficial to your positive future can be forgotten. And each time an old, useless memory fades away, you come a step closer to your goal.

As you continue to let go of those worries and tensions, you take control of your life. You take control of your choices. You take control of your good feelings. As you let go of the negative experiences of the past you take control of your future, of how you see yourself tomorrow, the next day, next week, a year from now.

But for now you can simply consider looking forward to the rest of this day. Bring to this day all that you desire for yourself. So in a moment you can take a very energizing, very refreshing breath and find yourself sitting alert and awake. But before you do that, just enjoy the quiet.

Now, take that very refreshing breath. And, in a moment, open your eyes, look around you, and, when you are ready, return to your day.

19

The Use of Medications

One of the most significant contributions of Western medicine has been the creation and use of medications to reduce patients' suffering. In recent years, a growing number of medical researchers have been investigating the benefits of medication for individuals who experience panic. The research efforts thus far have focused on two diagnostic categories: panic disorder and agoraphobia, which I described in Chapter 3.

As this book goes to press, in 1986, the Food and Drug Administration has not approved any medication for use in the treatment of panic disorder or agoraphobia. Therefore, any use of drugs specifically for these problems should be considered experimental and investigational.

The FDA withholds approval until a medication has been shown to be safe and effective, based on extensive and well-controlled research studies which consistently establish its benefit. The primary reason that no medication has been sanctioned yet is clear: the diagnosis of panic disorder and agoraphobia has eluded mental health professionals for years. In fact, panic disorder was not classified as a distinct problem in the American Psychiatric Association's *Diagnostic and Statistical Manual* until its third edition, in 1980. Therefore, major research efforts were begun only within the last decade.

The early years of research in any new area usually lack the coordinated efforts needed to clearly establish the facts. Each scientist is a pioneer, investigating territory never before explored. However, once patterns begin to unfold, replication of study designs can be used to verify benefits or limits of a specific medication. This period of replication is now under way.

The edicts of the FDA primarily restrict the manufacturer of the medication from advertising the benefits of that drug for any particular disorder until the agency grants approval. However, physicians are able to prescribe these medications, based on their professional judgment of the risks and benefits to the patient, when the medications have been approved in the treatment of other disorders.

Four kinds of medications appear to help reduce symptoms in some individuals who experience panic attacks, based on current research findings. Each of these four is described at the end of this chapter. Other drugs are currently being investigated, but it is too early to determine their effectiveness.

The greatest benefit that medications can provide is to enhance the patient's motivation and accelerate progress toward facing panic and all of its repercussions. For a drug to help in this area, it must help in at least one of the two stages of panic. The first stage is anticipatory anxiety: all the uncomfortable physical symptoms and negative thoughts which rise up as you anticipate facing panic. The second stage is the symptoms of the panic attack itself. Both current research and clinical experience suggest that these four medications may help reduce symptoms during one or both of these stages for some people.

A number of other medications are widely prescribed for anxiety or nervousness. However, no reliable studies support the use of minor tranquilizers such as Valium, Serax, Librium, Ativan, or Tranxene for panic disorder. Although these drugs may make the patient feel somewhat calmer, some of them can actually add to the difficulties of the panic-prone individual.

If you would like to consider medication as a form of assistance in conquering panic, here are a few suggestions which may make your decision easier.

Begin by Obtaining an Accurate Diagnosis. The medications described here are considered options for individuals diagnosed as experiencing panic disorder or agoraphobia. If you are having panic-like symptoms, follow the instructions outlined in Chapter 2 to determine first if there is any physical cause. If no physical diagnosis can be made, your physician should refer you to a licensed mental health professional who specializes in anxiety disorders for an evaluation.

There Is No Magic Pill. Among clinicians who specialize in anxiety disorders, there is general agreement that medication can be beneficial for some panic-prone patients when used in conjunction with a treatment approach similar to the one outlined in this book (that is, one which is directed toward altering your dysfunctional thoughts and encouraging your ability to face those situations that you fear). Although treatment must be based on the specific problems and resources of each patient, the key to successful cure lies in each individual's sense of his personal ability to face and overcome panic. All professional interventions, whether individual therapy, group therapy, medication, behavioral techniques, or practice exercises, should have but one purpose: to stabilize your belief that you are able to exert personal control over your body and your life.

It is within this context that medications are used. Medicines are designed to be used as a beneficial short-term crutch to help out while you heal yourself. Medications do not heal you any more than a cast heals a broken leg. The body heals itself, given the proper support.

Complex problems do not have simple solutions, although many people will look for a quick cure and a magic pill. If they can find a sympathetic physician, they will begin a regimen of medications as a means of removing all discomfort. They often do this because they believe that they suffer from some genetic disease which predestines them to a life managed by chemical treatment. Unfortunately, their beliefs are reinforced by reports in the media which present a limited analysis of a complex problem. By deciding to believe that they have a physical disorder, these patients surrender themselves to panic. And in the process, they lose self-esteem, determination, and the willingness to trust in the healing power of their body and mind. They remain dependent on medications, physicians, friends, and family as they continue to limit their personal freedom.

Be Willing to Tolerate Some Side Effects of Medications. Each of these medications can have side effects. Some will be minor symptoms that may be bothersome to you but do not require medical attention. These side effects may also diminish as your body adjusts to the medication. Other side effects should be reported to the prescribing physician. Prior to using one of these medications, ask your physician about the possible side effects: which are to be expected, which might diminish over time, and which should be called to his or her attention.

I suggest that you educate yourself about the possible side effects, not because these medications are more powerful or more harmful than other drugs, but so that you will then be better prepared to tolerate some of the minor symptoms. For instance, the symptoms of dry mouth, blurred near vision, constipation, and difficulty with urination are called "anticholinergic effects" and are common side effects in a number of drugs. Often they diminish in a few weeks as your body adjusts, or when the dosage is reduced. In the meantime, your prescribing physician may suggest ways of relieving the discomfort. A dry mouth is best relieved by frequent rinsing or by sucking on hard candy or chewing gum (preferably sugarless). Mild constipation can be counterbalanced by increasing your intake of bran, fluids, and fresh fruits and vegetables.

Another possible side effect is "postural hypotension." This is a lowering of the blood pressure as you stand up from a sitting or lying position, or after prolonged standing. This disequilibrium can cause sensations of dizziness or lightheadedness, especially in the morning when you get out of bed. These are simply signs that your circulatory system needs a little more time to distribute blood equally throughout your body. You may also notice an increase in your heart rate (tachycardia or palpitations) to compensate for this brief hypotension.

When this side effect is mild, doctors advise that you get out of bed more slowly in the morning, sitting at the side of the bed for a full minute before standing. In this same way, take your time rising from a seated position during the day. If you feel dizzy, give your body a minute to adjust to the standing position.

If You Decide to Use a Medication, Give It a Fair Trial. In order to evaluate the benefit of a medication, you must give it enough time to provide its therapeutic effect. Work with your physician, especially in the early weeks of your medication trial, in order to adjust the dose and to relieve any worries you might have. Each of these drugs is initiated at a low dose and then increased slowly according to your response. Several weeks' trial at full dose is needed to determine the benefits.

You Will Not Remain on Medication Indefinitely. Although it may take from three weeks to three months to establish the proper dosage of one of these medications, most investigators suggest that a six-month to one-year drug treatment is sufficient. Within this period you should actively face your panic-provoking situations, using the skills described in this book.

You Must Taper Off These Medications Gradually. Once you have begun treatment with one of these medications, you should never abruptly discontinue your daily dose. Instead, your prescribing physician will direct you in a safe withdrawal process, which may take several days to several weeks.

Medications Are Optional. You always have a choice regarding the use of medication. Do not let anyone persuade you that drugs are required in order to overcome panic or that they offer the only cure for anxiety attacks. As you have read throughout this book, many forces come to bear on your episodes of panic. Anxiety attacks are symptoms which can reflect any one of several different psychological disorders and a number of physical problems. Keep your mind open to all your options in resolving this difficulty. If you choose to use medications as part of your treatment, do so because of your values and beliefs and your trust in your physician. If medications do not benefit you, continue to give your other options a fair trial. We know from research and clinical experience that these medications are of no benefit to some people and can make matters worse for others.

TRICYCLIC ANTIDEPRESSANTS

Tricyclic antidepressants are traditionally used in the treatment of severe depression or depression which occurs with anxiety. Of this family, *imipramine* has been the focus of most of the research on the treatment of panic. (Other heterocyclic antidepressants are still in the early stages of research on their benefits for this disorder.)

Possible Benefits. May reduce panic attacks, elevate depressed mood.

Dosages Recommended by Investigators. Since some panic-prone individuals become overstimulated on very low dosages of a tricyclic, the medication trial can begin with as little as 10 to 25 milligrams (mg) per day. If the patient adjusts to the side effects, the dosage is increased by 25 mg every two or more days until the preferred dosage is reached.

Although some patients require a smaller or larger dosage, the usual maintenance dosage is between 150 mg and 250 mg per day. Experts recommend taking the full daily dosage at one time, usually at night before bed. In this way, the patient will be less bothered by daytime sedation or other side effects.

Possible Side Effects. Dry mouth, blurred vision, constipation, difficulty in urination, postural hypotension, tachycardia. Sometimes these side effects will disappear with the passage of time or with a decrease in the dosage. Some people may experience side effects on dosages as low as 10 mg per day: jitteriness, irritation, unusual energy, and difficulty falling or staying asleep.

ALPRAZOLAM

Alprazolam (trade name Xanax) is a fairly new medication in the benzodiazepine family, which are anti-anxiety drugs. Other medications in this family, such as diazepam (Valium) and clorazepate (Tranxene), seem to have no benefit. The slight difference in the molecular structure of alprazolam appears to account for its benefit.

Possible Benefits. May reduce anticipatory anxiety and panic attacks; is rapid-acting and has few side effects.

Dosages Recommended by Investigators. Alprazolam is usually started using 0.25 mg (¼ mg) or 0.5 mg (½ mg) three times a day. If taken after meals, the side effects such as drowsiness are diminished and the therapeutic effects can last longer. This dosage may be increased by adding 0.5 mg to one of the three daily doses until 2 mg three times per day is reached. From that level, any additional increases are given at bedtime or applied equally during the day. The dosage range is 2 to 6 mg per day.

Possible Side Effects. Tiredness (sedation), unsteadiness of gait (ataxia), slurring of speech and, occasionally, headache. Some patients may experience a depressed, irritable mood in the early weeks of the trial. Usually the side effects of alprazolam are not serious and will disappear with the passage of time or with a lowering of the dosage.

MONOAMINE OXIDASE INHIBITORS

Monoamine oxidase inhibitors, commonly called MAO inhibitors, are the other major antidepressant family. Phenelzine (trade-named Nardil) has been the MAO inhibitor most researched within the treatment of panic.

Possible Benefits. May reduce panic attacks, elevate depressed mood, and increase confidence.

Dietary Restrictions. The patient using an MAO inhibitor must be quite responsible, since this medication requires significant dietary restrictions. No cheese, red wine, beer, chocolate, yeast extracts, meats prepared with tenderizer, pickled herring, sour cream, yogurt, chicken livers, canned figs, raisins, soy sauce, bananas, avocados, fava beans, or lima beans are to be eaten while on this medication (cottage cheese is acceptable). These foods contain a substance called tyramine, which when combined with an MAO inhibitor can cause dangerously high blood pressure and severe headache.

Medication Restrictions. The patient using an MAO inhibitor should always consult the prescribing physician prior to taking any additional medications. This especially includes over-the-counter cold medicines (including nose drops or sprays), amphetamines, diet pills, tricyclic antidepressants, and certain antihistamines.

Dosages Recommended by Investigators. Each tablet of phenelzine is 15 mg. Dosage is three to six tablets per day, usually based on body weight.

Possible Side Effects. Postural hypotension, difficulty sleeping, increased appetite, orgasmic dysfunction, drowsiness, dry mouth, and hypertensive crises.

PROPRANOLOL

Propranolol (trade-named Inderal) belongs within the family of medications known as beta-adrenergic blocking agents, or "beta-blockers." It is traditionally used to treat high blood pressure, angina, certain heart conditions, and migraines.

Possible Benefits. May reduce some peripheral symptoms of anxiety, such as tachycardia and sweating, and general tension; can help control symptoms of stage fright and public-speaking fears; has few side effects.

Restrictions on Use. Propranolol should not be taken by patients with chronic lung disease, asthma, diabetes, and certain heart diseases, or by patients who are severely depressed.

Dosages Recommended by Investigators. Usually propranolol is taken three to four times per day for a total of 40 to 160 mg. The prescribing physician may determine dosage, in part, by monitoring the patient's resting heart rate. This medication can be used in combination with imipramine or alprazolam.

Possible Side Effects. Dizziness or lightheadedness, short-term memory loss, unusually slow pulse, lethargy, insomnia, diarrhea, cold hands and feet, numbness and/or tingling of fingers or toes.

20

Experience: The Greatest Teacher

Here are a few guidelines which may prove helpful when you begin to face panic. They are designed as principles to be used by anyone who desires to control anxiety attacks, whether their episodes of panic occur within panic disorder, a phobia, asthma, premenstrual syndrome, depression, or any of the other physical or emotional difficulties mentioned in this book.

GUIDELINES FOR CONTROLLING ANXIETY ATTACKS

Find a supportive ally

We humans are social beings. We operate best when in communication with others. We change ourselves based on our relationship with others. When it comes to solving problems, there is no benefit to working in isolation and secrecy. You will make your most productive advances when you are supporting your own efforts and when you spend time with others who support you. It is essential that you develop a Supportive Observer within you as you face panic. One way to encourage your own Supportive Observer is to develop relationships with people who have those qualities.

Find at least one ally: someone who cares about your well-being and values your worth, someone who respects and supports your goals. In choosing supportive allies look for these traits: They remind you of your freedoms and choices. They give you permission to feel safe. They support all your efforts and invite you to feel confident. They trust you. They believe you can change, so they expect a positive future. They know there is always more than one option in any decision. They help you focus more on solutions than on problems.

An ally may be your spouse, some other family member, a close friend, someone who has struggled with these problems before, or a trained health professional. Often a person is willing to support us but doesn't know the best way to go about it. Most likely you will have to explain to your allies how they can help. For instance, you might want them to read this book so that they can better understand the problems you face. Or you mght need to explain how the Supportive Observer sounds, as described in Chapter 18.

This is not to imply that your allies must always be available to help you every step of the way. The most important role they play is to let you know you are not alone. When you know that someone in the world understands you, then you can feel you have a choice: you don't have to do this by yourself. You can feel safe: someone will be there to listen to you. You can feel supported: you don't have to be strong and independent 100 percent of the time. And you can feel confident: with the support of your allies you can learn to do most anything you desire.

When you have to depend totally on yourself, the pressures can be great. When you depend totally on someone else, your self-esteem and pride are diminished. But when you have someone in your life who is committed to a supportive relationship, then your personal power is greatly enhanced. Some days we are in no mood to pick ourselves up by the bootstraps, put on a smiling face, and meet the world head on. How nice it is to call someone and say, "Tell me everything's going to turn out OK." Hearing that supportive voice can literally be a life-saver. And, over time, those supportive voices teach you how to talk to yourself in a sometimes gentle, sometimes firm voice that keeps this current problem in perspective as you explore solutions.

Always fight for, not against

Taking control of panic is a positive process. We all have images of how we would like our lives to turn out. We consider tasks we wish to accomplish, pleasures we hope to enjoy, relationships we want to prosper. By gaining control over panic you get to turn your sights toward the positive future.

Panic, however, has other plans for you. It invites you to stop whatever else you are doing and fight against it. Panic would like you to halt your life and think of nothing else except your struggle with it. In a paradoxical way, panic lives off of your willingness to fight it or run from it.

Don't fall for this trap. Never fight against this invisible enemy. Turn your eyes toward your positive goals, whether for today, this week, this year, or your life. Then fight forward, toward them. When you become anxious, tense, or panicky, you then find ways of taking care of those feelings in order to continue moving forward. Always keep one eye on your positive future.

Let me give you an analogy to illustrate this point. Let's say that you have had a busy, active week. It's now Friday afternoon. Tomorrow, company will arrive for a weekend visit. You would like to prepare by cleaning the house and doing some laundry but at the same time you feel physically fatigued from the week.

What do you do? One choice is to focus on your fatigue. "I'm not going to let this exhaustion beat me. I'm going to fight that couch, because I want so much just to lie down and sleep." Notice how your attention now turns to the negative: how to stop exhaustion from setting in, how to keep yourself from taking a rest. Energy is wasted in this struggle.

Another choice is to look toward the positive future. "I would like my home to appear clean tomorrow. I also want to feel rested. Most important, I want to enjoy my guests over the next two days." When you look forward to your desired goals, your attitude shifts. Perhaps in the long run it is best that you take that nap right now so that you will feel more like cleaning in a couple of hours. Or maybe doing a quick pick-up and hiding that dirty laundry in a closet will give you more time to relax and enjoy your friends. Fighting exhaustion is no longer the issue. Straightening up a bit, feeling rested, and having a pleasurable weekend are much more important.

When panic arrives, keep one eye on your positive goal while you respond. In essence, your attitude is, "I am going to continue in this direction. Right now I need to see how I can support myself while I'm feeling uncomfortable. I'll take as long as I need to support myself so that I can continue heading toward my goal."

Face panic paradoxically

While you are moving forward toward your positive goals, assume that you will face panic along the way. When we set our sights on a challenging task we usually expect that we will work hard to achieve it. We make sacrifices and sometimes deny ourselves the easy way out of problems, because we know that is the cost we must pay. Struggle and effort, then, are part and parcel of working toward a positive goal. There are no surprises in that logic.

The twist comes when we face our anxieties along the way. During these moments, the work that is often required is actually to stop working so hard. The strategies described in this book are all designed to help you *not* struggle with panic. You can use any one of the several Calming Response skills while facing panic. But these are not designed so that you can better "fight" panic or "banish" panic at that moment. Instead, consider them ways of passing the time while panic tries to pick a fight with you. By changing your attitude toward panic, you withhold its nourishment. It dies off from lack of attention. This same principle is involved when you purposely try to produce your symptoms, as explained in Chapter 16. Whenever you permit panic to exist while you keep moving toward your positive goals, you weaken panic's grip on your life.

This, then, is the paradox. You must always work actively toward your goals. However, when panic stands in your way, you take control of it by not pushing or struggling. You slow down long enough to regain control, then continue on your way.

Set your Intentions

Panic exerts a force over you. It attempts to push you into a corner where you feel trapped and afraid. To confront this force you must place some target in front of you, some short-term goal to reach.

In Chapter 17 I listed a sampling of long-term, positive goals, such as:

"I will feel safe in restaurants and comfortably enjoy my meals with friends."

"I will feel in control at parties and not need to drink alcohol to relax."

"I will remain calm and keep within my normal breathing pattern as I climb the steps to my apartment" (for the patient with post-myocardial infarction or a chronic obstructive lung disease).

Creating your own goal will give you a clear sense of purpose. When you feel lost or confused, this goal can remind you of your positive direction.

Mastering panic, however, will require an additional goal, a short-term objective which I call your "Intention." Your Intention will be your immediate task, which when accomplished moves you closer to your long-term goal.

To understand the difference between a long-term goal and an Intention, consider this example. Imagine that you are thirty years old and have worked as a typist for the past six years. After much soul-searching you feel a strong need to become more independent in your life's work. You decide to establish this as your long-term goal: greater job independence. Now what?

Your next step is to create a short-term task which will help move you toward independence. You ask yourself, "What can I do today, this week, or this month about that goal?" The answer to this question is your Intention: "This month I will investigate what kinds of jobs might give me greater independence." This Intention now gives you a concrete and specific task to accomplish in the short term. Once you set your Intention, you always have some positive task to direct your actions.

Let's say that after a month of exploring options, you take another step closer to your goal: "I think there is room in this city for a word-processing service. With my experience I know what it takes to provide quality typing to customers. I think I am capable of managing a small staff of typists. But I don't know much about business." You set your next Intention: "I'll take a 'small business' course at night this fall at the technical college." This Intention gives you a short-term focus. You must select the best course, register, buy the materials, attend class each week, complete your homework assignments, and so forth.

It is far easier to motivate yourself when your goal is almost within reach. Small decisions can now seem important, because they influence your immediate-future goals. If you have difficulty applying yourself to your studies because owning your own business seems so far in the future, then set your Intention closer to your reach: "By the end of this course I want to be able to say that I applied myself every week to complete the assignments of that week. Therefore, I will start by finishing my paper due this Friday."

This is the process to use in overcoming panic. For instance, some people might have the positive goal of "looking forward to the adventures of life without fearing panic." You will reach that goal by setting dozens of short-term goals, one after the other. As you accomplish one Intention you will set your sights on the next.

In order to look forward to the adventures of your life without fearing panic, one short-term goal must be to tolerate mild to moderate symptoms of anxiety. If you can accept those symptoms arising on occasion, and if you can trust in your ability to manage them, then your fear of them will diminish.

Once you set this Intention of learning to tolerate symptoms, you can establish short-term tasks. Practicing the breathing and Calming Response exercises in this book is a good first start. During this same early stage of learning you can begin listening for your Negative Observer comments. Once you discover how your thoughts consistently reinforce your sense of fear, you can begin to practice Supportive Observer comments or other disruptive techniques. In this way you slowly chip away at panic.

Don't be in a rush to reach your long-term goal. By focusing too much of your attention on the distant future, you can feel demoralized and frustrated, as though you will never arrive at your destination. Instead, create images of your positive future, but work actively on accomplishing immediate tasks.

At any point in your day, you should be able to set your Intention. This is done not as a way to evaluate your progress, to point out your failures or to criticize your weaknesses, but as a way to keep yourself motivated. Use your Supportive Observer to establish Intentions, and be careful of the Negative Observers, who are always just around the corner. The biggest troublemakers here are the Critical Observer and the Hopeless Observer.

You can spot the Critical Observer by its tendency to talk about the past: "I said on Monday that I was going to get out of the house for an hour's walk each day. Here it is Thursday, and I haven't done it yet. I'm doing terribly." Such comments are not only useless, they are damaging to your self-esteem. When working on the task of conquering panic, set your Intentions with your Supportive Observer. Often the words will be similar, but your tone will reflect a supportive, future-oriented attitude. The Supportive Observer isn't interested in yesterday or even the last hour. It pays attention to the present and the near future, in this manner: "On Monday I decided to walk an hour a day. Now it's Tuesday, and I haven't started yet. *What do I need to do in order to take a walk today?*" Not fulfilling your agreement yesterday is unimportant. Don't waste time focusing on the past. You are not in control of yesterday, but you *are* in control of today.

Once again, paradox comes into play as you set your Intentions and work toward them. The paradox is this: you should set a concrete, specific short-term goal, with every intent to fulfill that goal. At the same time, it does not matter whether you actually reach your goal in the way you expected.

For instance, let's say your long-term goal is to comfortably shop in stores again. You have been taking a number of steps to prepare, such as practicing the Calming Breath a dozen times each day, spending quiet, meditative time for twenty minutes each day, and learning to give yourself Supportive Observer comments during stressful times. Now you decide to set a new Intention: "to walk around inside the South Square Mall today, looking in store windows with a friend, for thirty minutes." Once you commit yourself to that Intention, you take as many steps toward that goal as you can manage. It is unimportant whether you accomplish that goal today. Your task is to set an Intention and move toward it to the best of your ability. And no further. Tomorrow you will simply review your learning from today and set a new Intention.

We all deserve to feel a sense of pride and success. Don't rob yourself of those good feelings by labeling anything you do as a failure. Do not define your personal success in terms of reaching your Intention. In conquering panic, you are successful any time you are actively moving toward your goal, regardless of whether you reach it.

Make your tasks reachable

As I am writing this chapter, our daughter is about fifteen months old. Since she is our first child, we watch with amazement as she grows in front of our eyes. It seems that each evening my wife tells me of another "breakthrough" in her development. Today she learned how to stack one peg on top of another. I watch her face contort as she tries to send messages of control to her hand, sliding the top peg around on the surface until it finally drops into position. She probably expended as much mental energy as the Apollo astronauts did in making the first lunar landing. Then, the expression of glee spreads across her face as she hears the applause and hollers of these two grown-ups next to her.

As hard as it is for me to imagine, in another couple of years Joanna will be talking in sentences, picking out her own clothes, and eating with a fork and spoon. And I will be able to stop washing diapers. To me, there is nothing more remarkable than the physical and intellectual development which takes place between conception and a child's fifth birthday. From just two cells comes the most incredible creation ever contemplated.

Child development is a slow, step-by-step process. One way that parents can negatively influence that process is by attempting to speed it up. A good parent is patient with the child, introducing just enough challenges to stimulate the child's growth, but not so much as to overwhelm. All good things come in time.

Many people who suffer from episodes of panic have been struggling for years and feel as though the struggles they face in the future will be too much to bear. To you I offer the same hopes and expectations parents have for their young children. The body is a phenomenal healing machine. It requires your faith, your commitment, your love, and your patience. With those qualities in place, it heals itself.

Just as your Critical Observer will pay attention to the past, your Hopeless Observer will think too far ahead. It looks at the distant goal and says, "I'll never get there. It is out of reach. I don't have what it takes to change." The Hopeless Observer has lost all curiosity; it never wonders about possibilities. Instead it uses your powerful skill of imagery to conjure up a picture of failure, and concludes, "I can't."

Your Supportive Observer isn't wearing rose-colored glasses, looking through to impossible dreams, unrealistically imagining that you can do anything in the world. But its positive attitude is clearly distinct. The Negative Observer will look toward a distant goal and comment, "I can't." Your Supportive Observer will say, "I'm not ready for that, yet."

These two comments may appear to be quite similar, but when you say, "I can't," you are essentially closing the door on your ability to make a difference in your own life. When you say, "I'm not ready, yet," you are presupposing that some day you will be ready. Your Supportive Observer keeps the door open for further growth and improvements, regardless of how long it takes.

There is always a step that is within your reach. If you feel incapable of accomplishing any of your tasks, you must create smaller and smaller steps until you find one to which you can say, "I wonder if I can do that? It seems within my reach." For instance, you don't begin learning public speaking skills by placing yourself at the podium in front of a thousand people. You learn by talking into a tape recorder and then listening to your voice, by telling more stories to your friends during dinner conversations, or by imagining yourself comfortably addressing a small group of friends.

If you are fearful of panicking while you drive, the thought of taking a cross-country trip might be overwhelming. What can you imagine doing? Can you sit in the driver's seat of a car, with the ignition off, parked safely in a driveway, while you practice your Calming Response skills? If so, can you start the engine, back the car to the end of the driveway, then return it to its parked position, even if you feel somewhat anxious? Can you do that ten times? Once you feel in control of that step, can you drive around one block, with a supportive friend as passenger? If not, practice driving to the corner and back. If that is not yet within your reach, let your friend drive the car to the corner, then exchange places and drive back yourself.

Regardless of what you fear, there is always a step small enough for you to take toward overcoming that fear. Whenever you run into difficulty, simply back up to a smaller step. The size of your step can never be too small. As the Chinese philosopher Lao Tsu wrote in the sixth century BC, "A tree as great as a man's embrace springs from a small shoot; a terrace nine stories high begins with a pile of earth; a journey of a thousand miles starts under one's feet."

Plan each task in advance

Some of my clients tell me that they feel most comfortable with activities if they can wait until the last moment to decide to participate. Often this is true because these individuals let their negative images and thoughts run wild. If they commit themselves to an activity seven days in advance, they subject themselves to a week's worth of anxiety, fear, and grandiose negative fantasies.

To take control of panic you must take control of planning your safe, enjoyable future. As you learn once again that you can indeed plan activities in your life, then you will also be able to pleasantly dream about your future. Our plans and dreams fill us with the sense of hope that we each deserve, no matter what our past may have been.

Before practicing any short-term task which moves you closer to your goals, consider each of these questions in detail. Perhaps you will benefit from writing your answers down, making them concrete.

1. What is my task?
2. When will I do this?
3. How long will I take?
4. What worried thoughts do I have about this task?
5. What self-critical thoughts do I have about accomplishing this task?
6. What hopeless thoughts do I have about this task?
7. What can I say (in place of those negative thoughts) to support myself during this task?
8. How can I increase my sense of safety while working on this task?

Mentally rehearse for success

One of panic's greatest weapons is its surprise attacks. Fear of the unexpected causes us to tense our body and remain mentally on guard. The best way to combat this weapon is to plan ahead for specific times when you are susceptible to panic. If you know what to expect and know how you plan to respond, you will strengthen your motivation and desire.

An essential part of this planning is mental rehearsals. I recommend considering two separate phases of this imagery. First, you should practice visualizing yourself as if you have already achieved your goal. In Chapter 18, The Guide, you read about this method of mentally projecting yourself far enough into the future to entertain an image of yourself after achieving your goal. In the second phase of imagery you will mentally rehearse the task itself.

The order in which you practice these images is important. It is much easier and more comfortable to see yourself after you have already finished your task than it is to see yourself in the middle of your work. However, once you have entertained all the good feelings, the pride, the sense of accomplishment and freedom that come with success, you can use those feelings to strengthen your resolve in facing the task. Furthermore, by voluntarily calling up images of success you begin to combat all the thoughts and fantasies of failure which have been so graphic in the past. You can replace the old, negative scenarios of your mind with new, positive ones.

I can remember an experiment we conducted in eighth-grade science class. The teacher gave us long bar magnets and a cup of iron filings and asked us to sprinkle the filings around the north and south ends of the magnet. In a few minutes' time we found that the filings formed the distinct pattern of the magnet's electromagnetic field. The energy field, of course, was always present. But it took those filings to make it visible.

By visually rehearsing your tasks, a similar process will take place. Your mind will begin to gather together the internal resources needed to overcome panic: your supportive thoughts, your calming behaviors, your sense of safety, and your trust in your body. The more you rehearse, the stronger you will become. Then, as you face the panic-provoking situation, these resources will surface to support you. Here are the procedures for each of these two mental rehearsals.

Success Imagery. Set aside about ten minutes for private, quiet reflection. Once you are comfortably seated, close your eyes and form a picture of the outcome you desire. This should be an image of yourself *after* you have successfully completed your task. Experience your success from all angles. see the satisfaction expressed on your face. Notice how you are standing, your posture, how you hold your head. How does success feel in your body? How do you feel emotionally? Let yourself feel that sense of relief and of comfort, knowing that you made it. Introduce someone else into your picture, someone who supports your accomplishment. Enjoy your time with that person. Now let your mental images drift to other positive changes that may come in your life after successfully overcoming panic.

There are a few guidelines to follow as you practice this "results" imagery. First, and most important, make certain that your outcome picture is of something that you desire, for this is the goal which will motivate you. Do not look for something you think you *should* want or that others say you should achieve. Continue to change the picture until you have one that reflects a pleasing personal goal. Second, develop your pictures in detail. Absorb yourself in the colors, textures, sounds. Spend time simply enjoying the many small details that make up the whole experience. Third, respond emotionally. Get to know how you feel physically when you are happy or proud. And, fourth, stay with the positive images. Don't rehearse how you accomplished your goal; keep yourself within the time period *after* you have succeeded.

The first few times you work on this success imagery you may want to use The Guide, Chapter 18. It provides you with a structure which is designed to elicit images in your mind while you are feeling relatively comfortable and safe. Once you have developed the skill of imagery to your satisfaction, you will be able to spend a shorter amount of time while you focus specifically on your goals.

Task Imagery. The second stage of rehearsal is imagining yourself going through your actual task. You should begin this imagery session after you have satisfactorily experienced your success imagery a number of times for that specific task. In fact, many of my clients say that the success imagery helps them even more than imagining how they will reach their goal. The more powerful your success images are, the stronger will be your drive to follow through to your goal.

There are several ways in which you can create your task imagery. Choose whichever one which seems most beneficial to you. You may want to experiment with each of these to find the best approach. Initially, start with Option 1 and work your way up to Option 3, since Options 1 and 2 help you build your skills more slowly and deliberately.

Begin each of these sessions in the same manner. Start by answering the questions outlined on page 254, under "Plan Each Task in Advance," preferably by writing them down. Then, set aside some quiet, reflective time in a comfortable setting. As you begin to unwind, sitting in that chair or couch, give yourself a few minutes to quiet your mind. Perhaps you will want to do the Meditation of One Hundred Counts or a few Calming Breaths. Simply take several minutes to help with your transition from the active day to a quiet, mentally restful period. Give yourself permission to feel comfort in your body. Then, begin one of the following procedures.

As you read these instructions, you will notice that I have worded them in a special way. I use phrases such as, "Allow yourself to . . . ," "Let your mind just . . . ," or "Invite an image of. . . ." These are ways of reminding you that you should not struggle with any images or work hard at creating an experience in your mind. Your conscious mind should concentrate on the task, but at the same time it must relax its control over your imagery. Let the visualizations come and go as they please. Even if you don't have a vivid picture of some scene, as long as you keep your mind focused on the topic, your unconscious will be working on your behalf.

Option 1: Turn your Observer quietly inward to the screen in your mind. Invite an image of yourself in some comfortable, safe place. Let yourself remain there for a few minutes, enjoying the pleasant experience. Continue in that scene until you can feel your body reflecting your comfort and sense of safety. Take a mental scan through your body; notice how that comfort feels.

Now, while you maintain that feeling, call up the image of your task. This transition is an important one. Only see the picture of the task in your mind, turn off the sound and turn off the feelings associated with the picture. You should take on the role of a detached Observer of the scene, as though you are the director reviewing the film clip. Keep your sense of bodily comfort from the previous scene.

While you are feeling physically relaxed, watch yourself, on that screen, simply float through the task. Don't bother making your actions realistic. Literally see yourself gliding through the entire experience, as if you are comfortably floating on a pocket of air. Do it with ease. Face no threatening moment. Have no difficulties. Take no more than thirty seconds to experience a half-hour task from start to finish. Always end your scene by reaching your goal and *enjoying it* when you get there. Spend as much of your imagery time enjoying your goal as you took to reach your goal.

When you complete that task in your mind, return to your first scene of that comfortable, safe place. Spend a few minutes experiencing that comfort in your body and mind again.

Repeat this complete process two more times before ending this session.

Option 2: Follow the instructions for Option 1. If you feel sensations of discomfort at any time while you are viewing your task, take a mental eraser and wipe away that scene completely. Return your comfortable, safe scene to the screen. Stay in that scene as long as you need to in order to regain your sense of ease. Then, maintaining those comfortable feelings, return to floating through your task from the beginning.

You can stop that task image as many times as you like for as long as you need to regain your sense of comfort. You don't even need to get through the task in your mind the first few sessions that you try. Consider that you are "playing" with these ideas and images. It doesn't really matter how far you get in any particular session.

It is important, however, that you take time to end each imagery session feeling at ease. When you are ready to stop, return to imagining your comfortable, safe scene until you feel that comfort reflected in your body.

Option 3: This session includes many steps. As you begin working with this design you can alter it to suit your learning style. Feel free to reduce the number of steps or to change any particular step in order to create a process which is specifically designed for your tasks. It is unnecessary to go through all the steps every time you rehearse.

Consider Option 3 an "advanced" rehearsal. Make sure you are able to rehearse with Options 1 and 2 before you begin with this one. Some people use only Option 1 or 2 in their rehearsals. Others never use process imagery at all. They find that the success imagery is enough to carry them through their task.

This session will require that you first write down your answers to the questions on page 254. Keep the sheet of paper in your lap as you begin shifting your body and mind into a more restful state. Spend a few minutes developing your quiet mind and body, using any of the Calming Response methods in this book.

1. Call up your success image. Give yourself a clear, positive goal. Take a nice Calming Breath as your body responds to that image.

2. Now, let that image fade away as you briefly visualize yourself somewhere in the middle of your task. See yourself totally in control of the situation, smoothly handling the scene, even if you can hold on to that sense for only a few moments. Take another nice Calming Breath as you let that image fade away.

3. Glance down at your answers to question 4, "What worried thoughts do I have about this task?" Take your answers one at a time. Look at your first answer, then close your eyes and repeat that one statement or question in your mind. If you can, visualize a few of the key words of that worried thought at the same time. Now, take a Calming Breath as you let that thought, and those words, fade from your mind. Don't bother responding to the thought or replacing it with a positive thought. Simply let it fade out, and let any of your associ-

ated tensions fade away. Use any of the Calming Response skills to return that sense of calmness to your body. Completely dissolve that negative thought without responding to it.

Once you have returned to that state of calmness and ease, glance down at your next answer. Proceed in the same fashion as above. After completing this process for each of your answers to question 4, use this same method with each answer to question 5, "What self-critical thoughts do I have about accomplishing this task?" and to question 6, "What hopeless thoughts do I have about this task?"

4. Spend as much time as you need to again develop your quiet mind and body. Consider this a "rest period": no work, no effort, just drifting comfortably, letting your body soothe itself.

5. Now, turn your attention to question 7, "What can I say to support myself during this task?" Reflect on your statements one at a time. Close your eyes and recite the first one to yourself. Think only about the statement, not about your task. Let the statement sink in. Let your body respond as though you believe the statement. Get to know how your body feels as it is supported. After you are satisfied with your response to that first statement, recite that second statement, let it sink in, and notice your body's response as you let yourself believe the statement to be true, if only for a few moments. Continue using this process with each of your supportive statements.

You may find that as you reflect on these statements a new and different supportive stance rises up in your mind. Reflect on that sentence and learn from it. If you like the way your body feels as you attend to it, jot down the new sentence for later use.

6. Begin to mentally rehearse your task. Start with any active preparatory steps you might want to take to increase your sense of safety. Then, see yourself moving through each stage of the task in the way that you have planned. Envision yourself at the beginning of the task, in the middle, and as you are finishing it. Finally, see yourself enjoying the completion of that task. (For example, if you are rehearsing an airplane flight, watch yourself enjoying that vacation or those friends you have gone to visit. If you are imagining your ability to exercise without having an asthma attack, see yourself sinking into a nice warm bath after the workout, enjoying that easy breathing as you rest those muscles, smiling to yourself at the accomplishment.)

You may take one of two approaches during this mental practice of the task. You can steadily watch the scene unfold in your mind's eye, even if you feel some anxiety during parts of it. Use your Calming Response skills during those times. The more you rehearse while allowing these small tensions to rise up, the more you will learn that our tensions come and go. As you tolerate them during imagery, they will become less debilitating in reality. Since your goal is not to be completely void of any tension but to reduce that tension to a tolerable level, this experience will increase your sense of control.

The second approach is to follow the imagery of your task without experiencing any anxiety. Each time you sense some tension in your body, simply "erase" the task image from your mind. Spend as much time as you need on any of the Calming Response techniques, as you continue to rest in that chair. Perhaps you will want to take a few Calming Breaths or to switch your imagery to some pleasant scene. When you are again feeling calm, return to the task image.

This method can take much longer than the first. In fact, you may not even get through to the end of your task rehearsal in your first sitting. Nonetheless, this can be just as effective as the first approach as long as you persist in your practice.

7. Always finish your sessions by taking a few minutes to become quiet and calm, without having to work on any task. Use that time to focus on a pleasant image, to experience comfortable body sensations, or to meditate on a calming word.

Practice your success imagery and task imagery as many times as you need to in order to begin practicing the task itself.

Always practice, never test

Experience is the greatest teacher. All the reading and talking and analyzing and planning that you do will be worthless unless you translate them into action. You must *act* against your Negative Observer beliefs in order to overcome them. Without doubt, your actions will provide you with your most valuable experiences.

Don't let your fearful thoughts stop you. And don't wait for some magical day when you will have mastered panic before you have even faced it. To resolve this problem you must start doing those things that you usually avoid, even if you have some symptoms of anxiety. So, begin by dispensing with excuses that stall your positive physical progress. You can chip away a little bit at your goal each day, if you choose to do so.

As you begin taking action, your attitude about the task will be a deciding factor in your progress. I instruct my clients to consider any activity they engage in as "practice." I take a firm stand on this point. Never view a future task as a "test" of your progress or of your ability to overcome panic. Never look back at an attempted task in order to label your efforts a failure. Never invest your self-worth in the positive or negative outcome of your plans.

I recommend this attitude not only for people who want to master panic, but also for all of my clients, regardless of their problem, and I attempt to maintain this attitude in my own life.

When you decide that all your experiences are practice, then you are, in effect, saying that you are willing to learn and that you are able to learn from each of those experiences. No one knows everything about any particular subject. Our greatest scientists continually create new questions to ask about their field of expertise. These brilliant men and women would be the first to defend the importance of maintaining the open, curious, exploratory mind of the student.

When you test yourself during every activity you inhibit your learning. If you say to yourself, "That action you took yesterday proves that you're never going to make it," then essentially you have said, "Don't bother learning from yesterday; it's too late for you." Of course, the truth of the matter is that making mistakes and studying them is one of our best learning tools.

It seems that people who are prone to panic attacks must pay close attention to this issue. I have watched clients improve steadily week after week. Then, one week, they inevitably have a small setback to their progress. From this one episode they become dejected, depressed, and demoralized. They are full of self-critical and hopeless thoughts.

Since everyone who takes on a challenge has setbacks, you can assume you will too. When you hear your Critical Observer and Hopeless Observer comments rise up, let them go. They are a distraction technique that panic uses to keep you from learning.

A FINAL NOTE

The trouble with our conscious mind is that it tries too hard.

Consider the performance of athletes. A professional athlete continually practices his drills and observes his techniques to improve his skill. But when it comes time to perform, the professional will stop paying attention to his body. Instead, he wants to trust his instincts, to trust his reflexes, to trust that all his practice has sunk in. He now looks outward, toward the game, toward the ball, toward the movements of the other players. When he engages in the event he stops questioning or doubting his ability. He stops watching his style. In short, he asks his critical mind to quiet down so that his body can do its work without disturbance.

Watch and listen to a professional musician performing a concert. He will play with abandonment, often without benefit of sheet music. All the necessary skills and memories flow out of the musician without conscious effort. With effort, certainly, but not *conscious* effort. Professionals trust themselves at another level of being.

Too much conscious attention interferes with our performance, regardless of the task. The human body is the finest, most sophisticated multisensory teaching machine in existence. Our conscious mind is but a minor player. In order to achieve our best performance we must not allow our conscious mind to become overly involved in the process. True concentration is effortless, but the hardest job during concentration is to quiet the conscious mind.

All of the dozens of ways in which I have approached the problem of panic pivot around the concept of trusting your body. Although many of the practice tasks I suggest in this book involve conscious thinking about each step, your final objective is to do very little conscious work. After you master the basic skills, practice keeping your mind off your body while you think very simply and slowly.

You will evolve beyond technique, all in good time. Your final goal can be to respond automatically and reflexively during times of trouble. You will know you have arrived when, one day, your conscious mind says, "Hey, what happened? I just handled that situation smoothly, and I didn't even know I was doing it."

Appendix

Don't Panic:
The Survivor's Guide

When panic becomes a repetitious experience, it follows a structured pattern. You can, therefore, follow a planned response when you notice the first signs of panic. This appendix summarizes some of the structured experiences described in *Don't Panic*. Feel free to copy these few pages and keep them in a suitable location for easy reference.

STOPPING THE NEGATIVE OBSERVER
(from Chapter 15)

1. Stop and listen for your worried, self-critical, or hopeless thoughts.
2. When you hear a negative thought pattern, decide that you want to stop it.
3. Reinforce your decision through supportive comments ("I can let go of these thoughts").
4. Begin the Calming Counts.

USES: *To disrupt recurring negative thoughts.*

TAKING CONTROL OF THE MOMENT OF PANIC
(from Chapter 15)

1. Listen for your worried, self-critical, or hopeless thoughts about your body and your circumstances.
2. Disrupt this negative pattern.
   - Use the Calming Breath or Calming Counts.

- Find some neutral or pleasant task to occupy your conscious thoughts.

3. As you are gaining control of your thoughts and your breathing, observe your physical sensations, your negative comments, and your surroundings.

4. Answer the question, "How can I support myself right now?"

5. Take supportive action based on your answer.

USES: *During panic or during panic-provoking times.*

SOME SUPPORTIVE COMMENTS DURING PANIC

- It's OK to feel this way, even though I'm uncomfortable.
- I can be anxious and still perform this task.
- I can manage these symptoms.
- This is not an emergency. It's OK to think slowly about what I need.
- I always have options, no matter what.
- I can trust my body.
- It's OK to feel safe.
- I deserve to feel comfortable now.
- I can take all the time I need to feel safe and comfortable.
- I can take as small a step forward as I choose. I can stop when I want. I can rest when I want. I don't need to constantly push.
- Everything is practice; there are no tests.
- I've survived this before and I'll survive this time, too.

USING PARADOX DURING PANIC
(from Chapter 16)

1. Take a Calming Breath, then begin natural breathing.

2. Don't fight your physical symptoms and don't run away.

3. Decide if you want to use paradox.

4. Observe your most predominant physical symptom at this moment.

5. Say to yourself, "I would like to take voluntary control of these symptoms. I would like to increase my (name the predominant symptom).

6. Consciously attempt to increase that symptom.

7. Now attempt to increase all the other symptoms you notice: "I would like to perspire more than this. Let me see if I can become very dizzy and make my legs into jelly, right now."

8. Continue natural breathing, while you consciously and fully attempt to increase all your symptoms of panic.

9. Do not get trapped in worried, critical or hopeless comments ("This better start working soon! I certainly must be doing this wrong. It'll never work.").

USES: *During panic.*

CALMING COUNTS
(from Chapter 14)

1. Take a long deep breath and then exhale slowly while saying the word "relax" silently.

2. Take ten natural, easy breaths. Count each exhale silently, starting with "ten."

3. During this time, notice any tensions, perhaps in your jaw or forehead or stomach. Imagine those tensions loosening.

4. When you reach "one," slowly return to your activity.

USES: *Any time that you want to encourage your body's Calming Response.*

To disrupt negative thoughts (also see "Stopping the Negative Observer," page 263).

To quiet the mind during meditation or relaxation (see "One Hundred Counts," page 190).

During panic or during panic-provoking times.

THE CALMING BREATH
(from Chapter 14)

1. Take a deep breath, filling first your lower lungs, then your upper lungs.

2. *Slowly* exhale, saying "relax" (or a similar word) under your breath.

3. Let your muscles go limp and warm, loosen your face and jaw muscles, quiet your thoughts.

4. Remain in this "resting" position physically and mentally for ten to fifteen seconds, or for a couple of natural breaths.

USES: *Incorporate this brief experience into your daily life. Use it six to eight times a day to reduce the buildup of normal tensions.*

To encourage the Calming Response.

During panic or during panic-provoking times.

NATURAL BREATHING
(from Chapter 11)

1. Gently and slowly inhale a normal amount of air through your nose, filling only your lower lungs.

2. Exhale easily.

3. Continue this slow, gentle breathing with a relaxed attitude, concentrating on filling only the lower lungs.

USES: *This should be adopted as your normal daily breathing pattern whenever you are not physically active.*

THE OBSERVER

- Takes time to collect all the relevant information
- Is detached from strong emotions
- May feel concern, yet thinks calmly
- Is devoid of prejudices
- Gains a perspective on the situation
- Sees problems in a different light
- Is objective

THE SUPPORTIVE OBSERVER

- Reminds you of your freedoms and choices
- Gives you permission to feel safe

- Supports all your efforts
- Invites you to feel confident
- Trusts you and lets you trust yourself
- Expects a positive future
- Points out your successes
- Looks around you for support
- Believes that you can change
- Knows that there is always more than one option in decisions
- Focuses more on solutions than on problems

THE WORRIED OBSERVER

- Anticipates the worst
- Fears the future
- Creates grandiose images of potential problems
- Expects and braces for catastrophe
- Watches, with uneasy apprehension, any small signs of trouble

Over time, the Worried Observer creates anxiety.

THE CRITICAL OBSERVER

- Makes certain you understand how helpless and hopeless you are
- Doesn't hesitate to remind you of the mistakes you have made and that you are lucky to have anything or anyone in your life
- Points out each of your flaws regularly, in case you might have forgotten them
- Uses any mistake to remind you of what a failure you are

Over time the Critical Observer produces low self-esteem and low motivation.

THE HOPELESS OBSERVER

- Suffers over your present experience
- Believes there is something inherently wrong with you

- Believes that you are deprived, defective, or unworthy—that you are missing what it takes to succeed
- Expects that you will fail in the future just as you have failed in the past
- Expects that you will continue to be deprived and frustrated
- Believes that there are insurmountable obstacles between you and your goals

Over time the Hopeless Observer leads to depression.

Bibliography

Abraham, G. E. "Premenstrual Tension." *Current Problems in Obstetrics and Gynecology* 3 (1981): 1–39.

Altesman, R. I., and Cole, J. O. "Psychopharmacologic Treatment of Anxiety." *Journal of Clinical Psychiatry* 44 (1983): 12–18.

American Psychiatric Association. *Diagnostic and Statistical Manual of Mental Disorders*. 3d ed. Washington, D.C.: American Psychiatric Association, 1980.

Ananth, J. "Physical Illness and Psychiatric Disorders." *Comprehensive Psychiatry* 25 (1984): 586–93.

Anderson, R. W., and Lev-Ran, A. "Hypoglycemia: The Standard and the Fiction." *Psychosomatics* 26 (1985): 38–47.

Arrick, M. C.; Voss, J.; and Rimm, D. C. "The Relative Efficacy of Thought Stopping and Covert Assertion." *Behaviour Research and Therapy* 19 (1981): 17–24.

Ascher, L. M. "Employing Paradoxical Intention in the Treatment of Agoraphobia." *Behavior Research and Therapy* 19 (1981): 533–42.

Asso, D., and Beech, H. "Susceptibility to the Acquisition of Conditioned Response in Relation to the Menstrual Cycle." *Journal of Psychosomatic Research* 19 (1975): 337–44.

Ballenger, J. "Panic Disorder and Agoraphobia." Conference on The Brain and the Heart: Psychiatric Complications of Cardiovascular Disease. Duke University Medical Center, November 14, 1985.

Bandura, A. "Self-efficacy: Toward a Unifying Theory of Behavioral Change." *Psychological Review* 84 (1977): 191–215.

Bandura, A.; Adams, N. E.; and Beyer, J. "Cognitive Processes Mediating Behavioral Change." *Journal of Personality and Social Psychology* 35 (1977): 125–39.

Beck, A. T. *Depression: Causes and Treatment*. Philadelphia: University of Pennsylvania Press, 1967.

———. *Cognitive Therapy and the Emotional Disorders*. New York: International Universities Press, 1976.

269

Beck, A. T., and Emery, G. *Anxiety Disorders and Phobias: A Cognitive Perspective*. New York: Basic Books, 1985.

Beck, A. T.; Rush, A. J.; Shaw, B. F.; and Emery, G. *Cognitive Therapy of Depression*. New York: The Guilford Press, 1979.

Benson, H. *Beyond the Relaxation Response*. New York: Times Books, 1984.

―――. *The Mind/Body Effect*. New York: Simon and Schuster, 1979.

―――. *The Relaxation Response*. New York: William Morrow, 1975.

Bernsted, L.; Luggin, R.; and Petersson, B. "Psychosocial Considerations of the Premenstrual Syndrome." *Acta Psychiatr. Scand.* 69 (1984): 455–60.

Biran, M., and Wilson, G. T. "Treatment of Phobic Disorders Using Cognitive and Exposure Methods: A Self-efficacy Analysis." *Journal of Consulting and Clinical Psychology* 49 (1981): 886–99.

Blanchard, E. B. "Psychological Treatment of Cardiovascular Disease." *Archives of General Psychiatry* 34 (1977): 1402–13.

Bland, K., and Hallam, R. S. "Relationship Between Response to Graded Exposure and Marital Satisfaction in Agoraphobics." *Behavior Research and Therapy* 19 (1981): 335–38.

Boston Collaborative Drug Surveillance Program. "Psychiatric Side Effects of Nonpsychiatric Drugs." *Seminars in Psychiatry* 3 (1971): 406–20.

Bowen, R. C., and Kohout, J. "The Relationship Between Agoraphobia and Primary Affective Disorders." *Canadian Psychiatric Association Journal* 24 (1979): 317–22.

Boyd, T. L., and Levis, D. J. "Exposure Is a Necessary Condition for Fear-Reduction: A Reply to De Silva and Rachman." *Behavior Research and Therapy* 21 (1983): 143–49.

"Breathing and Control of Heart Rate." *British Medical Journal,* December 1978, 1663–64.

Breier, A.; Charney, D. S.; and Heninger, G. R. "The Diagnostic Validity of Anxiety Disorders and Their Relationship to Depressive Illness." *The American Journal of Psychiatry* 142 (1985): 787–97.

Breier, A.; Charney, D. S.; and Heninger, G. R. "Major Depression in Patients with Agoraphobia and Panic Disorder." *Archives of General Psychiatry* 41 (1984): 1129–35.

Brown, B. B. *Between Health and Illness*. Boston: Houghton Mifflin, 1984.

―――. *Supermind*. New York: Harper & Row, 1980.

Burns, D. D. *Feeling Good*. New York: William Morrow, 1980.

Butler, G.; Cullington, A.; Munby, M.; Amies, P.; and Gelder, M. "Exposure and Anxiety Management in the Treatment of Social Phobia." *Journal of Consulting and Clinical Psychology* 52 (1984): 642–50.

Carr, D. B., and Sheehan, D. V. "Panic Anxiety: A New Biological Model." *Journal of Clinical Psychiatry* 45 (1984): 323–30.

Cassem, N. H., and Hackett, T. P. "Psychological Rehabilitation of Myocardial Infarction Patients in the Acute Phase." *Heart and Lung* 2 (1973): 382–88.

Chambless, D. L.; Foa, E. B.; Groves, G. A.; and Goldstein A. J. "Exposure and Communications Training in the Treatment of Agoraphobia." *Behavior Research and Therapy* 20 (1982): 219–31.

Chambless, D. L., and Goldstein, A. J., eds. *Agoraphobia: Multiple Perspectives on Theory and Treatment.* New York: John Wiley, 1982.

Clark, D. M., and Hemsley, D. R. "The Effects of Hyperventilation: Individual Variability and Its Relation to Personality." *Journal of Behaviour Therapy and Experimental Psychiatry* 13 (1982): 41–47.

Clark, D. M.; Salkovskis, P. M.; and Chalkley, A. J. "Respiratory Control as a Treatment for Panic Attacks." *Journal of Behaviour Therapy and Experimental Psychiatry* 16 (1985): 23–30.

Coryell, W.; Noyes, R.; and Clancy, J. "Panic Disorder and Primary Unipolar Depression: A Comparison of Background and Outcome." *Journal of Affective Disorders* 5 (1983): 311–17.

Cousins, N. "Anatomy of an Illness (as Perceived by the Patient)." *New England Journal of Medicine* 295 (1976): 1458–63.

———. *The Healing Heart.* New York: Norton, 1983.

Crowe, R. R.; Gaffney, G.; and Kerber, R. "Panic Attacks in Families of Patients with Mitral Valve Prolapse." *Journal of Affective Disorders* 4 (1982): 121–25.

Crowe, R. R.; Noyes, R.; Pauls, D. L.; and Slymen, D. "A Family Study of Panic Disorder." *Archives of General Psychiatry* 40 (1983): 1065–69.

Davidson, D. M.; Winchester, M. A.; Taylor, C. B.; Alderman, E. A.; and Ingels, N. B., Jr. "Effects of Relaxation Therapy on Cardiac Performance and Sympathetic Activity in Patients with Organic Heart Disease." *Psychosomatic Medicine* 41 (1979): 303–9.

De Silva, P., and Rachman, S. "Does Escape Behaviour Strengthen Agoraphobic Avoidance?: A Preliminary Study." *Behaviour Research and Therapy* 22 (1984): 87–91.

De Silva, P., and Rachman, S. "Exposure and Fear-Reduction." *Behavior Research and Therapy* 21 (1983): 151–52.

Dietch, J. T. "Diagnosis of Organic Anxiety Disorders." *Psychosomatics* 22 (1981): 661–69.

Di Nardo, P. A.; O'Brien, G. T.; Barlow, D. H.; Waddell, M. T.; and Blanchard, E. B. "Reliability of DSM-III Anxiety Disorder Categories Using a New Structured Interview." *Archives of General Psychiatry* 40 (1983): 1070–74.

Drachman, D., and Hart, C. "An Approach to the Dizzy Patient." *Neurology* 22 (1972).

Dudley, D. L.; Glaser, E. M.; Jorgenson, B. N.; and Logan, D. L. "Psychosocial Concomitants to Rehabilitation in Chronic Obstructive Pulmonary Disease." Part 1: "Psychosocial and Psychological Considerations." *Chest* 77 (1980): 413–20.

Dudley, D. L.; Glaser, E. M.; Jorgenson, B. N.; and Logan, D. L. "Psychosocial Concomitants to Rehabilitation in Chronic Obstructive Pulmonary Disease." Part 2: "Psychosocial Treatment." *Chest* 77 (1980): 544–51.

Dudley, D. L.; Glaser, E. M.; Jorgenson, B. N.; and Logan, D. L. "Psychosocial Concomitants to Rehabilitation in Chronic Obstructive Pulmonary Disease." Part 3: "Dealing with Psychiatric Disease (as Distinguished from Psychosocial or Psychophysiologic Problems"). *Chest* 77 (1980): 677–84.

Dudley, D. L.; Wermuth, C.; and Hague, W. "Psychosocial Aspects of Care in the Chronic Obstructive Pulmonary Disease Patient." *Heart and Lung* 2 (1973): 389–93.

DuPont, R. L., ed. *Phobia: A Comprehensive Summary of Modern Treatments*. New York: Brunner/Mazel, 1982.

Ellis, A. "A Note on the Treatment of Agoraphobics with Cognitive Modification Versus Prolonged Exposure in Vivo." *Behavior Research and Therapy* 17 (1979): 162–64.

———. *Reason and Emotion in Psychotherapy*. New York: Lyle Stuart, 1962.

Emmelkamp, P. M. "Agoraphobics' Interpersonal Problems: Their Role in the Effects of Exposure in Vivo Therapy." *Archives of General Psychiatry* 37 (1980): 1303–6.

———. *Phobic and Obsessive-Compulsive Disorders*. New York: Plenum, 1982.

Emmelkamp, P. M.; Kuipers, A. C.; and Eggeraat, J. B. "Cognitive Modification Versus Prolonged Exposure in Vivo: A Comparison with Agoraphobics as Subjects." *Behavior Research and Therapy* 16 (1978): 33–41.

Emmelkamp, P. M., and Mersch, P. P. "Cognition and Exposure in Vivo in the Treatment of Agoraphobia: Short-term and Delayed Effects." *Cognitive Therapy and Research* 6 (1982): 77–88

Emmelkamp, P. M.; Van Der Hout, A.; and De Vries, K. "Assertive Training for Agoraphobics." *Behavior Research and Therapy* 21 (1983): 63–68.

Fawcett, J., and Kravitz, H. M. "Anxiety Syndromes and Their Relationship to Depressive Illness." *Journal of Clinical Psychiatry* 44 (1983): 8–11.

Finnberg, E. A. "Anticipating Side Effects of Relaxation Treatment." Letter in *American Journal of Psychiatry* 140 (1983): 369–79.

Flannery, J. G., and Szmuilowicz, J. "Psychiatric Implications of the Mitral Valve Prolapse Syndrome (MVPS)." *Canadian Journal of Psychiatry* 24 (1979): 740–43.

Ford, C. V.; Bray, G. A.; and Swerdloff, R. S. "A Psychiatric Study of Patients Referred with a Diagnosis of Hypoglycemia." *American Journal of Psychiatry* 133 (1976): 290–94.

Frankl, V. E. *Psychotherapy and Existentialism: Selected Papers on Logotherapy*. New York: Simon & Schuster, 1967.

Freedman, R. R.; Ianni, P.; Ettedgui, E.; Pohl, R.; and Rainey, J. M. "Psychophysiological Factors in Panic Disorders." *Psychopathology* 17 (1984): 66–73.

Gannon, L. "Evidence for a Psychological Etiology of Menstrual Disorders: A Critical Review." *Psychological Reports* 18 (1981): 287–91.

Garssen, B.; Van Veenedaal, W.; and Bloemink, R. "Agoraphobia and the Hyperventilation Syndrome." *Behaviour Research and Therapy* 21 (1983): 643–49.

Garvey, M. J., and Tuason, V. B. "The Relationship of Panic Disorder to Agoraphobia." *Comprehensive Psychiatry* 25 (1984): 529–31.

Gendlin, E. T. *Focusing*. 2d ed. New York: Bantam, 1981.

Gittelman, R., and Klein, D. F. "Relationship Between Separation Anxiety and Panic and Agoraphobic Disorders." *Psychopathology* 17 (1984): 56–65.

Goldfried, M. R., and Robins, C. "On the Facilitation of Self-efficacy." *Cognitive Therapy and Research* 6 (1982): 361–80.

Goodstein, R. K., and Swift, K. "Psychotherapy with Phobic Patients: The Marriage Relationship as the Source of Symptoms and Focus of Treatment." *American Journal of Psychotherapy* 31 (1977): 284–93.

Goodwin, J. *Continued Readjustment Problems Among Vietnam Veterans: The Etiology of Combat-Related Post-Traumatic Stress Disorders*. Booklet. New York: Disabled American Veterans.

Gorman, J. M.; Askanazi, J.; Liebowitz, M. R.; Fyer, A. J.; Stein, J.; Kinney, J. M.; and Klein, D. F. "Response to Hyperventilation in a Group of Patients with Panic Disorder." *American Journal of Psychiatry* 141 (1984): 857–61.

Gorman, J. M.; Fyer, A. F.; Gliklich, J.; King, D.; and Klein D. F. "Effect of Imipramine on Prolapsed Mitral Valves of Patients with Panic Disorder." *American Journal of Psychiatry* 138 (1981): 977–78.

Gorman, J. M.; Levy, G. F.; Liebowitz, M. R.; McGrath, P.; Appleby, I. L.; Dillon, D. J.; Davies, S. O.; and Klein, D. F. "Effect of Acute Beta-Adrenergic Blockade on Lactate-Induced Panic." *Archives of General Psychiatry* 40 (1983): 1079–82.

Gorman, J. M.; Martinez, J. M.; Liebowitz, M. R.; Fyer, A. J.; and Klein, D. F. "Hypoglycemia and Panic Attacks." *American Journal of Psychiatry* 141 (1984): 101–2.

Gould, R. L. *Transformations: Growth and Change in Adult Life*. New York: Simon and Schuster, 1978.

Greenberg, G. D.; Ryan, J. J.; and Bourlier, P. F. "Psychological and Neuropsychological Aspects of COPD." *Psychosomatics* 26 (1985): 29–33.

Grossman, P. "Respiration, Stress, and Cardiovascular Function." *Psychophysiology* 20 (1983): 284–300.

Grunhaus, L.; Gloger, S.; and Weisstub, E. "Panic Attacks: A Review of Treatments and Pathogenesis." *Journal of Nervous and Mental Disease* 169 (1981): 608–13.

Gurney, C.; Roth, M.; Garside, R. F.; Kerr, T. A.; and Schapira, K. "Studies in the Classification of Affective Disorders: The Relationship Between Anxiety States and Depressive Illnesses—II." *British Journal of Psychiatry* 121 (1972): 162–66.

Hafner, R. J. "Behaviour Therapy for Agoraphobic Men." *Behaviour Research and Therapy* 21 (1983): 51–56.

———. "Predicting the Effects on Husbands of Behaviour Therapy for Wives' Agoraphobia." *Behaviour Research and Therapy* 22 (1984): 217–26.

Hall, S. M. "The Abstinence Phobias: Links Between Substance Abuse and Anxiety." *The International Journal of the Addictions* 19 (1984): 613–31.

Hallam, R. S. "Agoraphobia: A Critical Review of the Concept." *British Journal of Psychiatry* 133 (1978): 314–19.

Handley, R. *Anxiety and Panic Attacks: Their Cause and Cure.* New York: Rawson, 1985.

Harris, E. L.; Noyes, R., Jr.; Crowe, R. R.; and Chaudhry, D. R. "Family Study of Agoraphobia: Report of a Pilot Study." *Archives of General Psychiatry* 40 (1983): 1061–64.

Harrison, T. "Post-traumatic Stress Syndrome." Workshop presented at Eleventh Annual Spring Conference of Southeast Institute, Myrtle Beach, S.C., 1985.

Hartman, N.; Kramer, R.; Brown, W. T.; and Devereux, R. B. "Panic Disorder in Patients with Mitral Valve Prolapse." *American Journal of Psychiatry* 139 (1982): 669–70.

Haskett, R. F., and Abplanalp, J. M. "Premenstrual Tension Syndrome: Diagnostic Criteria and Selection of Research Subjects." *Psychiatry Research* 9 (1983): 125–38.

Hibbert, G. A. "Hyperventilation as a Cause of Panic Attacks." *British Medical Journal* 288 (1984): 263–64.

Hickey, A. J.; Andrews, G.; and Wilcken, D. E. "Independence of Mitral Valve Prolapse and Neurosis." *British Heart Journal* 50 (1983): 333–36.

Hillenberg, J. B., and Collins F. L., Jr. "The Importance of Home Practice for Progressive Relaxation Training." *Behaviour Research and Therapy* 21 (1983): 633–42.

Himadi, W. G.; Boice, R.; and Barlow, D. H. "Assessment of Agoraphobia: Triple Response Measurement." *Behaviour Research and Therapy* 23 (1985): 311–23.

Hoogduin, C. A. L., and Hoogduin, W. A. "The Out-patient Treatment of Patients with an Obsessional-Compulsive Disorder." *Behaviour Research and Therapy* 22 (1984): 455–59.

House, A. E.; Manelis, L.; and Kinscherf, B. M. "Vigilance as a Model of Self-monitoring Accuracy: Empirical Effects and a Conceptual Framework." *Behavioral Assessment* 5 (1983): 83–96.

Jacobson, E. *Progressive Relaxation.* 2d ed. Chicago: University of Chicago Press, 1974.

James, J. E.; Hampton, B. A.; and Larsen, S. A. "The Relative Efficacy of

Imaginal and in Vivo Desensitization in the Treatment of Agoraphobia." *Journal of Behavior Therapy and Experimental Psychiatry* 14 (1983): 203–7.

Kantor, J. S.; Zitrin, C. M.; and Zeldis, S. M. "Mitral Valve Prolapse Syndrome in Agoraphobic Patients." *American Journal of Psychiatry* 137 (1980): 467–69.

Katerndahl, D. A., and Vande Creek, L. "Hyperthyroidism and Panic Attacks." *Psychosomatics* 24 (1983): 491–96.

Kelly, W. *Post-traumatic Stress Disorder and the War Veteran Patient.* New York: Brunner/Mazel, 1985.

Kennedy, H. L.; Whitlock, J. A.; Sprague, M. K.; Kennedy, L. J.; Buckingham, T. A.; and Goldberg, R. J. "Long-term Follow-up of Asymptomatic Healthy Subjects with Frequent and Complex Ventricular Ectopy." *The New England Journal of Medicine* 312 (1985): 193–97.

Klein, D. F. "Anxiety Reconceptualized." *Comprehensive Psychiatry* 21 (1980): 411–27.

———. "Delineation of Two Drug-Responsive Anxiety Syndromes." *Psychopharmacologia* 5 (1964): 397–408.

Klein, D. F., and Rabkin, J. G., eds. *Anxiety: New Research and Changing Concepts.* New York: Raven Press, 1981.

Klein, D. F.; Zitrin, C. M.; Woerner, M. G.; and Ross, D. C. "Treatment of Phobias." Part 2: "Behavior Therapy and Supportive Psychotherapy: Are There Any Specific Ingredients?" *Archives of General Psychiatry* 40 (1983): 139–45.

Kraft, A. R., and Hoogduin, C. A. L. "The Hyperventilation Syndrome." *British Journal of Psychiatry* 145 (1984): 538–42.

Krantz, D. S. "Cognitive Processes and Recovery from Heart Attack: A Review and Theoretical Analysis." *Journal of Human Stress,* 1980, 27–38.

Kutz, I.; Borysenko, J. Z.; and Benson, H. "Meditation and Psychotherapy: A Rationale for the Integration of Dynamic Psychotherapy, the Relaxation Response, and Mindfulness Meditation." *American Journal of Psychiatry* 142 (1985): 1–8.

Lader, M. "Behavior and Anxiety: Physiologic Mechanisms." *Journal of Clinical Psychiatry* 44 (1983): 5–10.

Ladouceur, R. "Rationale of Systematic Desensitization and Covert Positive Reinforcement." *Behaviour Research and Therapy* 16 (1978): 411–20.

Lankton, S., and Lankton, C. *The Answer Within: A Clinical Framework of Ericksonian Hypnotherapy.* New York: Brunner/Mazel, 1983.

Leckman, J. F.; Weissman, M. M.; Merikansas, K. R.; Pauls, D. L.; and Prusoff, B. A. "Panic Disorder and Major Depression: Increased Risk of Depression, Alcoholism, Panic, and Phobic Disorders in Families of Depressed Probands with Panic Disorders." *Archives of General Psychiatry* 40 (1983): 1055–60.

Leggett, J., and Favazza, A. "Hypoglycemia: An Overview." *Journal of Clinical Psychiatry,* January 1978, 51–57.

276   *Bibliography*

Lehmann, H. E. "The Clinician's View of Anxiety and Depression." *Journal of Clinical Psychiatry* 44 (1983): 3–7.

Lehrer, P. M. "How to Relax and How Not to Relax: A Re-evaluation of the Work of Edmund Jacobson—I. *Behaviour Research and Therapy* 20 (1982): 417–28.

Ley, R. "Agoraphobia, the Panic Attack and the Hyperventilation Syndrome." *Behaviour Research and Therapy* 23 (1985): 79–81.

Liebowitz, M. R., and Klein, D. F. "Differential Diagnosis and Treatment of Panic Attacks and Phobic States." *Annual Review of Medicine* 32 (1981): 583–99.

Lum, L. C. "Hyperventilation and Anxiety State." *Journal of the Royal Society of Medicine* 74 (1981): 1–4.

———. "Hyperventilation: The Tip and the Iceberg." *Journal of Psychosomatic Research* 19 (1975): 375–83.

MacNeil-Lehrer-Gannett Productions. "My Heart, Your Heart." One-hour documentary shown Feb. 27, 1985, Public Broadcasting Corporation.

Marks, I. M. "Agoraphobic Syndrome (Phobic Anxiety State)." *Archives of General Psychiatry* 23 (1970): 538–53.

Mathews, A. M.; Gelder, M. G.; and Johnston, D. W. *Agoraphobia: Nature and Treatment*. New York: Guilford Press, 1981.

McMullough, C. J., and Mann, R. W. *Managing Your Anxiety*. Los Angeles: Tarcher, 1985.

Mavissakalian, M. "Pharmacologic Treatment of Anxiety Disorders." *Journal of Clinical Psychiatry* 43 (1982): 487–91.

Mavissakalian, M., and Barlow, D. H., eds. *Phobia: Psychological and Pharmacological Treatment*. New York: Guilford Press, 1981.

Mavissakalian, M., and Michelson, L. "Patterns of Psychophysiological Change in the Treatment of Agoraphobia." *Behavior Research and Therapy* 20 (1982): 347–56.

Mavissakalian, M.; Michelson, L.; and Dealy, R. S. "Pharmacological Treatment of Agoraphobia: Imipramine Versus Imipramine with Programmed Practice." *British Journal of Psychiatry* 143 (1983): 348–55.

Mavissakalian, M.; Michelson, L.; Greenwald, D.; Kornblith, S.; and Greenwald, M. "Cognitive-Behavioral Treatment of Agoraphobia: Paradoxical Intention vs. Self-statement Training." *Behaviour Research and Therapy* 21 (1983): 75–86.

Mavissakalian, M.; Salerni, R.; Thompson, M. E.; and Michelson, L. "Mitral Valve Prolapse and Agoraphobia." *American Journal of Psychiatry* 140 (1983): 1612–14.

Meyer, V., and Reich, B. "Anxiety Management: The Marriage of Physiological and Cognitive Variables." *Behaviour Research and Therapy* 16 (1978): 177–82.

Michelson, L., and Ascher, L. M. "Paradoxical Intention in the Treatment of Agoraphobia and Other Anxiety Disorders." *Journal of Behaviour Therapy and Experimental Psychiatry* 15 (1984): 215–20.

Milton, F., and Hafner, J. "The Outcome of Behavior Therapy for Agoraphobia in Relation to Marital Adjustment." *Archives of General Psychiatry* 36 (1979): 807–11.

Mullaney, J. A., and Trippett, C. J. "Alcohol Dependence and Phobias: Clinical Description and Relevance." *British Journal of Psychiatry* 135 (1979): 565–73.

Munjack, D. J., and Moss, H. B. "Affective Disorder and Alcoholism in Families of Agoraphobics." *Archives of General Psychiatry* 38 (1981): 869–71.

Neuman, F. *Fighting Fear*. New York: Macmillan, 1985.

Norris, R. V. *PMS: Premenstrual Syndrome*. New York: Rawson, 1983.

Pariser, S. F.; Jones, B. A.; Pinta, E. R.; Young, E. A.; and Fontana, M. E. "Panic Attacks: Diagnostic Evaluations of 17 Patients." *American Journal of Psychiatry* 136 (1979): 105–6.

Pariser, S. F.; Pinta, E. R.; and Jones, B. A. "Mitral Valve Prolapse Syndrome and Anxiety Neurosis/Panic Disorder." *American Journal of Psychiatry* 135 (1978): 246–47.

Pasnau, R. O. "Clinical Presentations of Panic and Anxiety." *Psychosomatics* 25 (1984): 4–9.

Pelosi, M. A. "Premenstrual Syndrome: Fact or Fantasy?" *The Journal of the Medical Society of New Jersey* 81 (1984): 303–8.

Pohl, R.; Rainey, J. M., Jr.; and Gershon, S. "Changes in the Drug Treatment of Anxiety Disorders." *Psychopathology* 17 (1984): 6–14.

Popler, K. "Agoraphobia: Indications for the Application of the Multimodal Behavioral Conceptualization." *Journal of Nervous and Mental Disease* 164 (1977): 97–101.

Price, W. A. and Giannini, A. J. "Premenstrual Tension Syndrome." *Resident and Staff Physician* 31 (1985): 34–38.

Quitkin, F. M.; Rifkin, A.; Kaplan, J.; and Klein, D. F. "Phobic Anxiety Syndrome Complicated by Drug Dependence and Addiction." *Archives of General Psychiatry* 27 (1972): 159–62.

Rachman, S. "Agoraphobia: A Safety-Signal Perspective." *Behavior Research and Therapy* 22 (1984): 59–70.

———. "The Modification of Agoraphobic Avoidance Behaviour: Some Fresh Possibilities." *Behavior Research and Therapy* 21 (1983): 567–74.

———. "The Return of Fear." *Behaviour Research and Therapy* 17 (1979): 164.

Rapp, M. S., and Thomas, M. R. "Agoraphobia." *Canadian Journal of Psychiatry* 27 (1982): 419–25.

Raskin, M.; Peeke, H. V.; Dickman, W.; and Pinsker, H. "Panic and Generalized Anxiety Disorders: Developmental Antecedents and Precipitants." *Archives of General Psychiatry* 39 (1982): 687–89.

Ross, J. "The Use of Former Phobics in the Treatment of Phobias." *American Journal of Psychiatry* 137 (1980): 715–17.

Rossi, E., ed. *The Collected Papers of Milton H. Erickson*, vols. 1 and 2. New York: Irvington, 1980.

Roth, M.; Gurney, C.; Garside, R. F.; and Kerr, T. A. "Studies in the Classification of Affective Disorders: The Relationship Between Anxiety States and Depressive Illnesses—I. *British Journal of Psychiatry* 121 (1972): 147–61.

Rubin, T. I. *Reconciliations: Inner Peace in an Age of Anxiety.* New York: Viking, 1980.

Rubinow, D. R., and Roy-Byrne, P. "Premenstrual Syndromes: Overview from a Methodologic Perspective." *American Journal of Psychiatry* 141 (1984): 163–72.

Schuckit, M. A. "Anxiety Related to Medical Disease." *Journal of Clinical Psychiatry* 44 (1983): 31–36.

Seidenberg, R., and DeCrow, K. *Women Who Marry Houses.* New York: McGraw-Hill, 1983.

Seligman, M. E. P. "Phobias and Preparedness." *Behavior Therapy* 2 (1971): 307–20.

Shader, R. I., and Greenblatt, D. J. "Some Current Treatment Options for Symptoms of Anxiety." *Journal of Clinical Psychiatry* 44 (1983): 21–29.

Shapiro, D. H., and Walsh, R. N. *Meditation: Classic and Contemporary Perspectives.* New York: Aldine, 1984.

Shapiro, D. H., and Zifferblatt, S. M. "Zen Meditation and Behavioral Self-Control: Similarities, Differences, and Clinical Applications." *American Psychologist* 31 (1976): 519–32.

Shear, M. K.; Devereux, R. B.; Kramer-Fox, R.; Mann, J. J.; and Frances, A. "Low Prevalence of Mitral Valve Prolapse in Patients with Panic Disorder." *American Journal of Psychiatry* 141 (1984): 302–3.

Sheehan, D. V. *The Anxiety Disease.* New York: Scribner's, 1983.

Shine, K. I. "Anxiety in Patients with Heart Disease." *Psychosomatics* 25 (1984): 27–31.

Simonton, O. C.; Matthews-Simonton, S.; and Creighton, J. *Getting Well Again.* Los Angeles: Tarcher, 1978.

Sommer, B. "The Effect of Menstruation on Cognitive and Perceptual-Motor Behavior: A Review." *Psychosomatic Medicine* 35 (1973): 515–34.

Stockwell, R.; Smail, P.; Hodgson, R.; and Canter, S. "Alcohol Dependence and Phobic States." II: "A Retrospective Study." *British Journal of Psychiatry* 144 (1984): 58–63.

Strain, J. J.; Liebowitz, M. R.; and Klein, D. F. "Anxiety and Panic Attacks in the Medically Ill." *Psychiatric Clinics of North America* 4 (1981): 333–50.

Stroebel, C. F. *QR: The Quieting Reflex.* New York: Putnam, 1982.

Suess, W. M.; Alexander, A. B.; Smith, D. D.; Sweeney, H. W.; and Marion, R. J. "The Effects of Psychological Stress on Respiration: A Preliminary Study of Anxiety and Hyperventilation." *Psychophysiology* 17 (1980): 535–40.

Suinn, R. M., and Richardson, F. "Anxiety Management Training: A Nonspecific Behavior Therapy Program for Anxiety Control." *Behavior Therapy* 2 (1971): 498–510.

Tearnan, R. H.; Telch, M. J.; and Keefe, P. "Etiology and Onset of Agoraphobia: A Critical Review." *Comprehensive Psychiatry* 25 (1984): 51–62.

Telch, M. J.; Agras, W. S.; Taylor, C. B.; Roth, W. T.; and Gallen, C. C. "Combined Pharmacological and Behavioral Treatment for Agoraphobia." *Behaviour Research and Therapy* 23 (1985): 325–35.

Telch, M. J.; Tearnan, B. H.; and Taylor, C. B. "Antidepressant Medication in the Treatment of Agoraphobia: A Critical Review." *Behaviour Research and Therapy* 21 (1983): 505–17.

Thorpe, G. L., and Burns, L. E. *The Agoraphobic Syndrome*. New York: Wiley, 1983.

Torgersen, S. "Genetic Factors in Anxiety Disorders." *Archives of General Psychiatry* 40 (1983): 1085–89.

United States Pharmacopeial Convention. *The Physicians' and Pharmacists' Guide to Your Medicines*. New York: Ballantine, 1981.

van Dixhoorn, J.; de Loos, J.; and Duivenvoorden, H. J. "Contribution of Relaxation Technique Training to the Rehabilitation of Myocardial Infarction Patients." *Psychother. Psychosom.* 40 (1983): 137–47.

Van Valkenburg, C.; Winokur, G.; Behar, D.; and Lowry, M. "Depressed Women with Panic Attacks." *Journal of Clinical Psychiatry* 45 (1984): 367–69.

Venkatesh, A.; Pauls, D. L.; Crowe, R.; Noyes, R., Jr.; Van Valkenburg, C.; Martins, J. B.; and Kerber, R. E. "Mitral Valve Prolapse in Anxiety Neurosis (Panic Disorder)." *American Heart Journal* 100 (1980): 302–5.

Weekes, C. "Simple, Effective Treatment of Agoraphobia." *American Journal of Psychotherapy* 32 (1978): 357–69.

———. *Simple, Effective Treatment of Agoraphobia*. New York: Bantam, 1979.

Weiss, K. J., and Rosenberg, D. J. "Prevalence of Anxiety Disorder Among Alcoholics." *Journal of Clinical Psychiatry* 46 (1985): 3–5.

Wilhelm-Hass, E. "Premenstrual Syndrome: Its Nature, Evaluation, and Management." *Journal of Obstetric, Gynecologic, and Neonatal Nursing* 13 (1984): 223–29.

Williams, S. L.; Dooseman, G.; and Kleifield, E. "Comparative Effectiveness of Guided Mastery and Exposure Treatments for Intractable Phobias." *Journal of Consulting and Clinical Psychology* 52 (1984): 505–18.

Wilson, R. R. "Interspersal of Hypnotic Phenomena Within On-going Treatment." In Zeig, J., ed., *Ericksonian Psychotherapy. Vol. 2: Clinical Applications*. New York: Brunner/Mazel, 1985, pp. 179–84.

———. "The Relationships Among Depression, Pain Perception and Therapeutic Activity in Chronic Low Back Pain Patients." Doctoral dissertation, 1981.

Wilson, R. R., and Aronoff, G. M. "The Therapeutic Community in the Treatment of Chronic Pain." *Journal of Chronic Diseases* 32 (1979): 477–81.

Wolpe, J. *Our Useless Fears*. Boston: Houghton Mifflin, 1981.

Yager, J., and Young, R. T. "Non-hypoglycemia Is an Epidemic Condition." *New England Journal of Medicine* 291 (1974): 907–8.

Zane, M. D. "Contextual Analysis and Treatment of Phobic Behavior as It Changes." *American Journal of Psychotherapy* 32 (1978): 338–56.

Zane, M. D., and Milt, H. *Your Phobia*. Washington, D.C.: American Psychiatric Press, 1984.

Zivin, I. "The Neurological and Psychiatric Aspects of Hypoglycemia." *Diseases of the Nervous System,* September 1970, 604–7.

Index

Goals (*cont.*)
  planning for, 253–54
  practicing vs. testing, 260–61
  reachable, 251–53
  rehearsal for achievement of, 254–60
  setbacks in achieving, 261
  short-term (intentions), 249–51
  Supportive Observer and, 250–53
Guide, The, 225–36
  audio recording of, 225
  decisions in, 231–32
  goals in, 225–26, 233–36
  images in, 233–36
  Observer in, 230–31
  Supportive Observer in, 226, 231–33
  surroundings in, 230–31
  use of, 227–30
Guillain-Barré syndrome, 14, 17

Hands, 148, 162
Headaches in panic attacks, 128
Head injuries, 19
Heart, 6, 128
  in Calming Response, 138
  disorders of, as cause of panic attacks, 13–18, 19, 21, 92–98, 117–18
  in Emergency Response, 127
  in hyperventilation, 148
  medications and, 240
  palpitations of (tachycardia), 13, 14, 148, 240
Heart attacks, 13, 15–16. *See also*
  Myocardial infarction, recovery from
Heartburn in hyperventilation, 148
Heart failure, 13, 15–16
Hematic disorders, 14, 23
Hemothorax, 17
Heterocyclic antidepressants, 26, 241–42
High blood pressure, 19
Hopeless Observer, 176–80, 198, 267–68
  decisions by, 194
  goals and, 250, 252
Hormonal disorders, 14, 21–23. *See also specific disorders and conditions*
Hormones, 25, 43, 80, 81
Humor in overcoming panic, 218
Hypertension, 19
Hyperthyroidism, 14, 22
Hyperventilation, 102, 147–50
  during breathing exercises, 152
  Emergency Response and, 149, 150
  mechanics of, 147–50
  panic attacks and, 149–50
  physical complaints caused by, 148–49
  psychological response to, 149

Hypoglycemia, 14, 22, 81–84, 88–89
Hypotension, postural (orthostatic), 20, 240

Illness, reaction to, 13, 15, 96–98, 117–18, 143
Images, 219–28
  in achievement of goals, 254–60
  Calming Response and, 137–38
  in Deep Muscle Relaxation, 156, 158–60, 164–65
  forecasting the future and, 133
  in The Guide, 233–36
  panic attacks and, 166
  problem-solving and, 221–25
  repetition and, 225
  self-fulfilling prophecies and, 220–21
  success imagery, 255–56
  task imagery, 256–60
Imagination, 233
Imipramine, 241–42
Inconsistent panic attacks, 111–13
"Incurability" of panic attacks, 119–21
Independence, development of, 67–68, 74–76
Independent observer. *See* Observer
Inderal, 243–44
Inferiority, feelings of, 52–55
Inhalation, 144–46
Intentions, 249–51
Interpretations, 133
Isoniazid, 25
Isoproterenol, 103

Jacobson, Edmund, 140, 154
Jaw in panic attacks, 128

Kennedy, Harold, 15

Labyrinth of the ear, 14, 19, 20
Lao Tsu, 253
Legs, 128, 163
Librium, 24, 238
Lips in Deep Muscle Relaxation, 163
Long-term goals, 225–26, 248–49
Loss of control, fear of, 29, 42, 110–13
  inconsistent attacks and, 111–13
  relaxation and, 137
Loss of a loved one, 68–71, 74
Low blood pressure, 20, 240

Medications. *See also specific medications and types of medications*
  as cause of panic attacks, 14, 24–26, 102–103
  side effects of, 24–26, 239–40, 242–44
  in treatment of panic attacks, 237–44
  withdrawal from, 241